Data, Disruption & Digital Leadership

Philipp Futterknecht • Tobias Hertfelder

Data, Disruption & Digital Leadership

How to Win the Innovation Game

Springer

Philipp Futterknecht
H&F Solutions GmbH – Experts
in Excellence
Bibertal, Germany

Tobias Hertfelder
H&F Solutions GmbH – Experts
in Excellence
Crailsheim, Germany

ISBN 978-3-658-41600-3 ISBN 978-3-658-41601-0 (eBook)
https://doi.org/10.1007/978-3-658-41601-0

This book is a translation of the original German edition "2030 - Strategieentwicklung für Innovation Leaders" by Futterknecht, Philipp, published by Springer Fachmedien Wiesbaden GmbH, DE in 2021. The translation was done with the help of artificial intelligence (machine translation by the service DeepL.com). A subsequent human revision was done primarily in terms of content, so that the book will read stylistically differently from a conventional translation. Springer Nature works continuously to further the development of tools for the production of books and on the related technologies to support the authors.

This Springer imprint is published by the registered company Springer Fachmedien Wiesbaden GmbH, part of Springer Nature.
The registered company address is: Abraham-Lincoln-Str. 46, 65189 Wiesbaden, Germany

Failure is an option. So is reading this book.
Philipp Futterknecht

You shouldn’t do things differently just to make them different—they should be better afterwards.
Tobias Hertfelder

Preface

Strategy guides are usually based in the past and often leave out the latest methods and technical tools. However, the world no longer works the way it did 30 years ago, and the people who have to implement strategies have different attitudes and values, and a different understanding of self-motivation. This book therefore incorporates all the important aspects of future-oriented innovation strategy development. Compared to traditional strategy guides, our approach is at least three times faster and more efficient, with its main focus on data analysis, associated agile methods, and the elimination of all redundancies. Many of the topics in this book can be found scattered among more than 100 individual publications. For our readers, we have summarized all the most important aspect of the subject and provided our own graphics to illustrate the content. The text also contains plenty of best practices to provide you not only with theory, but rather a complete package. We hope you have fun reading this book.

Bibertal, Germany — Philipp Futterknecht
Crailsheim, Germany — Tobias Hertfelder

Contents

About the Authors

Philipp Futterknecht and **Tobias Hertfelder** realized early on that you have to continually reinvent yourself to be better than everyone else. They have continuously perfected their methods since the foundation of their companies, and they now combine their collected experience as digitization and networking experts with a high level of management and innovation knowledge that they are keen to share with individuals and companies.

List of Figures

List of Table

Innovation Strategy 2030: One Step Ahead of Its Time

1

Developing and Implementing Strategies Using the Latest Data Analysis Methods

1.1 Our Digital Innovation Universe

Since Albert Einstein published his theory of relativity, we know that the gravity produced by massive objects attracts other objects. Einstein provided his proof in the early years of the twentieth century. Everything that approaches such massive objects is literally swallowed up by them. The greater the mass, the greater the force of attraction (see Fig. 1.1). It is the same in innovation strategy projects. Many things have to fit together in order to achieve an above-average result. Every participant in a project has their own mass and has an impact on team synergy. This situation isn't new and has been the case for several decades. Whoever best understands this interplay of forces will also be able to achieve the best result. In this book, we would like to introduce you to our universe of digital leadership projects.

What has changed dramatically, however, and is changing our priorities enormously, is the influence of data on strategic processes. This is not about designing a strategy for digitization, but about using existing data as part of a corporate strategy. If you don't take this into account, you will suffer huge losses in the future. As this change brings about a new equilibrium, the chances of success for the methods used also change. This book is about how you can master this change, and about the tools you need to do so.

► If you are interested in the topic of the universe and its interaction, you can make use of the freely accessible video platforms. There you will find many parallels to the processes in your company.

P. Futterknecht, T. Hertfelder, *Data, Disruption & Digital Leadership*,
https://doi.org/10.1007/978-3-658-41601-0_1

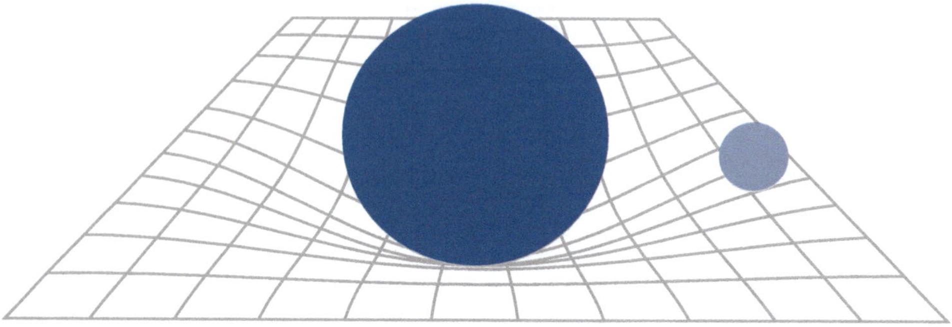

Fig. 1.1 The effect of gravity in digital leadership projects. (Source: H&F Solutions GmbH/www.hf-solutions.co)

1.2 Introduction

You are in charge of digital leadership in your company and you had a perfect plan for a new innovation strategy project, but now you find your project is already ruined and a lot of things need to be reworked. This is a real disappointment. And then there's that one colleague who always knows better and annoys the entire project team with his agile methods. This colleague is the only one who doesn't think he needs to have a proper plan, and management rewards him for it. Now you've had enough, which may also be why you bought this book. Is everything we used to do bad now?

In the past, there have always been changes due to things like technological progress or globalization that have forced us to think differently. As described above, we all inhabit a world where everything seems to be pulling at us and where we would actually have to clone ourselves to meet all the demands made of us. But that wasn't the case in the past, was it? Yes, it was—it's just that the process was slower back then and the mass of communication data was less significant. On closer examination of these changes, as is the case almost everywhere, the truth probably lies between these two extremes. Although a lot has changed, many things that worked in the past still work today. That's why we want to use this book to give you some guidance on things that will work today and in the near future in order to help you succeed in digital leadership creation and implementation. We can reassure you that there are not as many things that need adjusting as you might assume. Let's look together at our past projects, as we have had an interesting time with about 80 per cent of them. If you focus on a just a few things and follow them through consistently, you are very likely to achieve your goals. For experienced strategists this may sound trivial, but for younger colleagues this fact is by no means self-evident. To take this to heart, you need neither help nor instructions from us. What you do need, however, is the right combination of experience, composure, and specific techniques. In this regard, this book is intended to contribute much of the required experience through the shared experiences and techniques it describes. You can take care of the composure part yourself.

This book also serves to ensure that you can efficiently implement things that you recognize. This will help you to keep up the pace of the projects you want to work on one after the other. However, it is rare that you will save time doing this. But you'll get faster and, as a result, you'll simply be able to complete more projects than before in a given period of time (or implement higher-quality projects). Our experience has also shown that implementation projects tend to come down to the same things over and over again, regardless of whether they are digitized or not. It also doesn't matter whether the things you work on are hot topics covered by buzzwords such as agility, consistency, mindset, change, or performance culture. It is the well-known things like courage, focus, and action that need to be applied and executed.

Until now, we have imparted this knowledge to each of our potential customers individually in countless work sessions. However, since we ourselves are interested in keeping projects lean for everybody involved, we decided to pack this topic into a book and make it available to people like you.

This document is the result of the authors' project experience from over 200 individual projects and the reading of many specialist books about strategy. It is not a complete set of instructions or a guarantee of success, but rather an initial selection of techniques and experiences designed to save you a lot of potentially unnecessary effort. When working on strategy projects, for other companies in the past, we would have been very happy to have a guide like this to accompany us in the leadership work we did.

1.3 Building Blocks for Successful Disruptive Innovation Strategies

"Innovation strategy work could be so easy if it weren't for the implementation. The fact that the strategy still has to fit the goals is just the icing on the cake."

This is how many decision-makers feel about strategy work. Strategy work is the link that bridges the gap between defining goals and implementing plans. Without a successful strategy, the chance of being successful decreases. In this book, we are by no means trying to reinvent the wheel. Nevertheless, the field of strategy development has been expanded in recent years to include the topic of *knowledge from data sets and software tools*. We believe that today's strategy projects should therefore be handled differently. To make this combination of data and strategy tangible, we have developed the *H&F Strategy Pyramid* (see Fig. 1.2). With this approach we want to make a decisive contribution to successful digital leadership development in today's companies. *The H&F Strategy Pyramid* contains all areas that are necessary to enable today's decision-makers to carry out successful strategy work. It doesn't just include theoretical concepts, it also covers all the topics necessary to successfully complete a strategy project.

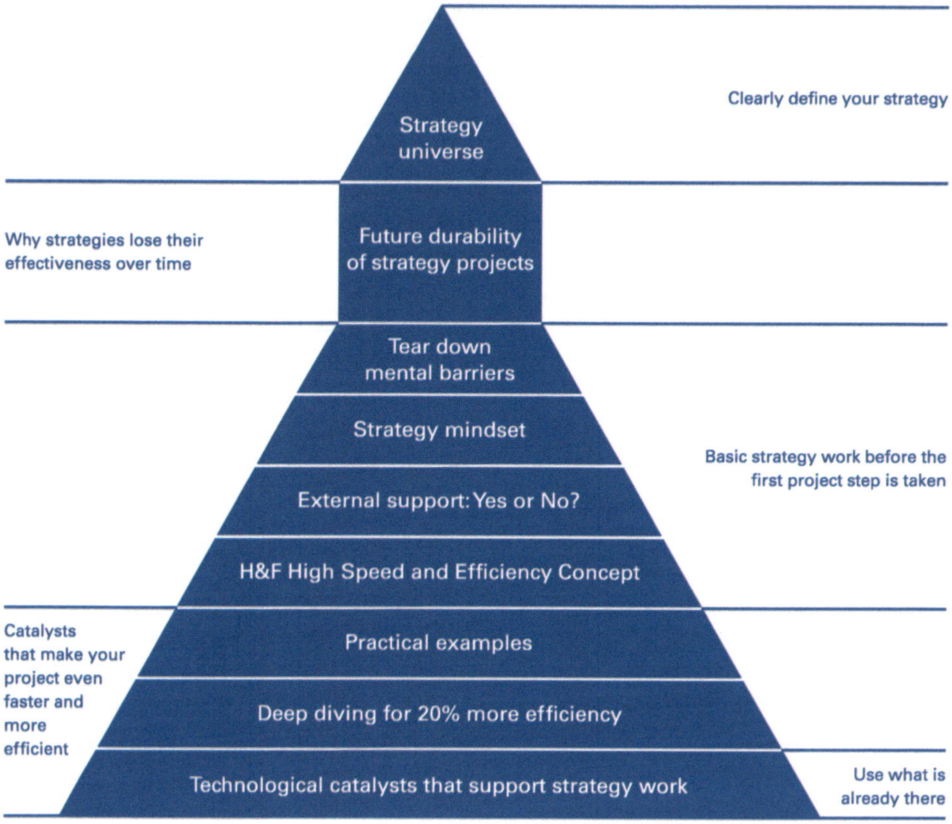

Fig. 1.2 The H&F Strategy Pyramid. (Source: H&F Solutions GmbH/www.hf-solutions.co)

1.4 Quick Start Guides

> In order to be able to act successfully in the future in spite of increasing complexity, we must pool our forces and increasingly limit ourselves to the bare essentials. To do this, it is necessary to prevent potentially time-consuming trouble spots from arising in the first place. (Philipp Futterknecht & Tobias Hertfelder, 2021)

Before we now turn to the topic of success-oriented implementation, it is important to clarify the areas in your company that present the greatest challenges. It may be a good idea to jump straight into the relevant chapter—after all, with the knowledge gained from this book, you may be better able to identify the important issues in your very next meeting. Especially for people with little available time, heading directly to the relevant chapter can be a worthwhile time-saver. Every topic might include the piece of the puzzle that can help you successfully and quickly reach your own personal goal. The basis for this is to stay focused—as soon as we mix too many topics together, we usually become less efficient and lose speed and agility as a result. Therefore, to get the most benefit from this book, start by focusing on one of the topics in the following illustration (Fig. 1.3). At this point, it's time choose between the following quick start guides.

If this is the first time you've encountered the topic of strategy development, feel free to work your way through this book from beginning to end and enjoy the full benefit, as you are sure to have done with other books.

1.4.1 Quick Start Guide #1: The Lifespan of a Strategy (Chap. 2)

The further you look back into the past, the longer strategies lasted and the fewer changes there were to the planned strategy period. Back then, everything was plannable, whereas today this is no longer the case, and this trend will continue in the future. The reasons for this are increasing complexity, shifting power structures in corporate leadership, and the changing mindset of the people doing the implementing. Increasing complexity will bring us to our knees if we fail to respond appropriately. Reducing complexity in your own view of a project and responding appropriately to the residual complexity will allow you to successfully manage important issues in the future. You will then no longer be the pacemaker that the team will follow blindly. Instead, you will serve as an impetus for teams with their own will and decision-making power. This is a paradigm change and will leave behind people who aren't prepared to accept this kind of change. Going forward, you'll split about 90 per cent of project participants into three relatively homogeneous attitude groups. If you learn to identify these, you will also succeed in giving the right impulses and channeling important strategic topics in a targeted manner.

1.4.2 Quick Start Guide #2: The H&F Strategy Process (Chap. 3)

Confusion Instead of Clout

You know where you want to go, but not how to get there? Your most recent ERP project implementations were less than satisfactory, or perhaps never even got finished?

There are different ways to make things successful, and you can achieve your intended results in many different ways. Once you have started and launched your project, you can quickly see whether the chosen methods are successful or not. Changing the fundamentals at this point is not impossible but is nevertheless very time-consuming. At this point, we would like to name 10 potential bottlenecks that you definitely need to eliminate. In this chapter, we provide clarity in areas that should not be negotiable in any project—because there are simply certain things you need to know to make your life easier. And no one can do without that.

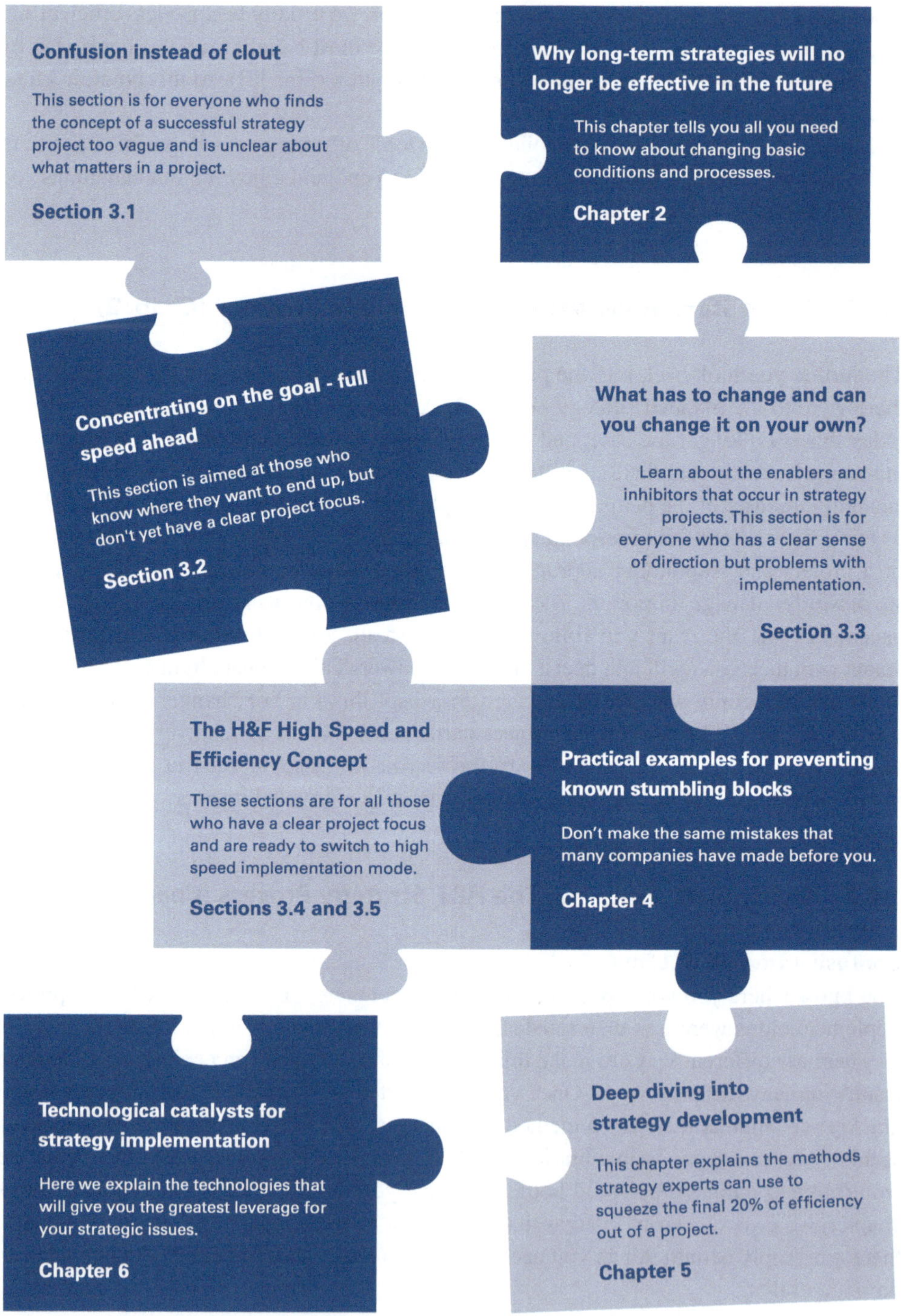

Fig. 1.3 An overview of our quick start guides. (Source: H&F Solutions GmbH/www.hf-solutions.co)

Full Speed Ahead with Your Eye on the Goal

You already have several successful strategy projects behind you. However, most of these projects turned into nightmares. As a 'lone wolf', you often ended up picking up the pieces yourself and – once again – everything hinged on the human factor. From a technical perspective, everything could have gone so well. In this chapter you will learn how to set up a project team and how to assign which activities to which team members. You can only deliver successfully if you have the right mindset. After working through this chapter, it should be clear to everyone that the project goal can only be achieved if you all pull together as a team.

Can We Make the Change on Our Own?

Can we save the world on our own or do we need help? This will become clear at the latest in the first half of a project. Most companies only call in external help when things have come to a long-term standstill. Out of frustration, they then sit back and let the external help do the donkey work. In this chapter, you will learn if and when it makes sense to bring in an external expert. In addition, you will learn whether the results achieved deliver real progress or only generate effort and may not even serve the actual project goal.

The H&F High Speed and Efficiency Concept

You know what's important and you have a dedicated project team, but your projects still drag on. If so, the project approach in this chapter will show you a way to effectively speed up the implementation process or significantly reduce the time required for the project. But beware, this is where things get a little unusual, and it will on average take one or two projects to really understand and think through this approach. However, it is doable from the get-go, so why not get started today?

1.4.3 Quick Start Guide #3: Practical Examples (Chap. 4)

In addition to all the technical aspects, we always get stuck in the same places in the course of our everyday work. With the help of practical examples, we would like to give you valuable insights into issues that were previously impenetrable to you. We would like to save you, the reader, from the worst mistakes and at the same time introduce you to the most interesting shortcuts for innovation strategy projects. Please note that not every practical example will be helpful for every situation in your own company. Sometimes it helps if you recognize early on that an idea is not applicable in your case.

1.4.4 Quick Start Guide #4: Deep Dive Expert Mode (Chap. 5)

This is a kind of digital leaders World Cup. In this chapter, you will learn about other important topics that will help you to advance your innovation strategy project even faster, to safeguard it even better, and to further increase your personal strategy performance. Please note that starting with this chapter without first mastering the basics probably won't produce the results you are hoping for. Nevertheless, a quick look at this chapter can't hurt – either as an extra stimulus on this topic or as a manual to help you become a true digital strategy champion.

1.4.5 Quick Start Guide #5: Technological Catalysts (Chap. 6)

If you have already read and understood Chaps. 2 and 3 and you think you can use the knowledge and techniques they contain to perform a successful implementation, Chaps. 4, 5, and 6 will provide you with further important information to help you become an even better digital leader. Alternatively, you can simply browse these chapters for individual approaches that inspire you.

> We would now like to ask you to sit back, relax, get yourself a nice cup of coffee (or something similar) and then take a relaxed look at your preferred chapter. You need to be calm and have a clear head if you want to absorb fresh input. In the end, the winner will not be the one who starts his project the fastest, but the one who makes the cleanest execution and has the best overview. We wish you every success as you work through the text.

Why Long-Term Innovation Strategies Will No Longer Be Effective in the Future

2

Innovation Strategies are plans that serve to achieve goals. The further you look back into the past, the longer strategies lasted, and the fewer changes there were during the planned strategy periods. Things used to be more plannable. This means that, in the future, things will probably become less plannable. Three things are largely responsible for this change:

1. Increasing complexity
2. Leadership power shifts
3. The mindset of those implementing the strategy

2.1 Increasing Network Density

One reason for decreasing plannability is increasing network density. Advances in digitization create more and more nodes that serve as information transmitters and receivers, and that influence the behavior of their environment (including people). We receive information and simultaneously send information to our environment at ever shorter intervals. If network density increases, non-linearity is automatically increased as well, which in turn generates increased complexity and momentum. It is easy to see how increased network density influences your behavior. As our environment and our businesses become more and more networked, business issues automatically become more networked too. Look back at your day so far and count the number of times you have interacted with your environment. When businesses become more and more networked, again complexity increases. This build-up of complexity ensures that simple, long-term strategies will have little effect in the future.

P. Futterknecht, T. Hertfelder, *Data, Disruption & Digital Leadership*,
https://doi.org/10.1007/978-3-658-41601-0_2

2.1.1 Connected Systems and Their Dynamics

At this point, we would like to focus clearly on the context of strategic work in a business environment. Many employees and the stakeholders they work with increase the density of information distribution. The ability to send information quickly also increases the number of changes to this information. It is not uncommon for employees to correct and revise their decisions faster than they can be processed by the recipient. This happens simply because they have the opportunity to do so. This process accumulates until things that were predictable and plannable in the past suddenly become unpredictable. In other words, you can no longer predict things today that you used to be able to predict better. This is due to the dynamics of networked systems described above. And now, in the middle of all this change, you have to work out an innovation strategy for reaching a goal in the distant future. This is now extremely difficult, because the influencing factors are becoming increasingly difficult to predict. This is the moment to look at an example from your recent past and see how well your predictions turned out. The automotive industry is a good example for increasing system dynamics. European car manufacturers have recently been overwhelmed by the momentum of the focus on alternative powertrains. This has only partly to do with the faulty strategies and is due much more to a failure to take increasing momentum into account. Now try to predict where the automotive industry is headed. This is incredibly difficult, and you can see the effect of industry dynamics in the statements made by the leading companies in the industry. The necessary developments over the next few years are perceived differently by each company. One manufacturer believes in further development of electric vehicles, while others are focusing on fuel cell technology, and still others see the car of the future as a software platform, irrespective of the type of powertrain.

Example.

As a manager or strategist, you are expected to be able to lead your company or division while simultaneously having a plausible answer to almost all questions—answers that ideally serve the company's goals. However, increasing momentum ensures that things are no longer predictable and, as a result, the answers given by decision-makers become more uncertain. When employees ask how the future is to be managed, you as the decision-maker will no longer have clear answers. It is not uncommon to hear managers say that in today's world you have to fly by sight. However, what this really means is that they themselves have no answers to the questions posed. Mastering complexity will therefore become one of the greatest challenges of the future. ◀

2.1.2 Dealing with Complexity

In the future we will still need strategies, but we will no longer be able to predict long-term outcomes. And this inevitably means a permanent adjustment of corporate goals and their associated innovation strategies, so we will have to learn to deal with continually increasing complexity. Politics is a good example. While a politician's word and opinions used to be valid for a long time, nowadays people almost exclusively act in the short term and with caution. This is because a decision could be outdated by the time it is fully communicated. Due to the unpredictability caused by increased complexity, it is no longer possible to predict things with certainty. However, we cannot change this situation by using tools or by changing our behavioral patterns. We have to learn to deal with complexity permanently and to accept it. On this basis, we have to align our behavior with real-world complexity.

2.1.3 The Effect of Decisions

In the past, decisions were distributed via communication channels that took several days or weeks to relay. When a director made a decision, a message was prepared by an assistant that was passed on to divisional managers. They in turn passed the decision on to the employees in the form of a printed announcement. It was not unusual for 4 weeks to pass before the announcement was read by everyone. Today this is done differently. A decision is made in a board meeting and at the latest an hour later, the first detailed information leaks out to stakeholders via channels such as email, social media, or privately organized departmental WhatsApp groups. People then begin to react to these messages, again immediately, and bat the pros and cons back to the board. This means that the decision-maker will enter the feedback loop about an hour after the meeting ends and actively responds. This is an obvious increase in communication density. As a result, the effect is completely different than it was 10–20 years ago. It is no longer clear whether this type of decision-making is still qualified or whether it is more like a compulsion to make decisions.

2.1.4 Success Through the Reduction of Complexity in Innovation Strategy Work

In order to continue to be successful in the midst of such high-speed communication, decision-makers have to be able to reduce complexity. This is because complexity has increased exorbitantly with the distribution of information and the backflow of information described in Sect. 2.1.3. To reduce complexity, you must understand the context and recognize recurring patterns. We discuss pattern recognition in Sect. 5.5.7. We believe that complexity reduction must be trained, and one tried-and-tested way to achieve this is to look at a question from as many perspectives as possible. Let's look at an example.

Example

In a sample strategy process, everything revolves around the decision to operate abroad in the European Union (EU) in the future. It isn't possible for you to evaluate all the influencing factors and make a rational decision based on them. However, after the first

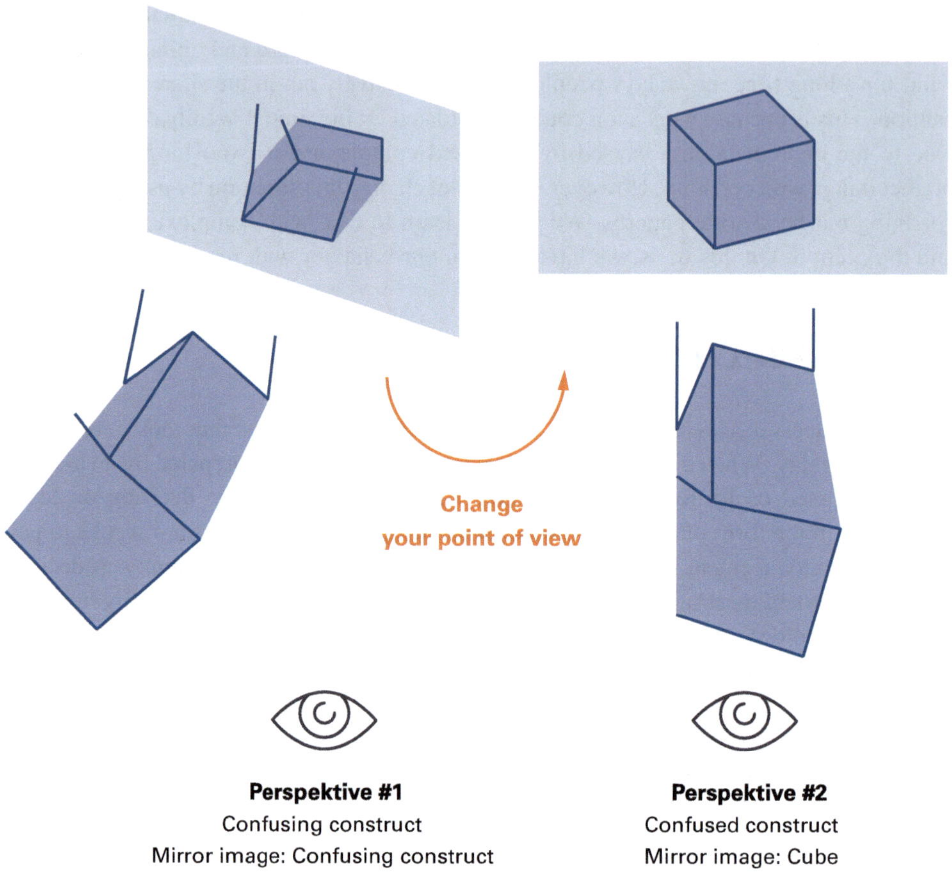

Fig. 2.1 Experimenting with different ways of looking at things. (Source: H&F Solutions GmbH/ www.hf-solutions.co)

management meeting, information has already leaked out to the extended management circle and initial feedback has already been received. In this feedback, specific pros and cons have already been fed back. You as the decision maker should now look at the situation from as many points of view as possible. If you have already looked at the situation from many angles, go back to your initial point of view. You will see that you now react differently than you did before. What has happened? By recognizing patterns, you have helped develop your sense of how to view the issue. Figure 2.1 illustrates this process.

If you are able to take a variety of viewpoints in a short period of time, you will be able to reduce complexity and make better decisions faster. In the case of the non-EU innovation strategy, this could involve starting a round of questioning with the stakeholders and subsequently looking at the challenge again yourself. You will see that your attitude towards this issue will change for the better. ◀

However, you shouldn't break complexity down too far. If you now separate the cube into its individual parts, it is virtually impossible to recognize the pattern that previously existed. Instead, you have to mentally break down the current situation in your company and reassemble it in such a way that the new strategy, including the non-EU countries, holds up. And all this must be considered in context.

Apart from the facts, in the future we must learn to constantly deal with complexity, as previously described. As humans, we are able to reduce complexity quite well using an ability we call intuition.

2.1.5 Experimenting with Complexity

In spite of reduction, complexity will still be so challenging that you will have to learn how to deal with it. To do this, you must learn to experiment with complexity. Certain aspects of complex processes you will recognize immediately, while you will have to look at other things for a while to see what is behind them. Experiments are nothing more than observations under controlled conditions, so you need to create an artificial environment to block out various external influences. In the case of innovation strategy, it has proved useful to mentally reproduce certain processes and scenarios in three or four different ways, in the form of pictures or text. In the course of an experiment, it is important that only one factor is examined at a time. This factor is then altered according to your various viewpoints. This approach makes it possible to determine quite quickly which influencing factors lead to which results. This type of experimentation can also be performed for questions about filling a position in the strategy team. You give different people the same task and observe the results they produce. Based on these results, we can then identify patterns. This is because the individuals implementing the strategy are likely to lead, or at least run in the same direction, as the experiment. Once these experiments are successfully completed, you have added another important piece of the puzzle to the overall picture of your strategic goal.

2.1.6 Future Actions

Due to the complexity described above, innovation strategy work in the future will no longer be primarily about implementing target definitions, but mainly about reducing complexity by recognizing patterns. Due to a lack of overall stability, we will therefore have to orient ourselves better, and in doing so, we cannot decide whether we want this or not. We can only decide whether or not to accept the challenge. In the future, successful strategies will therefore no longer be created behind closed doors in back rooms but will emerge within networks. In order to master this task successfully, we have created a basis in the form of the *H&F High Speed and Efficiency Concept*. In addition to the actual implementation concept, there are several basic conditions that support this approach. These are detailed in the following sections.

2.1.7 Emergence of the Basis for Future Innovation Strategies

In the future, successful strategies will largely be created by work collectives or networks in which every single participant can serve as an impulse generator. Unusual today, the transparency of this approach will create previously unknown momentum. In this context, the qualities and abilities of the individual project participants are a new factor.

2.1.7.1 Combining Individual Building Blocks into an Overall Innovation Strategy

In the future, only the consolidation and final strategy definition will continue to take place in a small group behind closed doors. During this process, all input factors are tabled in order to declare the future company (or division) goal in the course of a transparent process. Once this decision is made, it is announced as usual. The *H&F High Speed and Efficiency Concept* can then serve as the basis for implementation.

2.1.7.2 Knowledge Centers Instead of Planning Units

As already described, it is important to recognize and understand the interrelationships that occur in complex models, so people who have this capability are more valuable than people who are good at simply executing a plan. For this reason, contact points must be created to assist and provide orientation for the constantly decreasing number of planners and implementers.

2.1.7.3 Future Pattern Recognition Will Only Be Possible Collectively

The knowledge centers described in Sect. 2.1.7.2 will also no longer be sufficient in the future, and pattern recognition will have to be carried out from within the collective. This is because a single source of knowledge will no longer be able to master the overall complexity. For more information on pattern recognition, see Sect. 5.5.7. Pattern recognition by individuals is the basis for collective pattern recognition, and this collective pattern recognition is in turn the basis of networks, which are the basis for the strategy work of the future.

2.1.7.4 Organization Within the Company

You probably have existing hierarchical structures in your company, but we are now talking about how things can only be solved in the network and collectively. These two approaches are not contradictory and can be operated in parallel through appropriate communication processes. After all, everything that happens informally in today's companies is nothing other than the operation of a network. The only difference is that this type of communication is not legitimized from an organizational point of view. The awareness that not all processes can be based on official organizational structures is probably older than most organizational forms. We can thus view the hierarchical organization as the 'official' organization and the network as the informal organization. In the future, it will therefore be necessary to design innovation strategies that serve the formal organization but, at the same time, can be positively supported by networks. In order to master complexity in the future, the intelligence contained in informal networks must also be integrated.

Summary

The world is spinning faster and faster, which leads to an increase in the number of nodes in the communication of people and machines, referred to as networking density. While people used to communicate on a daily basis and machines not at all, both now communicate every minute. This creates a situation in which matters appear more complex due to the vast amount of information available. We communicate differently today than we did in the past, and every new communication receives responses from other participants after a very short time. If someone sends a message, he immediately receives a reaction, which in turn is answered quickly. This exchange pushes people who have no technical support to their limits. Especially in innovation strategy work, it is important to reduce this complexity with the help of different ways of looking at things. This complexity can be counteracted by creating different knowledge centers in companies. For example, an industrial company should in the future hire not only technology specialists, but also statisticians and data analysts. If you succeed in recognizing patterns within the plethora of available information and interpreting them collectively, these will form the basis on which you can build the corporate strategies of the future. ◀

2.2 Leadership Power Shifts

In hierarchical systems, it used to be the provider of knowledge or products who decided on the success of organizations. In a complex networked system—which your company is currently becoming—it is increasingly the network participants who are the decision makers. And they are also the ones who decide on the success of the implementation of future strategies. In the future, what a manager sends to his employees or what a company sends to its customers will no longer be of interest, and the decisive factor will be how employees or customers judge what is sent. If managers of the future no longer give instructions but instead only provide stimulus, all project participants will automatically become decision-makers. It will therefore be the collective that decides whether an innovation strategy is successfully implemented or not, rather than just the managers. It is therefore critical how well your information is received by its recipients.

2.2.1 Changing from the 'Sender Principle' to the Democratization of Companies

As already described, complexity forces us to network and to act as a collective. By 2030 this collective pattern will force us to democratize decision-making in companies. In other words, we are talking about a kind of resonance effect. Leaders send impulses and receive resonance in order to respond in turn in an appropriately adapted way. You can compare this principle with communication in and around meetings. Only a fraction of the communication on specific topics happens in the associated meetings, and more than 70 per cent of decisions on any given topic are made through informal communication channels. This inevitably leads to a shift in the balance of power away from the management team to the collective.

2.2.2 The Resonance Capacity of Networks

In order to successfully develop and implement an innovation strategy, you need to find out what resonates in your network. And resonance in most cases means the interference of many network participants in decisions. For example, when it comes to reorganizing production sites, decisions are no longer made behind closed doors. Almost all stakeholders are involved, and a kind of co-governance culture among all stakeholders is emerging in companies. In other words, we now have just as many national team coaches as citizens. To be able to implement a strategy successfully in the future, you have to operate successfully in networks, so it's no longer a question of how entrepreneurs and managers develop their companies, but how well the company can develop in the direction of the system's existing momentum. Within this type of system decision-makers are no longer masterminds but rather impulse generators, as already described. If you manage to find out which information evokes the appropriate resonances, you will have a much better chance of being able to successfully implement your strategic goals.

2.2.3 Competitors Lose Importance

Until now, the focus of many corporate goals and strategic development has been on satisfying the customer and positioning the company in relation to the competition. However, because this previously stable system has begun to waver, this view will no longer be sufficient in the future. A change of direction has begun, from focusing on two or three main focal points to focusing on a homogeneous network of stakeholders. It is possible to counteract this change by increasing cooperation. So, if we increase cooperation and network density, the processes that have supported us up to now continue to lose their effect. As a result, companies move from existing stability to a state of instability. Within this instability it is then no longer important to know who my leader is, but rather to know who the network nodes are that will help me to succeed in my task.

2.2.4 The Role of Project Stakeholders in Innovation Strategy Processes

If project participants are now no longer recipients of instructions but rather networkers, the question arises as to which success-related topics company leaders should pay attention to. If strategy processes are viewed from a democratized point of view, attractiveness and meaningfulness become the most important themes for the individuals involved, while legacy topics—such as the role model function of managers and corporate loyalty—lose significance. These last two are based on a formal organization, whereas the topics that will be important in the future are based on an informal organization—i.e., on the network. As you can see, here too the role of project participants is inevitably shifting to one of non-linearity. In the future, successful innovation strategy work can only take place if employees see meaning in the existing corporate network. This then gives rise to the bonds necessary to preserve the stability of the network.

2.2.5 Success Through the Intelligence of the Collective

In the future, innovation strategies can largely only be defined and implemented by the collective. For this to succeed, we need to create new forms of cooperation, and we are therefore forced to think step by step in this direction. Summarized in a single sentence, we are talking about the ability of companies to cooperate within smart networks.

Summary

In the future, power in companies will shift from executives to all stakeholders. In the process, executives will move from being decision-makers to being instigators, which also means that power will shift from the individual to the collective. In the future, successful innovation strategy work will only be possible if those involved understand its purpose. We are therefore forced to evolve step by step from individual decision-makers to collective decision-makers. ◀

2.3 Implementer Mindset

Companies and leaders are currently shaped by the past. This is because in the past, existing problems had to be overcome. The situation now in the early 2020s must be seen as a starting point for a development towards organizations that can successfully define and implement innovation strategy projects in the future. So far, we have refrained from presenting highly scientific analyses, and we have instead summarized the topic for you using various sources and our own surveys. At this point, it is simply a matter of understanding the overall context.

2.3.1 A New Generation of Digital Leaders

The topic of changing generations is nothing new. Every generation probably claims to the next that everything was better in the past. However, what is happening in the current situation—which began in the 2000s—is truly astonishing. In the past, if you asked certain groups of people about specific issues, the responses were often varied but nevertheless homogeneous, or at least clustered. If you ask successful leaders or strategists about a specific topic, you will get a clear idea of how they think about strategy and what they see as factors for success. However, if you ask the younger generation today, this clustering effect seems to have disappeared, and the answers to the same questions head off in a wide variety of directions. In the past, the younger generation had a different but nevertheless clustered opinion to the older generation. If you talk to young people, you will see these tendencies within certain groups. However, as you increase the number of respondents, you will begin to see a large crowd that sees a single issue in very different ways. If you apply these observations to strategy and ask how future decision-makers see the topic of strategy, the answer you will get from some of the respondents is that strategy needs to be independent, experimental, networked, and meaningful from within the group. At the same time, however, there will be another group that thinks strategy should be predetermined, thoroughly organized, and professional. The first group thus represents the informal organizational approach, while the second group tends toward a formal organization approach. Moreover, it is surprising to find that what one group sees positively, the other sees negatively, and vice versa. Thanks to the rapid exchange of good information, indifference is rarely present. In any case it becomes clear that you cannot attribute a specific behavior pattern to the coming generation. This is often the case, and it is generally assumed that the younger generation wants only freedom and self-determination. It is precisely this lack of clustering and the increasing network activity described above that our *H&F High Speed and Efficiency Concept* is designed to address.

2.3.2 Significant Clusters

Here too it is astonishing that, following clustering, groups of largely the same size are formed. Once again, no clear trends can be identified. At this point, we would like to highlight three clusters which you must take into account in the course of your innovation strategy work.

2.3.2.1 Defense of the Status Quo

You will always encounter stakeholders who feel threatened by new innovation strategies. It does not matter where the new strategies are headed—this group of people will try to prevent all innovations. They feel threatened by all innovations and fight to keep everything as it is.

2.3.2.2 Satisfaction in the Present

People who are satisfied with the present situation are mostly career-oriented. They don't deal much with the past or the future, but accept the present and try to make the best of all the innovations that the future may bring. This group will support you in all your plans for the future, and will use them specifically to aid their own careers.

2.3.2.3 Desire for Permanent Change

People with a constant urge for change will be grateful for every innovation that future strategies bring, but they will not be satisfied with this situation and will demand even more progress. This group of people will therefore always create a kind of positive unrest.

2.3.3 Significant Issues for the Strategic Work of the Future

Over the past 30 years, we have experienced an ever-increasing difference between what individuals understand as successful strategy and how strategies are actually applied. If you look at studies in this area, the topics of agreeing on goals, controlling key numbers, increasing efficiency, and maximizing profits are what a majority of those involved are willing to work hard for. In turn, these tendencies form an important piece of the puzzle in the mechanics of implementation.

After reading the previous sections, the question now is: do you want to continue as before, or do you want to change something? If you want to take the change route, you should start with small projects that enable you to experience the effects of the approaches we will describe in the following chapters. If you want to dive in at the deep end and comprehensively develop or adapt your corporate innovation strategy, we will be happy to support you in the process.

Summary

If you interviewed successful strategists in the past, you always got similar answers. If you ask this question today, you get such different answers that you can no longer see any clustering. It is therefore no longer possible to pin the next generation down to a particular type of behavior. The *H&F High Speed and Efficiency Concept* was developed in response to this distribution. It allows for highly flexible innovation strategy work that takes the most diverse views and attitudes of those involved into account. ◀

3 The H&F Strategy Process

3.1 Confusion Instead of Clout

People who are closer mentally to their goals than to the start of their path are demonstrably more successful. Instead of harboring doubts, it is better to consistently believe in your own goals and the goals of the company. To begin with, we would like to point out what we consider to be the 10 most important obstacles that currently prevent successful innovation strategy work.

3.1.1 The 10 Obstacles that Prevent Companies from Becoming High Performers in the Implementation of Management and Innovation Strategy Projects

Most of the time, our weaknesses lie not in what we see and address incorrectly, but in the issues we don't see and thus cannot focus on, address, or incorporate in our work. The great thing, however, is that this situation affects all companies and no one is exempt. Although data is an elementary part of today's innovation strategy work, dealing with it is still mostly assigned to IT departments. Because of this, companies tend to see it as an IT issue and don't consider it as part of their strategy work. We have highlighted 10 topics that were the main reasons for low performance in this area during the last 5 years. The interesting thing is that, at a first glance, 90% of these topics have nothing to do with data or strategy.

3.1.1.1 Incorrect Assessment of Future Market Power

Market power is the decisive factor for the success of any company. However, since the late 1980s, this factor has switched from being a company internal to an external factor (see Fig. 3.1). In the early 1960s, many companies didn't have to worry about the market. At

P. Futterknecht, T. Hertfelder, *Data, Disruption & Digital Leadership*,
https://doi.org/10.1007/978-3-658-41601-0_3

Fig. 3.1 Changes in market power. (Source: H&F Solutions GmbH/www.hf-solutions.co)

that time, the customer had to purchase what was available and wasn't able to decide between different versions of a product. It wasn't until the manufacturers' suppliers decided to bring new raw materials to the market that something new became available to the manufacturers. In the late 1970s, this market power passed to the manufacturers, who told their suppliers what materials they needed to produce certain products. Then, in the early 1990s, market power passed to distributors, who decided what products the manufacturers should produce in order to make the best possible deal. However, the customer still predominantly bought what retailers offered. It wasn't until the end of the first decade of the twenty-first century that customers came into play as decision-makers throughout the market. Retailers began to understand that customers would like to have products tailored to their needs. This behavior still holds true today. Nowadays, strategies are developed not for today, but for tomorrow. By the year 2030, market power will have migrated further in the direction of the forecasters.

In the future, those who—based on today's events—can predict which things customers will want to buy tomorrow can generate a decisive competitive advantage.

Example

Imagine a pump manufacturer who puts his product portfolio together based on customer demand. However, he also produces other products for a range of specialist applications. The products sold are divided into categories and can be evaluated later on the basis of sales figures. It is also common to analyze materials used in order to optimize the purchasing process. These two views enable the manufacturer to make a forecast for the future. However, today's companies have many more options for analysis at their disposal.

Let's look at another company. A manufacturer of specialized parts produces custom parts in small batches. This previously highly profitable business is facing difficulties due to price pressure. In terms of forecasting capability, the company has begun to analyze not only raw materials and part types, but also 100 additional parameters to provide a more accurate forecast. In doing so, the company noticed that there were many dependencies between part types, machine usage, the profitability of individual parts, machine breakdowns, and even employee turnover. Appropriate software was able to use machine learning to analyze which types of service could provide the greatest benefit to the customer in the future, while also providing the company with the best opportunities. As a result, the service portfolio was changed. At the same time, due to the increasing demand for short-term deliveries, a new machine was purchased which offered fewer processing options but increased production speed and reliability. This was ultimately the focus that enabled the company to achieve further growth and profitability, and all without customer input. It's not impossible to make this kind of change based on gut feeling but, unfortunately, very few companies are able to do this. However, software tools can and, in most cases, are able to deliver above-average results in the short term. ◀

In your innovation strategy work, you should therefore focus not on the here and now, but on tomorrow. This is because your market power may lie somewhere completely different than where you would have suspected before reading this book.

3.1.1.2 Target Chaos Across All Hierarchical Levels

Our times are becoming increasingly digitized, in the truest sense of the word. Most companies are still controlled by a few decision-makers. This reduces complexity and is a clear advantage when formulating company goals. In contrast, a small proportion of companies are controlled by many decision-makers or by decision-making bodies, and therefore tend to be less focused and at the same time less willing to make decisions. This situation can be compared to an endless piano keyboard. Individual decision-makers are not able to keep track of everything, while too many decision-makers focus right down to the last detail, but as an organization they are usually very sluggish. Between these two extremes there is a small number of companies that manage the corporate balancing act, even if they are a dying breed. So what is special about the companies that manage to stay in the middle? These companies often show common interests in the immediate environment of the decision-makers, who all pull largely in the same direction. They fight for the same goals. As a result, energies are focused, and maximum progress is generated. This progress feels even more effective today than in the past because this kind of behavior is becoming more and more of a unique selling point in most industries. Make sure you have clear ideas about this issue and form a innovation strategy project team that unites behind your main goal.

3.1.1.3 Clear Strategic Results Can Only Be Achieved by Analyzing Complicated and Complex Processes

People generally want nothing more than simple answers to complex questions. Unfortunately, we have to disappoint you at this point. There are no simple answers to complex questions. Or are there? We believe—at least in innovation strategy work—that there are some simple solutions (see Fig. 3.2). However, you can only achieve these if you approach tasks in a certain way. If you want things to be simple, you have to derive them using a complex process of disassembly. You can only get a good result by breaking down the

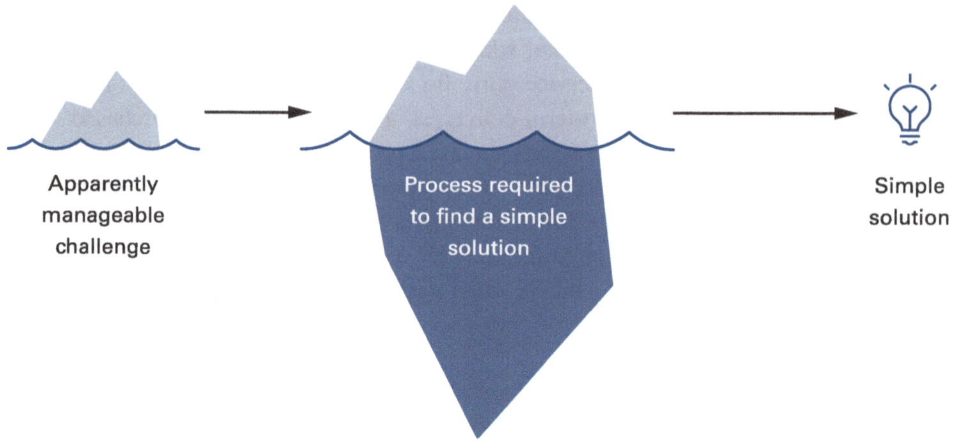

Fig. 3.2 Solving complicated or complex problems. (Source: H&F Solutions GmbH/www.hf-solutions.co)

target state into virtually all its individual parts, examining them and then presenting the whole as a simple result.

When faced with a strategic challenge, the solution often seems easy to achieve. After all, your company's goals are clear to everyone. You start a strategy development process, bring in a couple of external consultants to back it up, and you can come up with a simple solution. After all, that's the goal: a simple and manageable solution. Unfortunately, innovation strategy work doesn't function like that, and simplicity doesn't forgive mistakes. Every detail must be right if you want to achieve a simple result. Everything must be self-explanatory, and this process takes a lot of patience and time. If we look generally at strategic development in companies, not even 20% of the companies that have begun developing a sound strategy manage to develop and implement it successfully. In more than 50% of cases, strategy processes fail without the participants knowing why. In order to prevent failure at this stage, everyone involved must be aware that strategy work is hard, painstaking work. In-depth processes must take place that break down the topic being worked on into all its individual parts. The main focus here is on the methodical derivation of multiple possible solutions. To do this, you have to work out a complete network of potential solutions and estimate the probabilities of their success. It is only possible to obtain clear strategic results once you have developed this extensive network. At the beginning of this process, many aspects appear complicated but, the more you work your way into the subject, the more comprehensible the work environment will be and the clearer the possible solutions will become.

How Do I Approach a Complex Task in Order to Obtain a Simple Solution?

Take your apparently simple challenge and start to break it down into individual building blocks. To do this, it is a good idea to record the individual connections that come to light in some kind of mind map on a whiteboard (or using your preferred medium). After the fourth or fifth branching at the latest you will encounter conditions and dependencies that you cannot simply ignore. However, you will still have to solve these details to get a simple solution to the challenge. You may get lucky and immediately find an isolated solution to a detailed problem, but this will not happen in most cases. Identify the problem that has occurred and begin your thought process anew, but take a different mental route or adopt a different viewpoint. In pursuing your second problem, you will likely recognize dependencies on the first problem, and the same is true when thinking through a third possible path or detailed process. Gradually, as you go through the process, a network of possible solutions and solutions begins to form. Many connections that were previously hidden begin to become clear. If you now think through this process long enough and begin to refine your solutions to include the increasing number of interdependencies, you will overcome the seemingly unsolvable, complex approach and obtain a simple solution that nearly everyone can deal with. And remember: Don't give up, even if it feels like you are already going through hell.

3.1.1.4 "You and I" Instead of "We"

We humans are a reflection of our thoughts. If we think using a "You and I" attitude, then we will subconsciously also act this way. This is usually already apparent at the start of a cooperation. Poor understanding of each other costs an enormous amount of money and, above all, time in the course of a strategy project.

Especially in the service industry and corporate supply chain environments, where consultants work, the wrong attitude can have a huge impact on output (see Fig. 3.3). This is because, as a decision-maker, you don't want to play both sides. You will probably want to achieve your goal with as little effort as possible. In adopting the "I" attitude, project participants are often only interested in satisfying their own interests and not in efficiently achieving a common goal. In fact, the pursuit of the common goal should be everyone's top priority, based on a strong "we" culture. In order to strengthen this "we"

Fig. 3.3 "Me" vs. "Us" attitudes. (Source: H&F Solutions GmbH/www.hf-solutions.co)

culture, we have spent the past few years developing the *H&F High Speed and Efficiency Concept*. This concept is characterized by the application of strategic target management, performance culture development, and performance enhancement methods, thereby providing an active contribution to the achievement of specific objectives. Within this concept both sides pursue the same goal together. We will provide more detail on this later on.

3.1.1.5 The Industrial Age Has Given Up Its Throne

Welcome to the world of digitization! For some, it may still seem like a fad, while for others, it is the only way to remain successful. There is no denying that, with the advent of smartphones, the industrial age is finally on the decline. On the positive side, the industrial age brought prosperity, convenience, and health, while on the negative side, it has given rise to pollution, exploitation of the working class, and modern warfare. We now need to understand that these issues are no longer the things that will determine corporate success in the future. Today, issues such as environmental protection, ownership of information, networking, and changes in the labor market are at the forefront. In the future, we will have to deal with these issues and generate opportunities from them. To do this, it is worth pausing for a moment and reflecting on yourself or your company (see Fig. 3.4):

No matter what your current status, in the course of your innovation strategy work your future goals should include a large share of assets from the digital age. Figure 3.5 provides a forecast of the topics that will play a key role in the next 20 years.

You could also add digital health and enterprise content management to this list. With regard to the success of your projects and your company, it is now important to learn to deal

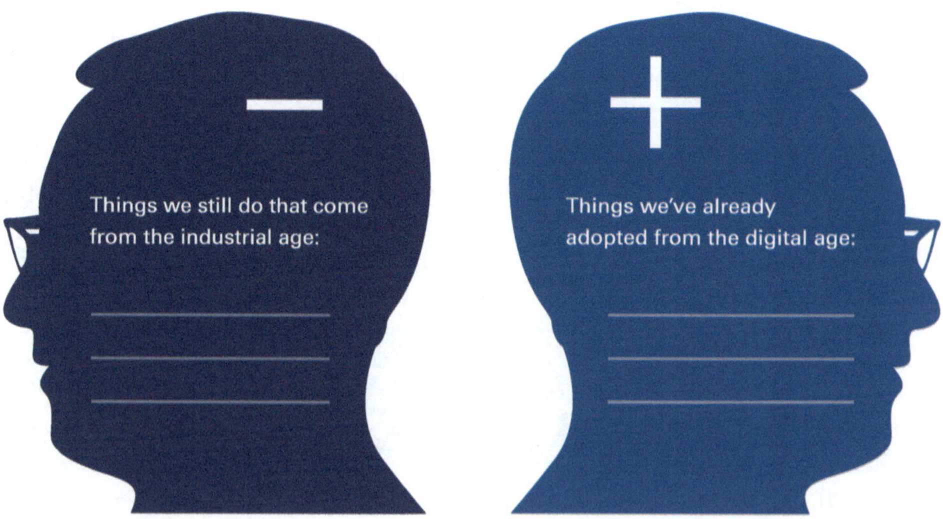

Fig. 3.4 The industrial age vs. the digital age. (Source: H&F Solutions GmbH/www.hf-solutions.co)

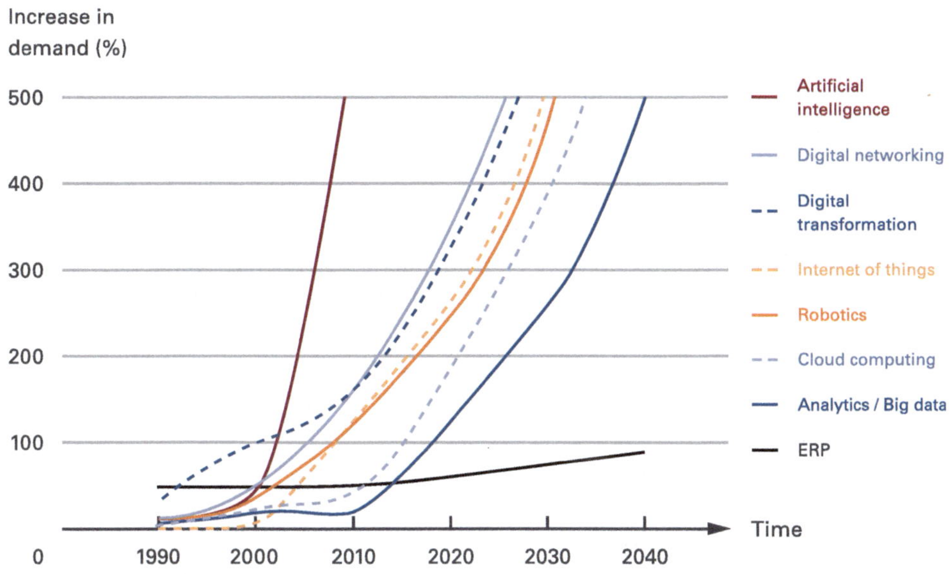

Fig. 3.5 Forecast of growth rates for major themes in the digital age. (Source: H&F Solutions GmbH/www.hf-solutions.co)

with these themes and look for the opportunities they provide. Digitization won't wait and requires you to actively embrace it.

3.1.1.6 We Are No Longer Wandering Through Our Imaginary Universe—We Have Arrived in the Midst of Global Competition

Networking not only brings people and companies closer together, it also rearranges all of our processes, all the way from the customer to the raw material supplier. This creates transparency and automation in places that would have been unthinkable just 10 years ago. In the future, knowledge and technology can be brought to almost any place on Earth, and this will help to ensure that nearly all developing countries have the opportunity to participate significantly in the global economy by 2050. In the past, every company knew almost all of its competitors but, in the future, this will no longer be the case in spite of increasing digitization. This is because competitors will regularly disappear and new ones will emerge. This also means that companies will have to face new challenges in the coming years, especially then it comes to speed and momentum. The box below lists what we think are the most important challenges facing innovation strategy development.

Effects of Global Competition on Corporate Innovation Strategies

- Increase in the speed of technology transfer
- Rapid emergence of new markets
- Abrupt disappearance of existing markets

- Working against an invisible corporate environment
- Shorter half-lives due to the new throwaway society

Increase in the Speed of Technology Transfer
Due to new telecommunication media, information today spreads many times faster than in the past. As a result, knowledge also spreads faster, and knowledge is the basis for technological development. If we then combine this knowledge with cultural influences, technologies will emerge somewhere in the world that would not have emerged elsewhere. This leads to a further increase in the speed of development, which in turn replaces existing structures faster. Ultimately, an innovation strategy shouldn't contain technological restrictions, but should remain sufficiently abstract so that the strategy can follow technological change and, ideally, further expand its existing competitive advantages.

Rapid Emergence of New Markets
Where markets used to be meticulously analyzed over a period of perhaps 1 or 2 years, nowadays new markets are created or existing markets collapse over the same period. It is important to understand that major global growth markets are not to be found in the western world, but rather everywhere else. If your business is looking to grow, taking a close look at growth markets should provide you with plenty of opportunities.

Abrupt Disappearance of Existing Markets
Just as new markets emerge, today's markets also disappear within 2–5 years. The internal combustion engine is probably the best-known example that is slated to disappear within the next few years. The majority of companies will still be able to delay this process, but they will not be able to stop it. Just as microfilm, drawing boards, and floppy disks disappeared in the past, things like landline telephony and PCs will disappear in the next few years. Your products may not be directly affected today, but it is highly likely that your environment will change fundamentally. For example, many countries around the world have simply skipped the era of landline telephony and their citizens' first phone was a mobile phone. It is therefore important to ensure that your strategic direction is balanced in the respect too.

Working Against an Invisible Corporate Environment
While your competitors perhaps used to have their offices across the street or a couple of blocks away, today there is usually no-one sitting around nearby. Competitors are also not necessarily to be found at the leading trade fairs that still exist. For many of today's companies, amongst the huge number of orders being processed, it is no longer clear who got the orders they lost. Even worse are the losses of potential sales that a company doesn't even get to bid for. In global markets, competition is even less transparent, and your competitors become completely invisible. There are many reasons why this is the case, and addressing them here is beyond the scope of this book. In the same way, it is beyond the

scope of any business to search for invisible competitors, and companies simply have to learn to deal with the market in a different way. It is therefore important that future strategies don't focus too much on the competition, but rather on the maximum benefit for the customer. There are numerous experts in this field in their respective markets. And remember, always be on the lookout for the best people for your team so you can generate an edge and start working against the invisible corporate environment.

Shorter Half-Lives Due to the New Throwaway Society
With the advent of global competition, values and norms have been remixed. The trend is increasingly toward a throwaway society and a corresponding shortening of product half-lives. This is particularly noticeable not in the type and duration of strategies, but rather in the lifespan of companies. Whereas 20 years ago the average lifespan of a company was more than 30 years, today it is only 10 years. If you see your company and its divisions as self-sufficient units, it won't make much sense in the future to develop innovation strategies with a time horizon of more than 3 years. It is better to introduce appropriate thinking, actions, and product cycles that are adapted to this state of permanent change and shorter half-lives. The same also applies to employee churn and, today, about one third of all new employees switch employers again within 2 years.

3.1.1.7 Generation Y and Individual Biorhythms

Today we have different challenges than 20–30 years ago but the core problem is the same as it was back then. The generation of decision-makers (usually aged 30-plus) is followed by a young adolescent generation whose assumptions lead to a different understanding of values and different views. The times of orderly working hours and clear instructions seem to be over. As is well known, fixed working hours and strict rules date back to the time of industrialization. Now, however, we are in the age of digitization. IT systems are becoming interactive, applications are becoming more and more standardized, and the ten-finger typing system has probably become obsolete in many places. It is now a matter of adapting to issues such as flexible working hours and clear targets for 'Generation Y' employees. After taking up this challenge at H&F Solutions, the first major effect was that sick leave dropped to zero days within 12 months. Everyone was allowed to decide for themselves when and when not to work, and how. This resulted in a completely different perception of sick leave, so that our employees reduced their own workload during weak phases in order to go full throttle again once they felt better. Now no-one has to rush to clock in at 7 am, and each employee can integrate his work into his daily routine in the best possible way. Later in this chapter, you will learn why shared values, emotions, and feelings play a major role in all of this, and to what extent they are a help or a hindrance to your ERP projects.

3.1.1.8 Silicon Valley Working Practices Are Leaving Us behind

Have you ever wondered how a company like Facebook could grow so fast and become so large in just a few years? It is obvious that marketing alone cannot create such a successful network in this form. How did they manage it? In the industrial age, there were no such success stories. And if there were, they were companies backed up by big, physical factories that you could touch. Huge numbers of employees walked through the factory gates in the morning to make these successful products. Today, companies are emerging that make things you can't touch, and these companies are growing even faster than the factories of the industrial age. But how is that possible? New employees have to be trained, so how can companies with more than 10,000 employees emerge within 24 months? Facebook and other Silicon Valley startups were able to do this by creating a vision and a clear mission statement to back it up. They were literally able to convince new employees to give the company the shirt off their back. Obsessed by images of the stated mission, employees adapted the new status quo with the help of cleverly developed strategies. Everyone aligned their actions with the given status quo and everyone in the organization was able to orientate and organize themselves around it. With the help of our strategic goal management method, it is possible for you, too, to align your organization or your project with this methodology and to adapt it to your needs. You can find out how this works in detail in Sect. 3.5 *The H&F High Speed and Efficiency Concept.*

3.1.1.9 China's Secret Weapon Is Still under the Radar

What does China do differently, other than vastly outnumber us? It pursues strategic target management. We would like to refrain from discussing the socialist system at this point and concentrate on China's entrepreneurial actions. How is it that in China large airports, megacities, and huge dams are built at a record pace? In extreme cases, entire villages are relocated to make these projects possible. The answer lies in reducing bureaucracy to a minimum. The amount of energy that goes into achieving these goals is much higher there than in Western countries. The result is a highly efficient and effective way of working. Run a quick self-check on your last two projects or tasks. Can you see any parallels? Companies that are managed in an agile and goal-oriented manner can easily make the transition to this kind unbureaucratic working practices. This might not work immediately for you and your next innovation strategy project, but you can still try removing layers of bureaucracy one slice at a time while you are implementing it. It is a very liberating feeling.

3.1.1.10 Gains in Efficiency Are Cancelled Out by Disproportionate Consumption

Promising increased efficiency is today's favorite mantra for virtually all areas of human endeavor. This ranges from saving materials, through employees using the latest machines, to sales structures in which almost the entire field sales force can be eliminated. Theoretically, companies should hardly be able to save themselves from mass efficiency and the corresponding limitless success. Such increases in efficiency are being implemented in practice but, unfortunately, humans are still driven by their basic instincts. In this case, this means striving for maximum consumption, and it is this instinct that nullifies gains in efficiency faster than they occur. Ironically, it is relatively easy to economize modestly and do a few selected things perfectly rather than trying to improve everything at once—and you only have everything if you consume on a large scale. If you manage to be modest in your strategic choices you can achieve independence and entrepreneurial freedom fairly quickly, and also react flexibly to digital change.

Summary

It is not uncommon for companies or people to generate more confusion than commercial clout in their strategy processes. To counteract this situation, we have highlighted 10 thematic questions that should not be overlooked in any innovation strategy process:

1. Who will wield market power in the future?
2. Goal chaos—is everyone fighting for the same goal?
3. Has the strategy team derived a sufficient number of solution paths?
4. Does the strategy team have a 'we' rather than a 'you/me' attitude?
5. Are the company's goals aligned with the digital age?
6. Has any thought been given to increasing global competition?
7. Is the strategy suitably oriented toward the next generation?
8. Does the strategy contain enough 'Silicon Valley' philosophy?
9. Are our work methods efficient enough to withstand permanent change?
10. Are our gains in efficiency sufficient to offset disproportionate consumption?

◀

3.2 Concentrating on the Goal: Full Speed Ahead

Isn't it simply good manners to go over budget and over time on a project? We think that's part of the story, but why is this so? This is simply because only projects in which budget and time are tight can be taken seriously. In companies where this is not the case, slack is a major driver of inefficiency. A few weeks into a project we are often asked by our clients whether we shouldn't perhaps generate more effort in order to achieve the project goal. The answer is 'No'. We have to strive for a state in which a shortage of resources, time, and money results in a concentrated work rhythm. Anyone who is always on schedule with their projects has definitely set their goals too low.

The following sections work step-by-step through the individual topics that we think form the indispensable basis of every innovation strategy project. At this point, you can double check your project performance. If only one of the following topics is poorly addressed, it will eat away at your performance. Generally speaking, you can subtract about 5% from the intended 100% maximum performance for each poorly staffed topic (see Fig. 3.6). This kind of summary is sure to please your management.

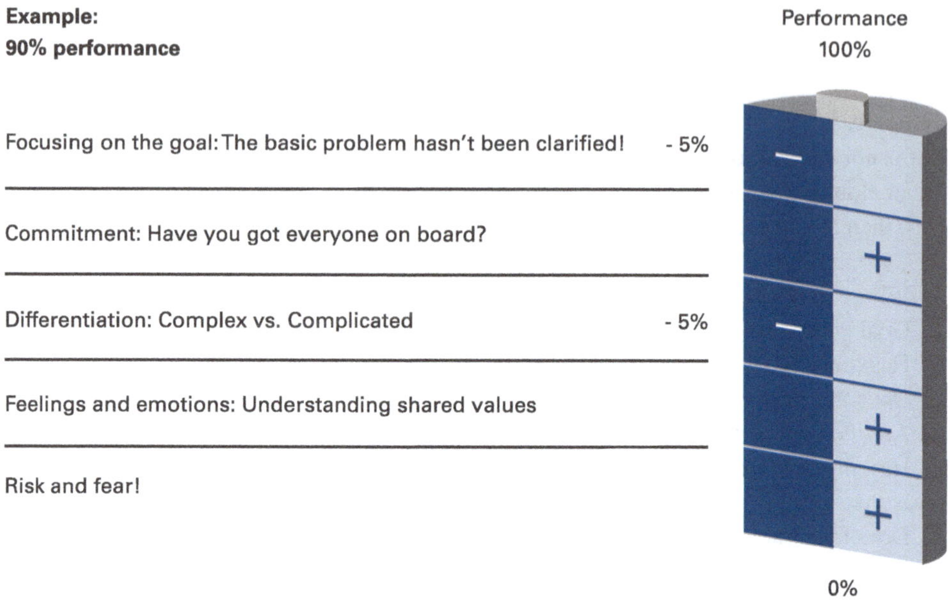

Fig. 3.6 Focusing on the goal—output vs. input orientation. (Source: H&F Solutions GmbH/www.hf-solutions.co)

3.2.1 Does a Strategy Project Have to Be a Nightmare? Why Complex Projects Will Always Fail in Terms of Planning and Timing

If a project becomes too complex it will fail. This is why strategy projects often turn into a farce. In order to be able to solve complex problems, you have to delve deeper and deeper into the details. If you are input-oriented, you will drift ever further toward questions of detail, whereas if you remain output-oriented, questions will already be addressed and corrected at a medium level, so that you will rarely drift off into detail-heavy nirvana. The following section tells you in concrete terms how to implement this idea.

3.2.1.1 Focusing on the Goal: The Basic Problem Has Not Been Clarified!

"Mr. Hertfelder and Mr. Futterknecht, we have invited you here today so that we can discuss our new ERP and networking strategy with you." Initial discussions with new customers often begin this way. The customer has outlined a project and has already determined its rough path. He now wants to take the safe route and buy in any missing expertise from outside the company. In principle, there is nothing wrong with this approach. The important thing to consider is that external consultants are bound to focus on creating value. In order to find out more, it is essential when initiating proceedings that we start by questioning precisely this benefit. Why do you want to carry out the release upgrade? Why are you doing it at all? Why do you want to achieve this goal? A qualified answer is not usually forthcoming. Having said that, it is hard to imagine that companies want to implement projects without being able to derive a profitable benefit from them. Or is it? In the case described, the customer answered that the software manufacturer demands a new release. A new version is available and the old version is only supported until the end of next year. The customer had no reason of his own to push ahead, and therefore no 'fundamental benefit'. This means that no matter what implementing the release will cost, it will be a bad project for the customer because it lacks a tangible benefit. We don't need to go into detail here about how such projects are handled in terms of acceptance by those involved, even if they are handled correctly from a technical point of view.

We regularly find that the justification for the project has not been clarified and that conviction is lacking because no clear goal has been defined. How can a project be successful if the benefit is not clarified from the outset or—even worse—simply doesn't exist? The answer "Because it has to be done" is not sufficient justification at this point. In cases like this, you will see that project participants lose interest in the project shortly after it starts and that the quality the project delivers will be suboptimal.

In this case, however, we knew that about 20% of the software manufacturer's customers were still running the old version, and that a medium-term phase-out of support for the old version was not even possible. In the workshop we ran, we were able to work out with the customer that a changeover within a timeframe of 12–15 months would make the most sense. During our discussions, it became apparent that eliminating more than 400 customizations before the changeover would be far more beneficial than switching to the new version immediately. This strategy was implemented and, in the end, 14 of the custom features remained and the effort involved in implementing the new release was reduced by more than half.

Without our persistent questioning, the customer would have headed straight into the release change and would never have realized the benefit of reducing the number of customizations. This brings us directly to our *Performance Booster #1*:

Important

Performance Booster #1:

NEVER START A PROJECT WITHOUT FIRST CLEARLY DEFINING THE EXPECTED BENEFITS. ◄

As soon as the goal and the benefit of a project are clearly defined, acceptance on the part of the project participants increases and thus also efficiency and the degree of success (see Fig. 3.7).

In this case, if we had directly fulfilled the client's requirement, the following conflict of interest would probably have arisen:

The employees would want to carry out the release change as diligently as possible without clarifying why they are doing it (i.e., aiming for perfection and a correspondingly large effort), whereas the boss would like to execute the project using the fewest means possible (i.e., as few resources as possible).

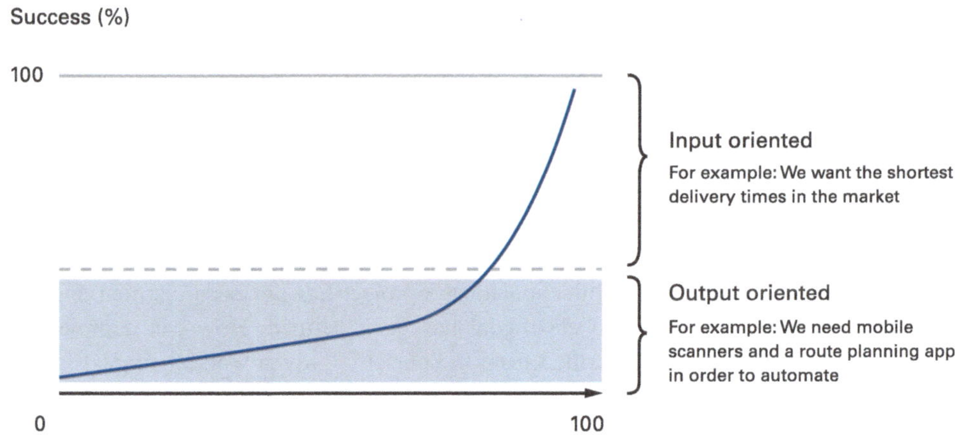

Fig. 3.7 The relationship between success and the clarity of your goals: output vs. input orientation. (Source: H&F Solutions GmbH/www.hf-solutions.co)

3.2.1.2 Commitment: Do You Have Everyone on Board?

As with any journey, employees need a basic understanding and benefit of any contribution they make to a project, and all project participants need to have an equally high level of understanding. Everyone needs to believe strongly that what they are doing will provide a benefit. If this is the case, everyone involved will feel closely connected to your project.

Your employees, project participants, management team, and everyone else involved will therefore need the same (or at least a similar) level of conviction regarding the achievement of the project goal. As a manager, you will only be able to implement projects quickly and efficiently if you can instill this feeling in your team. In doing so, it is important not to fall back into familiar patterns of top-down leadership. After all, employees without their own inner drive rarely feel compelled to go beyond their limits. We don't need to explain to you at this point how a project turns out if running it feels like fighting a losing battle.

But please don't start by trying to solve this problem with money alone. If you think money is a motivator, you are on the wrong track. Money cannot motivate in the long term. True motivation can only be achieved by providing challenging tasks and corresponding feelings of success. Such success can then be financially rewarded later on.

To help you visualize this idea, simply assign yourself to one of the quadrants illustrated in Fig. 3.8.

Important

Performance Booster #2:

MAKE SURE YOUR TEAM UNDERSTANDS THE GOAL AND IS COMMITTED TO IT (EVERYONE SHOULD BENEFIT). ◄

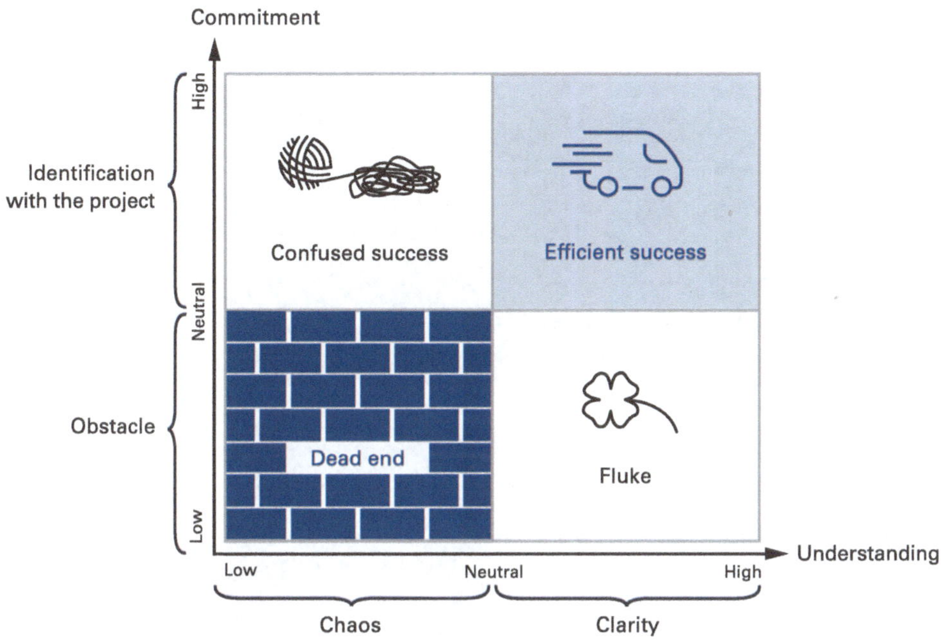

Fig. 3.8 Commitment and understanding as success factors. (Source: H&F Solutions GmbH/www.hf-solutions.co)

To conclude this section, we would like to point out that you should never approach innovation strategy topics with logic and rationality. Positive output only comes from a purely emotional discussion, and you have to deal with this aspect first in order to move forward. Build on emotions and feelings! This way you can motivate people and actively gain their commitment.

3.2.1.3 Differentiating Between Complicated and Complex Systems

Now things get a little complicated. Or perhaps complex? At this point it is sufficient if you understand the basic difference. If a large system can be abstracted and structured, and the factors influencing it are known, it is described as "complicated". However, such a system can still be described on the basis of our knowledge of it, and we can control it by manipulating the factors influencing it.

A system that we can describe, but whose influencing factors are not known, and which can therefore neither be controlled nor planned, is described as complex. We also talk about complexity when the influencing factors are known but the relationships between them cannot be described. This means that the system in question cannot be fully interpreted.

Why is this distinction so fundamentally important for an ERP project? Because different measures have to be taken when addressing these distinct types of challenges. Many decision makers are not aware of this difference. People often try to make complex projects and schemes manageable using a rigid plan. But how can you set up a plan for

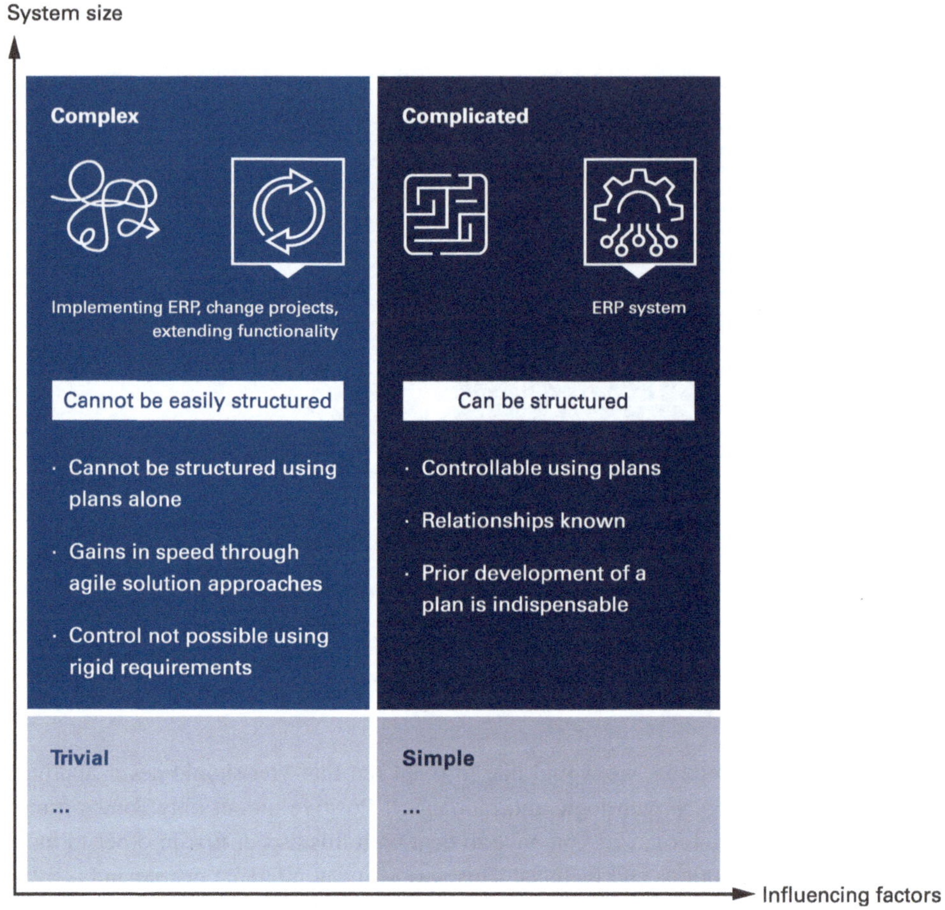

Fig. 3.9 Complex vs. complicated. (Source: H&F Solutions GmbH/www.hf-solutions.co)

which you understand neither the dependencies nor the relationships? This is simply not possible for complex projects. In this case, you have to react to situations as they arise and solve the challenges they present.

As Fig. 3.9 shows, software, strategy, and management projects are typical complex projects. They have such a large number of influencing factors that cannot be addressed using a rigid plan or a fixed methodology. Here, approaches such as agile management or OKRs (see Sect. 3.5.1) are beneficial, as they allow short-term situational intervention.

You will need some kind of roadmap for these kinds of projects, so that you know roughly where you are headed and you can define some basic cornerstones. However, creating an elaborate plan would be completely superfluous, since the necessary control measures and ongoing changes would require disproportionate effort. It is better to apply your energy to achieving project progress from day one.

Important

Performance Booster #3:

IN COMPLEX PROJECTS, DON'T WASTE TIME AND ENERGY ON UNNECESSARY PLANNING. INSTEAD, USE YOUR ENERGY TO PRODUCE TANGIBLE PROGRESS. ◀

3.2.1.4 Emotions and Shared Values

The Effect of Emotions

At this point, take a couple of minutes and listen to yourself thinking. What thoughts are going through your mind right now? Researchers have found that about 95% of our thoughts do not result from reflection or consideration, but are instead guided by our emotions, which can trigger positive or negative reactions. Here, we would like to take a little excursion into this fascinating topic.

Basically, emotions are either primary or secondary. The approach we are familiar with names seven primary emotions: fear, happiness, anger, sadness, curiosity, disgust and contempt. From these, in turn, a variety of secondary emotions can then be derived. These can be emotions such as pride, confidence, security, shame, guilt, or courage. So why is understanding these emotions important for successful projects? Because the most important factor in any project is the human factor, and humans are largely controlled by emotions, or at least they act based on their emotions. Our brain is responsible for this, although if you take a closer look, the brain is simply an organ that performs its function, just like our other organs. Our brain continuously evaluates what is right or wrong, guided the whole time by our emotions. Anyone who can master their emotions will be able to focus fully on a project and thereby make real gains in speed and quality.

As shown in Fig. 3.10, it is optimal if the emotional boosters outweigh those that step on the brakes. Such a relationship thus generates additional speed and, in turn, faster achievement of your goals. And this means success, which leads to a better return on investment, and so on.

Important

Performance Booster #4:

DON'T TURN PROJECT MEETINGS INTO PURELY CRITICAL EVENTS. ENSURE CLARITY AND ACCEPTANCE. PRODUCING INSIGHT MAKES IT EASIER TO GENERATE LEARNING PROGRESS. WORK WITH ONE ANOTHER INSTEAD OF AGAINST ONE ANOTHER. ◀

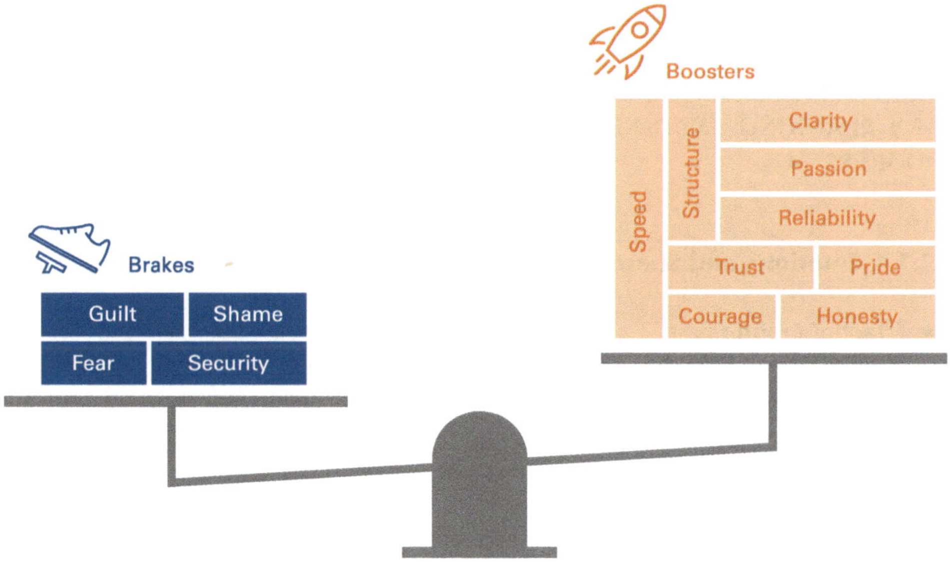

Fig. 3.10 Emotional boosters vs. emotional brakes. (Source: H&F Solutions GmbH/www.hf-solutions.co)

Decision Makers and Fear

The worst thing that can happen to your decision-makers is that they get scared, mainly because fear can rarely be suppressed. The best way to counteract this is to create meaning for the decision-maker—a fundamental element in any strategy project. This is because the process of transformation creates the precise opposite of security, namely uncertainty. If you succeed in dispelling your team's fears, you will be able to avoid potential flashpoints.

However, a degree of courage is essential. You simply cannot plan the effects and results of innovation strategy projects, and you have to consciously make a 'bet' on which risks will turn into major suppliers of results. You have to consciously get your team to make this bet with you.

This process is often led by external personnel who are experienced in this kind of work and are thus able to approach the topic with a clear view that is free from team-internal interrelationships.

Consistency

For us, consistency in this context means sticking to commitments and obligations. More precisely, it is about being able to rely on each other. Especially in management, most decision-makers find it difficult to make agreements and stick to them.

▶ An agreement is an arrangement or binding understanding regarding an expectation or agreement that is to be fulfilled by a predefined future point in time.

The goal is for employees and management to **bilaterally** adhere to the agreements that they previously made **together**. This is the only way to develop a performance culture that everyone reliably adheres to and that works toward a mutually planned goal.

Example

We ask a highly specific question: "Ms. Doe, your job is to take care of implementing work package ABC by next week. Do we have an agreement on topic XY?" You will quickly notice if someone is happy to 'sign off' on this kind of verbal agreement or whether they express concern. The following week, when you ask Ms. Doe if the work package was successfully implemented, she may tell you early on that she couldn't implement the work package for some reason or other. You can then act on this and say: "But we had an agreement. . ." The essence of this scenario is that you can demonstrate to Ms. Doe that she should have adhered to the agreement or should have given timely notice of any change to the agreement. However, Ms. Doe clearly decided not to communicate (e.g., she showed unreliable behavior) and thus gave the other team members no opportunity to **jointly** work on the agreed goals. ◀

If employees do not adhere to agreements, they become unreliable, and you need to appropriately and clearly address such unreliable behavior. Initially, this creates a sense of shame and consternation in the employee, but the next time an agreement is made, the employee will not want to get into such a situation again. This engenders increased reliability in your employees and your organization, and helps to generate a corresponding performance culture.

▶ It is important that you always make agreements in advance or at the outset of the work so that everyone involved always has clear expectations. This way, when an obligation becomes due, you can clearly state it and demand its completion.

Discipline

In this context, we associate discipline with implementing a culture of change using our efficiency concept so that the planned goal cannot be supplanted by external influences (such as day-to-day operations, for example). By adhering to intelligently selected targets, task packages, appropriate project organization processes, and strategy targets, an implementation should be driven forward consistently and with discipline, and a high probability of successful implementation should be achieved through the previously generated acceptance.

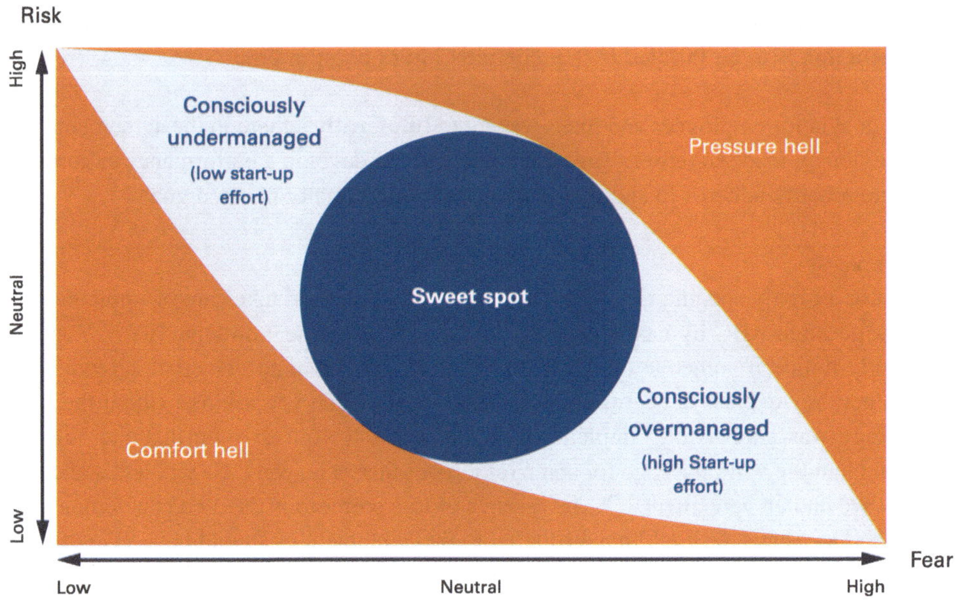

Fig. 3.11 Risk vs. fear. (Source: H&F Solutions GmbH/www.hf-solutions.co)

3.2.1.5 Risk and Fear

If you still have major doubts at this point, you should possibly consider turning back and not starting the project. There is nothing worse than crashing and burning under pressure. Let's compare this experience to building a house. By the time you sign the loan agreements at the latest, you should have made up your mind whether you want to go through with it. From that point on, there is no turning back and the only thing left for you to do is to accept the risk and the fear that comes with it.

However, don't ignore your gut feelings when making this kind of decision. Innovation strategy is not rational and therefore not always precisely evaluable. At this point, you should try to assemble the necessary pieces of the project puzzle (or at least those that you currently recognize) into an overall picture, within the context of the uncertainty that still exists. To make it easier, use Fig. 3.11 to help arrange your overall project, your subprojects and, if necessary, your project participants.

Important

Performance Booster #5:

IF YOU MANAGE TO STRIKE A BALANCE BETWEEN RISK AND FEAR, YOU WILL GENERATE A CATALYST THAT WILL GIVE YOUR PROJECT AN ENORMOUS FORWARD BOOST. ◀

Defining "Hope"

"Hope" is the desire that a specific event occurs without actively doing anything to encourage it. This is, at least, our understanding of the term. The probability that ERP projects will "hopefully" turn out well without active management is close to zero. Never rely on hope, but instead try to work out and prepare your issues accordingly. Try to provide clarity from the very beginning. Sometimes, simply not starting a project too soon can be seen as a success. A common alternative is to prepare a project in advance and push the start date 4–9 months into the future. This gives you time to finish current projects first, so that you can then focus more effectively on the new (planned) project.

3.2.1.6 Practical Example for Self-Reflection

Example

One of our first strategy projects involved introducing ERP at a mechanical engineering company. We were quickly able to establish a basis of trust with the customer, who soon handed over the project management role to us. Thanks to our agile project team and our ability to decipher complex issues (we are, after all, mechanical engineers), we were able to clarify the following points in advance:

- Development, together with management, of clear goals
- Commitment from the project team to ensure the achievement of the planned goals
- Advance elimination of many doubts through many conversations
- Setting a roadmap for the first 6 weeks with associated (sub-)goals

◀

Do you see how you don't need to do an awful lot of work up front to lay the groundwork for a project? Nevertheless, some of the remaining unanswered questions are as follows:

Questions

- Do I have to act differently and ask different questions for larger projects?
- Is there a danger of losing the overview in a large project team?
- Is it necessary to completely convince every member of a project team?
- Will I manage to eliminate all negative emotions (fear, despair, insecurity, and so on)?
- Will the project be successful if management doesn't back up the project team's decisions?
- Is there a high probability of failure, even if all tips are considered?

All these questions can be answered "No" at this point. If you as digital leader, project manager, or team member have done your homework, the project will most likely be successful. The following sections will show you how to successfully implement strategy projects using our guidelines.

3.2.2 The Mechanics of Management: Why Traditional Methods Will No Longer Be Effective in the Future

You are probably familiar with the scenario: the boss sets the goals and communicates them to the next hierarchical level down (i.e., middle management). They are then passed on to the responsible department heads and subsequently to individual members of staff. This is a classic example of the waterfall principle, as we know it in most German companies. Halfway through the project at the latest, no-one knows anymore what project goal the organization is actually working on. The result is that, without interaction, long-term focus cannot be maintained. The goal should be that every employee can contribute to the success of the company and understands how and with what he or she can make a contribution. A variety of tools and methodologies have been developed for this purpose in recent years, and we would like to give you a few tips on how to apply them:

3.2.2.1 Direction of Thinking vs. Direction of Working (Goal → Start vs. Start → Goal)

Humans are creatures of habit and live in the here and now. Scientific studies have shown that it is easier for humans to deal with things from the past (i.e., to fall back on existing knowledge) than to work creatively and to create new knowledge in the future. However, if you only operate using past knowledge, you will not be able to innovate. Likewise, you will never be able to carry out successful innovation strategy projects, as these are always related to the future.

Hence the following question before we go into more detail on how to differentiate the two points mentioned above:

Are you more likely to be able to innovate or cause a revolution based on past experience, or is this more likely to happen if you work on a goal that lies in the future?

We want to clarify that you have to proceed differently with your direction of thinking and your direction of working (see Fig. 3.12):

Experience: Based on the Past But in the Here and Now (Start → Finish)

Let's discuss in more detail what past experience means in this context. Experience is practical work based on knowledge gained from the past, which could also be referred to as routines. These can be further optimized with the gain of further experience.

Optimization: Based on Experience

We are talking here only about optimizing existing things. Whether this meets the requirements of the future, however, is not certain. If you look at the past, you only work on optimizing existing things. And what do you get out of it? You will only be able to make tiny adjustments that advance your company in very small steps. To create the same effect from a deductive goal -> start thought process, you have to complete many optimization steps to reach your goal. You should be on the lookout for things that will solve the problems you need to overcome, whether these are factors that come from the future or

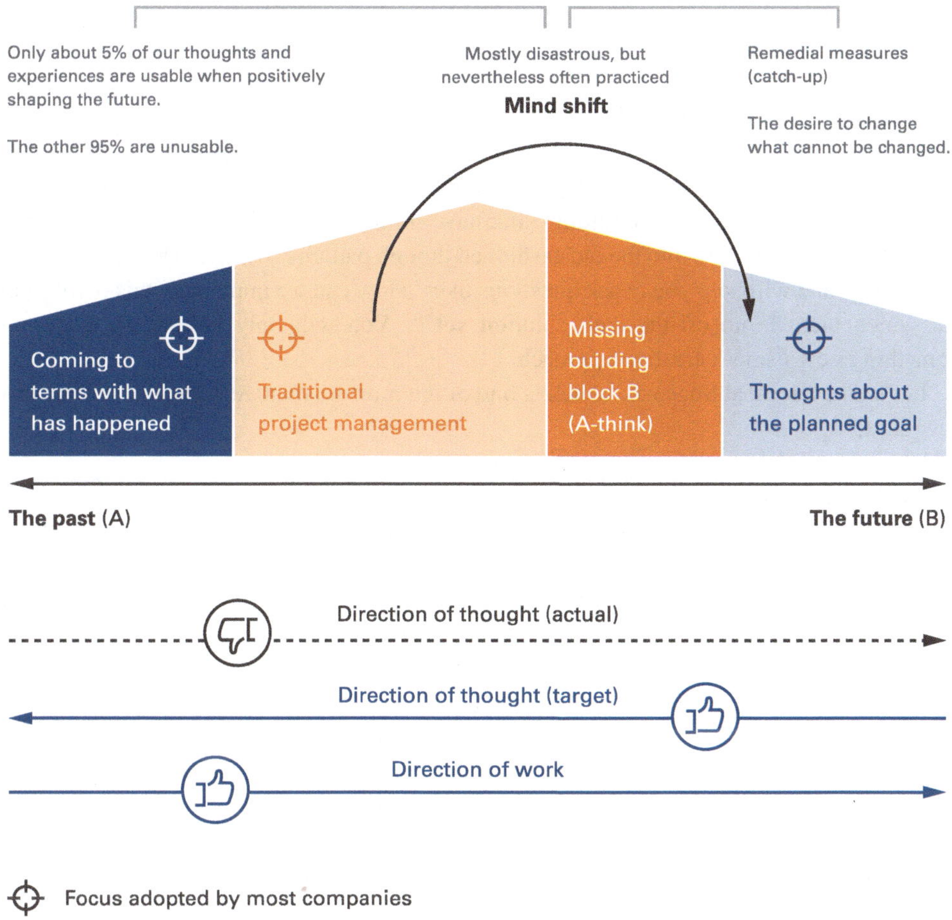

Fig. 3.12 Direction of thinking vs. direction of working. (Source: H&F Solutions GmbH/www.hf-solutions.co)

from the past. Your starting point is the question of how to make today's state better than yesterday's. You will then build on this experience and use it to deduce how not to do things and how to do them better in the future.

Back to the Future: Vision-Led (Goal → Start)

The core of an innovation strategy project is usually future-oriented. An attempt is made to achieve a target state that doesn't yet exist in the medium term (approx. 1–3 years) or in the long term (4–7 years). The target state should be clearly different from the current state. And should be a significant improvement on the current state of the business. A strategy project doesn't exist to optimize the current state, but rather to realize a mission statement through visionary or emotional forces that create a momentum for implementation.

Strategy projects that are exclusively related to the past are no different to a tranquilizer pill for management that is happy with minimal advances.

Revolution/Innovation: Based on the Future!

How can I generate a fresh, innovative wind for my strategy projects? In contrast to start -> finish thinking, you can always derive greater effects from target -> start thinking, which forces you to think about things that have no reference to the past. This approach prevents you from falling into the old-fashioned though patterns such as: "How did we used to do this?" and will help you to ask questions like: "How can we implement this revolution for which there is no off-the-shelf solution yet?". You will only be able to work out something new using a creative approach.

Let's take a look at Space-X, which is one of the most innovative companies of the last few decades.

The Space-X Example

Elon Musk's Space-X program is a great example. Space-X has the goal of getting people to Mars. Using NASA's current technology (which sends expensive rockets into orbit and then lets them burn up) it is virtually impossible to bring thousands of tons of necessary payload into orbit for the space glider to Mars. Elon Musk formulated the requirement for cheaper rockets that can transport material into space like a kind of 'space taxi' and that can be recycled by bringing them back to Earth and re-using them. To do this, the team at Space-X turned conventional thinking on its head, with the result that more than half of the required rocket components can be easily and quickly ordered on today's market. Tests that have been broadly covered by the media show that these 'space taxis' already work and generate 'only' fuel costs. This is a truly innovative approach that massively reduces manufacturing time and costs. This example makes it clear that the goal would have been impossible to reach using NASA's existing technology. Space-X has achieved a revolutionary result using the innovative approach of low-cost re-usable rockets. ◀

3.2.2.2 Push vs. Pull Management

The core of push management is a focus on 'how'. How do I implement something? What methods do I use? How do we rectify things if something does not work out as planned? In contrast, pull management is concerned with the 'what' and the 'why'. The focus is on the goal and, until this is clarified and defined, there should be absolutely no discussion of the 'how'. Figure 3.13 provides an overview of this topic:

Push Management: Focusing on 'How'

Traditional and weak project sessions always focus on the 'how'. How do I achieve a planned state? The actual discussion is usually no longer about the actual subject (i.e., the project goal or planned result), but rather about how I can achieve a specific thing.

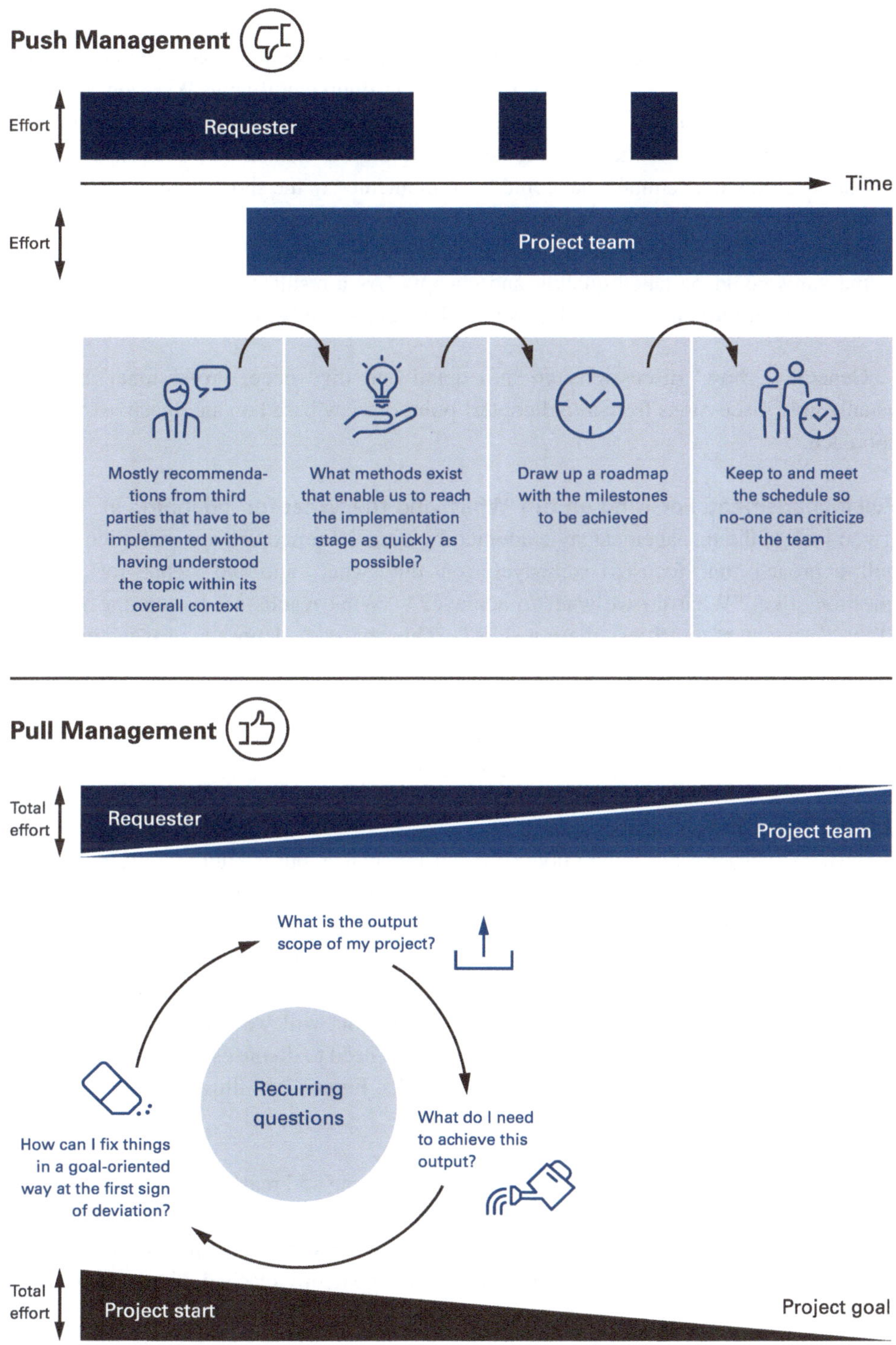

Fig. 3.13 Push vs. pull management (Source: H&F Solutions GmbH/www.hf-solutions.co)

Example

Some time ago a customer asked us to join their in-house digitization committee. The very first meeting was about how to implement digitization now. We soon asked the question: "What for?", which obviously irritated everyone present. After a short pause, the committee chair replied that the decision to digitize had already been made and the plan was now to examine what could be implemented in the shortest possible time. The questions of what goal was being pursued through digitization, or of what impact these measures could achieve wasn't voiced. The meeting was all about how digitization measures could be taken quickly and cheaply. As a result, the committee drew up a catalogue of measures of which less than 10% ended up being implemented. ◀

Generally, 'how' discussions go into detail and dive deep. Professional managers usually hold discussions from a 'helicopter' point of view based on an objective, detached approach.

Pull Management: Focusing on the 'What' and the 'What for' (Planning vs. Results)
If you look at the management style adopted by successful people, you will often find the pull approach that focuses exclusively on the 'what' and the 'what for', asking questions like: "What do we want to achieve?", "What results are we aiming for?", or "Why do we want to achieve these results?". This approach defines a clear picture of the planned goal that every project participant is able to follow, and the additional derivation of added value rounds it out. This allows for the creation of a clear idea of a goal that can be strived for as an anchor in the future. Once such a clear target has been defined, the decisions made automatically have a higher quality.

3.2.2.3 Planning vs. Outcome

In most cases, success or failure doesn't occur by chance, but is rather a reflection of our own behavior. We are guided by our thoughts, and we think constantly without having to actively do anything about it. However, many people simply keep their thoughts to themselves, and the same happens with our plans. We plan something without really knowing what effects it will actually have on the results we achieve. Only when we underpin our planning with the power of our thoughts will we succeed in putting our plans into action. In order to do this successfully, we need to do the exact opposite and plan less. Our focus must be clearly on achieving results. Figure 3.14 illustrates this principle:

Planning and Control
In the planning and control cycle, the focus is on defining and reaching milestones. After a short time, project control is shifted away from results to a culture of adherence to plans, and delivering results at status meetings becomes a fundamental element. Data may even be glossed over so that, on the surface, milestones are apparently reached. Non-compliance is

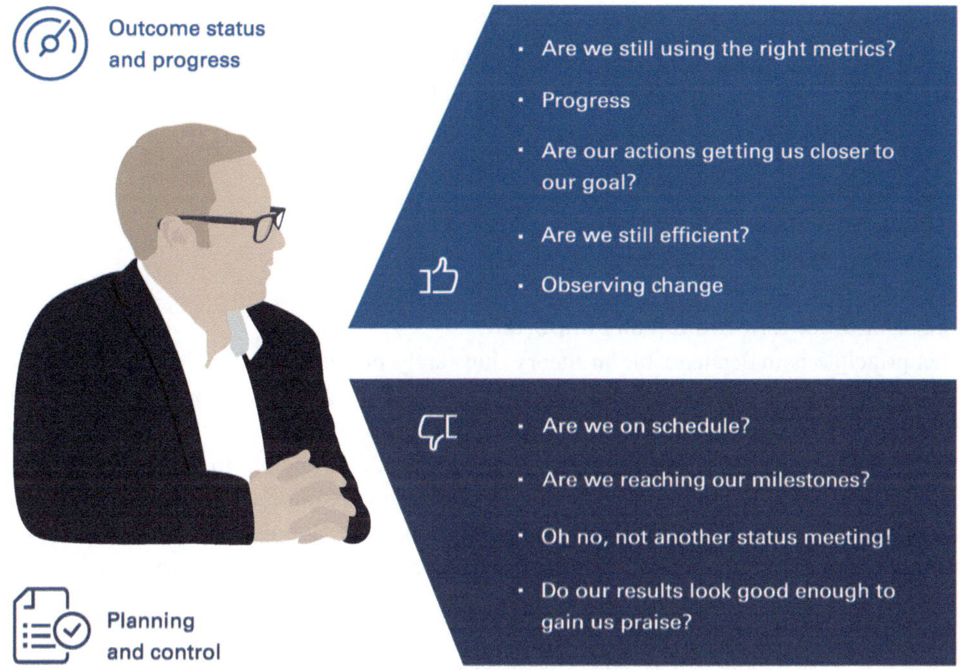

Fig. 3.14 Planning vs. action. (Source: H&F Solutions GmbH/www.hf-solutions.co)

punishable, and a culture of pure justification prevails. Endless controlling builds an atmosphere of permanent pressure and mistrust, and a downward spiral begins.

Outcome Status and Progress

Every question is based on the idea of goal fulfillment. "Does this decision or this milestone still contribute to the achievement of the desired result?" The focus here is on generating above-average progress. Progress made leads the project via predefined progress and outcome metrics. By the way, it doesn't actually matter how much progress is made over a specific period of time. The only important thing is that progress is permanent, which in turn generates pride and motivation to achieve the next (partial) result. It is less important to slavishly reach the next milestone—you may reach two milestones in 1 month and none in the next 8 weeks.

3.2.2.4 Security vs. Speed

If possible, we all want maximum speed for our projects, and we certainly don't want to sacrifice security in the process. However, we know that it's impossible to achieve both, so the only solution is to change the way we look at things. Security is an emotional state—for one person it may mean having enough money in the bank to cover all costs for the next 5 years, while for someone else it is less about money and more about being able to afford bread on a daily basis. What does security mean to you? Planning security, financial security, or security to achieve your project goals? The tension between security and speed is, in a manner of speaking, the accelerating force in your project, and the more security you give up, the more speed you attain. In order to provide you with something tangible at this point, we would like to share three considerations:

- Speed and content are equally important
- Projects that take too long lose value
- Always hold on to useful things

Speed and Content Are Equally Important

This principle is understandable in theory, but rarely put into practice. If you can't get a project up to speed, even the best content won't help. After all, you can only work effectively if you go fast. You can still get the best results under mild pressure, because that's when you're most focused. You can compare this principle to a major inventory check that usually takes place once a year within a tight timeframe, and no serious mistakes are allowed. In other words, everyone involved is focused. You need to work in compact, highly-focuses sprints and allow yourself short breaks between sprints to recover.

Projects That Take Too Long Lose Value

When things drag on they lose value. People can only be motivated to do certain things for a certain amount of time. Once a project has begun to drag it becomes difficult to get it back up to speed. Therefore, you need to either keep your foot on the gas pedal or deliberately pause your project. If you do pause a project, it is essential to communicate it that way. Nothing is worse than running too many projects in parallel and failing to complete a single one. This is the exact opposite of speed and achieves zero progress.

The Pareto Principle

How much security you are prepared to give up in concrete terms is something you have to decide for yourself. Our experience has shown that you get the maximum benefit from your projects if you apply the Pareto Principle. If you have already achieved 80% of your planned result, you should set yourself new goals as soon as possible. This is true at least for strategy development and implementation. However, if you set your expectations too high, your project will quickly become inefficient (see fig. 3.15).

(Fake) Security

After reading the previous section, you may be thinking that a well-developed plan provides a high degree of certainty of success. This is not the case. A plan creates an instrument with which your dynamic environment is difficult to depict. It cannot solve complex issues and cannot make them any more plannable. Ninety-nine per cent of project plans are therefore a collection of things that will never happen anyway. As we see it, plans therefore usually only represent a form of apparent certainty—i.e., a plan is more of a depiction of habits than an added value for your project. If you work for an organization

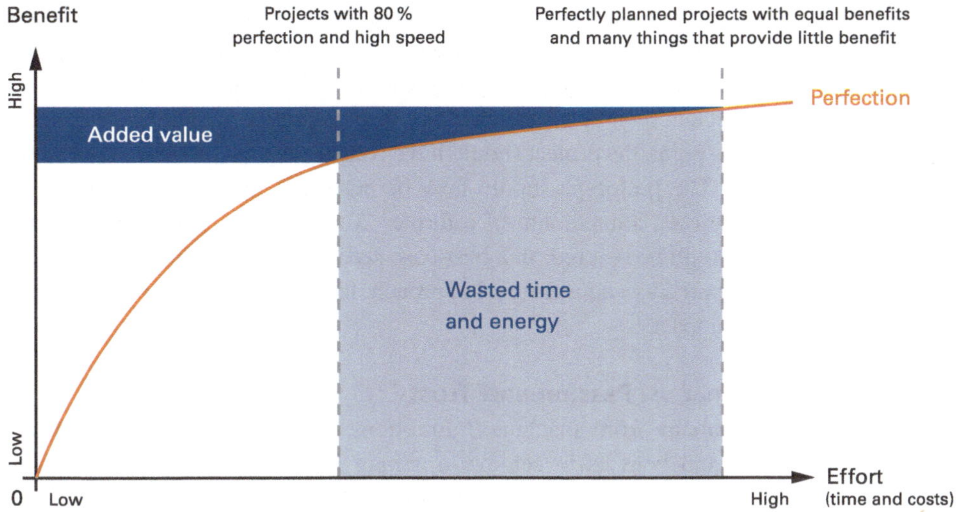

Fig. 3.15 Cost/benefit leverage. (Source: H&F Solutions GmbH/www.hf-solutions.co)

where project plans are always fulfilled, you should start crosschecking during regular project meetings. Take a look at how many of the topics revolve around goal achievement and how many revolve purely around plan compliance.

Speed/Agility

The opposite of planning is the agile project management approach. Using this approach, you always know where your project is headed, but fine-tuning is performed on the fly. Avoiding the use of detailed plans enables you to go faster. Compare this to flying a plane: unless your company has a built-in autopilot, you should forget rigid structures and simply fly by sight. In an agile business context, this means you should try to reach your intermediate goal as quickly as possible and only act when an obstacle arises. Permanent progress leads the way, and the goal is maximum achievement of objectives without getting bogged down in details.

During our own projects, we try to achieve 80% of the planned result as quickly as possible using the available means. This approach will be familiar to those involved in software development, but can also be applied to other types of projects too.

We often find that large numbers of analyses, concepts, plans, calculations, and so on were carried out at the start of a project and that, in the process, 80% of the energy used was wasted on things that didn't generate any useful progress. Implementation was then slated to be performed using the remaining 20 percent. Welcome to the world of inefficiency! The *H&F Strategy Approach* does away with a lot of this up-front activity. We start with a sketched-out concept and flesh it out with current insights as the project progresses. A maximum of five to six slides are sufficient. At the start, you should refrain from any kind of activities that do not directly contribute to the success of the project. These are topics such as the creation or formatting of documents, the creation of elaborate presentations, and so on. These are real time wasters that no one needs at this stage of the project's progress.

The basic concept is followed by prototype creation and testing. Based on this, the feasibility of the project can then be clearly derived. This prototype should cover all basic requirements. Up to this point, the project should have consumed a maximum of 20% of the total available energy. The prototype should now be perfected and fine-tuned using the same amount of energy (i.e., a maximum of a further 20%). Following that, the targeted 80% project success should be secured. In a best-case scenario, the remaining 60% are the savings you make compared to a conventional approach. Isn't that great? You have already achieved a significant impact!

3.2.2.5 Emotions: Fear vs. Passion and Trust

What distinguishes humans from machines? Emotions, intuition, and feelings. These protect us from risks and help us to achieve a certain level of inner security. At this point, we would like to limit ourselves to emotions and show you how they can help to generate passion and trust. Take a look at the two images shown in Fig. 3.16.

When the Primary Emotion Is Fear of Implementation

As already mentioned in Sect. 3.2.1.5, the last thing you need in a project is fear, as this often blocks the potential of project participants. Instead, it would be great if we could motivate our fellow human beings to generate a continual upward spiral. The remarkable thing about fear is that it cannot be suppressed at all. We can only learn to keep it in check or to deal with it. The main trigger of anxiety is the thought of making mistakes. However, the best results are achieved when we are close to this limit, and it is extremely rare that we achieve good results without making mistakes. If you don't allow mistakes, a culture of justification will quickly creep into your company. Your employees will become increasingly anxious and will generate increasingly little progress. They will become insecure, and your project team will find itself in a downward spiral as a result. Status meetings are rehashed to reflect what the project owner wants to see, but end up leaving out reality—due to fear. According to the guiding principle "I only trust statistics that I invented myself", presentations become farcical and a potential performance culture is transformed into a team of frightened yes-men.

The Pulling Power of Passion and Trust

You will get maximum traction in your innovation strategy project if you foster passion and trust. Don't force your employees into a specific way of working, but instead let their own inner drive decide what they want to do (and how) in order to make a project successful. Everyone should do what drives them. You can't motivate employees, only they can motivate themselves. Show your confidence by allowing them to make mistakes, because we can all only learn and gain insight by making mistakes. Only employees who you demonstrably trust will take responsibility and continue project work on their own, driven by inner motivation. To do this, however, management has to hand over responsibility to

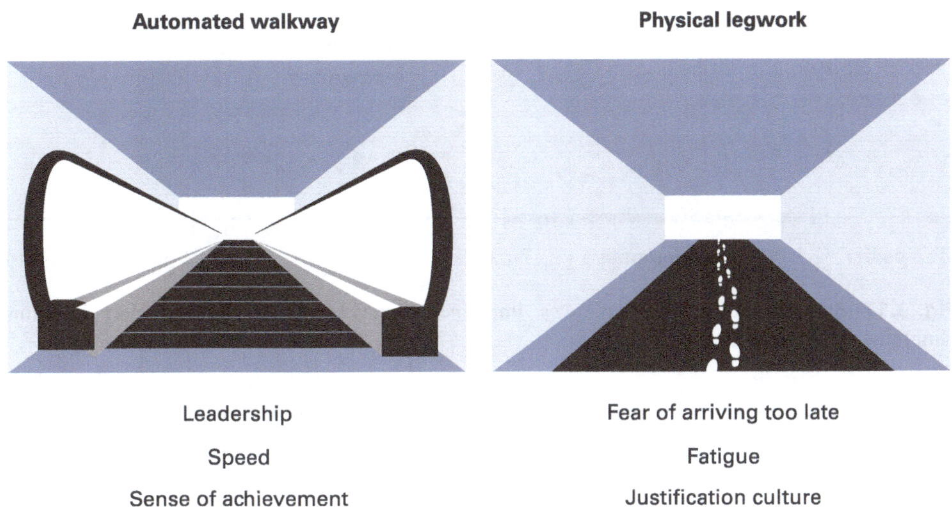

Fig. 3.16 Emotional impact. (Source: H&F Solutions GmbH/www.hf-solutions.co)

the project team and transform itself from a central management body (executive board and management) into a decentralized management body (employee level, team leaders, department heads).

One sure sign of this kind of change is the performance the team produces, which becomes clear at regular project status meetings. Give employees the opportunity to celebrate successes that they have achieved. We do this using the *Scrum* method of packaging work. Each successfully completed package represents a step towards success, and even the smallest steps represent progress in the context of the project. Every employee can identify with the project goal by completing a small task and thus contributing to the overall success of the company. And by the way, it is by no means 'normal' for this kind of project to succeed. There have simply been too many abandoned IT and ERP projects in the past to think that way.

Using this approach, you will quickly determine whether you are on the right track—for example, when your project participants look forward to the next status meeting. Once this approach is defined and implemented, your thoughts can turn to how you can drive project progress even faster (e.g., "How do I enable my colleagues to achieve the focused project state even faster?").

3.2.2.6 Implementation Technocracy vs. Implementation Momentum

Every day we work with our customers on highly complex topics, and they are often far greater experts in their specific field than we are. They are usually people who base their actions on scientific and technical methods. However, this knowledge draws exclusively on past experience and projects it into the future. After all, what has worked in the past is likely to do so in the future. We refer to this approach as implementation technocracy.

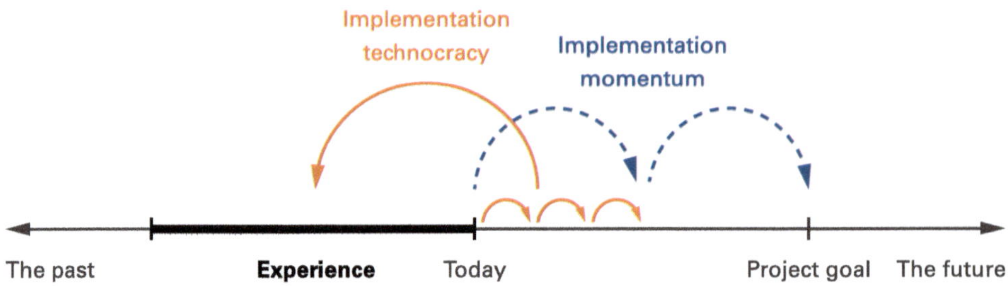

Fig. 3.17 Implementation technocracy vs. implementation momentum. (Source: H&F Solutions GmbH/www.hf-solutions.co)

However, strategic topics and agile methods deal with things that lie in the future. In order to progress, it is necessary to also deal with topics from the future. At this point, it therefore makes much more sense to deal with topics from the present and the future. What are the means available to us today? How can I solve a problem using the latest methods? If you manage to project this momentum into the future, and work hard to implement it, you will be able to drive the issue further toward the project goal than if you invest more of your energy in the past. This is what we call building implementation momentum (see also Fig. 3.17).

Implementation Technocracy: Guilt, Shame, and Justification Culture

"Where are we up to in our project?"; "Why are we behind schedule?"; "But others have done it faster in the past." If these kinds of questions or statements arise, you have already lost your team. A project is fundamentally about progress and, if you are in technocracy mode, you will be permanently confronted with the question: "How far have we got?", or with statements such as: "Others have already done stuff like that", or "You're the implementation expert . . .", or "It was you who set the schedule".

What is actually happening here? You are focusing on the reasons why a milestone hasn't been reached. However, at the beginning of the project not all influencing factors that are necessary to achieve the milestone are usually in place, thus making a precision landing impossible. So why do you do this to your team? Because it's easy to work with starting points. If you use blame and justification, you will develop a culture that is no fun for anyone and brings about more shame than motivation for everyone involved. Ergo, performance culture is a no-go.

Implementation Momentum: Pride and Motivation through Permanent Progress and Success

Who doesn't want to be proud of what they do? Pride motivates, and we are most proud when we make progress. And making progress is not as hard as you think. What is hard, however, is measuring progress, so you need to use appropriate progress metrics. The key to the success of progress metrics is to decouple the time reference. This is because without a time reference, there can be no counterproductive pressure that will curb motivation.

However, this doesn't mean you can't demand performance from your project participants, it just happens in a different way. Assigning blame is no longer an option, since there is no deadline or schedule, but only the rule of achieving permanent progress. At this point, you turn the tables on the participants, because employees are pleased and proud when they can achieve independent results and solve tasks on their own. In this case, pride acts as a booster for team motivation. Since you show your trust in the team by exercising less control, this also has a corresponding positive effect, and a performance culture will begin to develop. This motivational power ensures implementation momentum that provides you with the necessary progress and success in your project.

3.2.2.7 Transparency

You can only give employees the chance to take responsibility if they can inform themselves independently about important projects or situations within the company. Information must also be made available so that it can be used independently and further insights can be generated from it. You can see this in companies that provide dashboards specifically for deriving important information with the most important key and control values. Figure 3.18 shows our own H&F Technologies cockpit. In digital leader companies, the information it contains also includes targets that can be compared with one another. This way, companies generate the requirements necessary to bring each business unit to an appropriate level through the use of KPIs (key process indicators).

There is thus complete transparency, and everyone involved can thus pursue the goals they have set themselves. In the case of a strategic project, this means measuring and monitoring the progress of the project. As a result of this transparency, everyone can contribute their ideas and contribute to progress.

▶ If you don't provide transparency, you won't be able to motivate your employees to take ownership.

3.2.2.8 Knowledge Transfer and Wording

Another issue you need to take care of is knowledge transfer. For strategic projects, the main challenge lies in the transfer of the project vision and its goals. These are usually difficult to transfer to all project participants, as things are often understood differently and information is then passed on incorrectly. The 'Chinese Whispers' principle means that information is often interpreted wrongly or simply gets lost along the way.

It is therefore essential to make sure that all project participants are informed as well as possible about this process and that awareness is heightened, especially in the initial phase. There are no automated tools to help you do this, so leadership skills are required. Always use identical wordings so that everyone involved is talking about the same thing when it comes to the crucial issues.

We were inspired by a well-known author, who points out that information must be presented in a way that everyone can understand—in a kind of *kids' board of management*

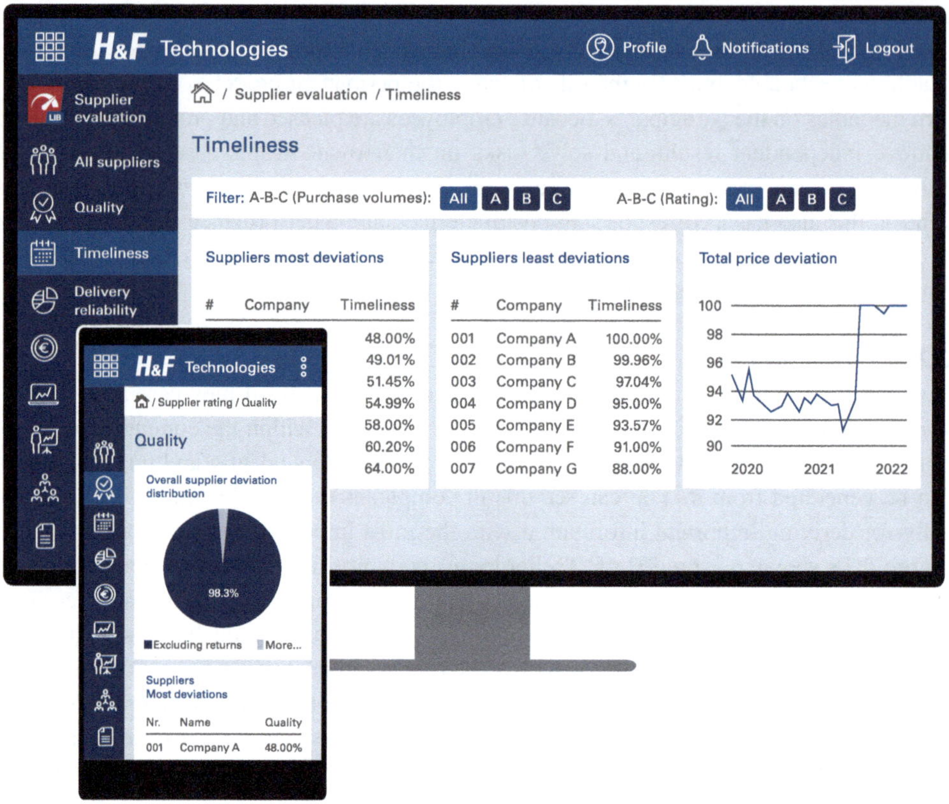

Fig. 3.18 The H&F Technologies cockpit. (Source: H&F Solutions GmbH/www.hf-solutions.co)

language. This means reducing the complexity of specialist terms to a minimum. After all, information transfer is all about precise dissemination (see Fig. 3.19). Keep what is said simple and to the point, and use the recipient's language. Your own large vocabulary won't help you at all if the other party isn't able to interpret it.

It has long been proven that many actions are largely dependent on habits—for example, eating regularly, getting up in the morning, or working through project topics. These habits are often described as automatism or auto-suggestion.

Summary

Anyone whose project stays on budget and on schedule has set their goals too low. High-quality work only gets done under pressure. You have to pay attention to a number of factors if you want to be successful, and some specific behaviors have proven to be particularly beneficial while others have not. Applying the following five behaviors will give your project a chance of success in spite of any uncertainty in your future dynamics.

The five boosters that provide a (theoretical) chance of sticking to your plan:

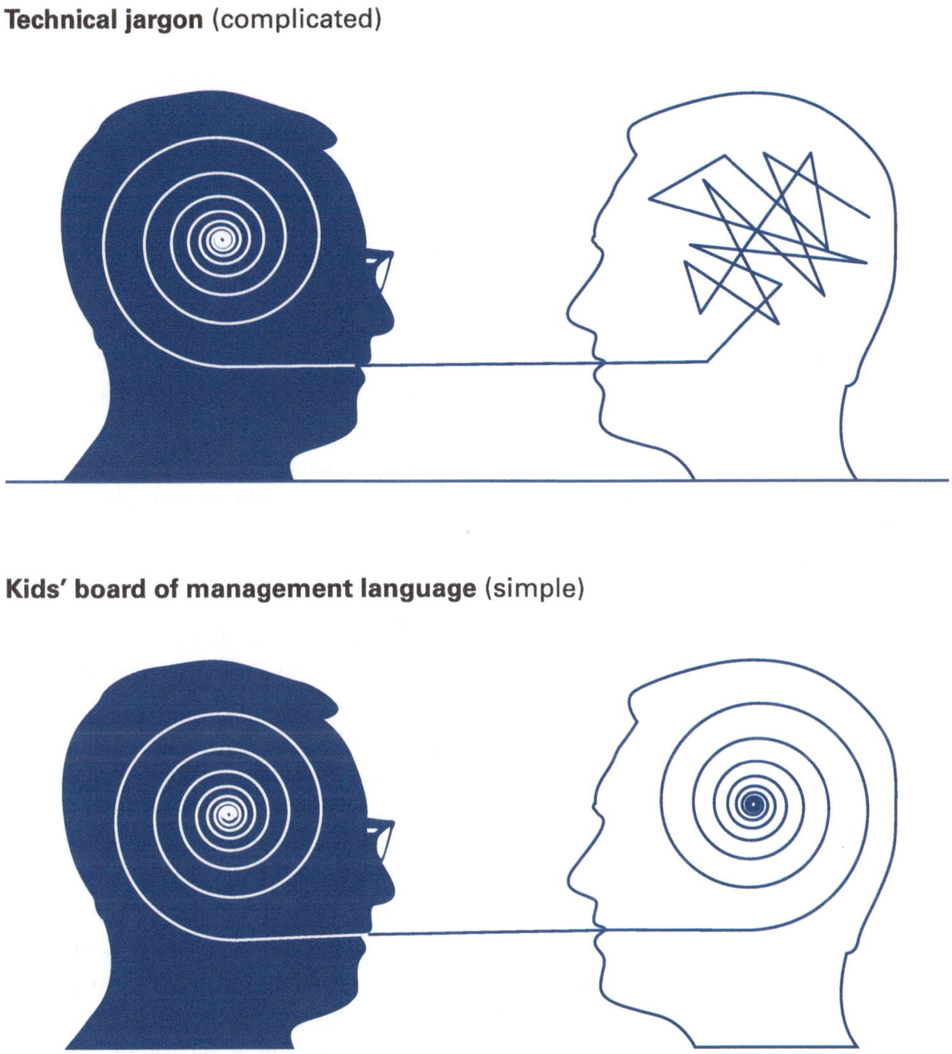

Fig. 3.19 Knowledge transfer in strategy projects (H&F Solutions GmbH/www.hf-solutions.co)

1. Never start a project without having clearly worked out the benefits
2. Ensure understanding and commitment in your team. Everyone should benefit from the project.
3. Don't waste time and energy on unnecessary planning for complex projects. Use your energy to put the available resources to practical use.
4. Don't turn project meetings into purely critical events. Ensure clarity and acceptance. Producing insight makes it easier to generate learning progress. Work with one another instead of against one another.

5. If you can successfully balance risk with fear, you will provide a catalyst that will give your project enormous forward momentum.

At the same time, there are existing behaviors that will no longer be effective in the future or that require a rethink. The following considerations must be urgently reconsidered for this:

- The direction of thought must always start with the goal, whereas the direction of work must be from the start of the project.
- While push management focuses on the 'how', in the future the 'what' will be the focus of the (pull management) action.
- Success and failure are the result of our actions. In order to be successful in the future, we need to plan less and achieve results more quickly.
- The tensions between security and speed create an accelerating force for your project. The more security you give up, the more speed you get. Things that take too long tend to lose value. Always divide your project into easily measurable, 'easy-to-digest' sub-units.
- Implementation technocracy (based on the past) contrasts with implementation momentum (goal-oriented). If you simply continue to using habits from the past, the future won't turn out future-proof. If, on the other hand, you redefine the future and decouple it from the time reference, you will create a motivational environment in which unprecedented progress can emerge.
- Create transparency. You can only give employees the chance to take responsibility if they can inform themselves independently about important projects or situations within the company. Information must also be made available so that it can be used independently and further insights can be generated from it.
- In innovation strategy projects, it is imperative that there is a transfer of knowledge vis-à-vis the target image and the vision. If you hold back important details, the room for interpretation is too large and the results will degenerate. Keep things simple and get to the point. Use the language of the information's recipients. Your own large vocabulary won't help you at all if the other party isn't able to interpret it. ◄

3.3 Can You Manage Change on Your Own?

Time and again, you will find yourself wondering whether you should go through an issue alone or whether it would be better to get help. We feel the same way as you do. We constantly want to learn and develop. However, we do not want to copy others completely, but remain true to ourselves. In the following section, we will present you with an approach that allows you to reduce external support to a minimum. This doesn't mean choosing the cheapest external provider, but instead finding the optimal cost-benefit ratio from working with external service providers like us.

3.3.1 Change

▶ In our context, change means making lasting changes to structures, processes, and behaviors. Change always begins within ourselves.

Companies that want to carry out a strategic project naturally follow the goal of something being different once the project is complete. However, to achieve this most companies resort to methods that optimize what already exists. In other words, they continue doing the same thing they have done in the past, just optimized. This is not change. In a successful change project, the state at the end of the project is different from the state at the start, and there has to be a discernible difference. The target state must support the business goal more than it did before. This kind of change never happens in a linear way, and success usually manifests itself in discreet jumps. Here, we refer to individual levels of success, as show in Fig. 3.20.

When a company reaches the next level of success, it functions on a different level than before, where things work differently.

The difficulty with this is that anything that took your business from one of the lower levels of success to a middle level of success will never take you to a higher level of success. Other measures and behaviors are necessary to take the next step. Climbing four levels of success requires four separate change processes. The results are different and the work required to achieve them is different. To reach this higher level, however, you must do different things or adopt different habits than on the level below. If you continue to work in the 'here and now' and only optimize, you will not be able to innovate and reach the next level of success.

3.3.1.1 Thinking in the Future, Not the Past

You have to adopt a certain basic attitude if you want to achieve clear increases in success, especially when you are on the lookout for efficient ways to achieve your goals. You need to have been mentally at the target state before starting the project in order to be able to make the decisions that pave the way to your goal. Many decision-makers focus too much on input variables. As already mentioned in the previous chapters, this is a much weaker approach to deriving or abstracting your goal. Only strong focus on a target state—including considering potential outcomes—enables you to concentrate on the 'what' and the 'why'. And precisely this is the basis for climbing to the next level of success.

▶ **Caution**

Many managers solve problems using an input mindset (recognizable by the classic 'how' questions, such as: "How do we solve this now?" or "How can we

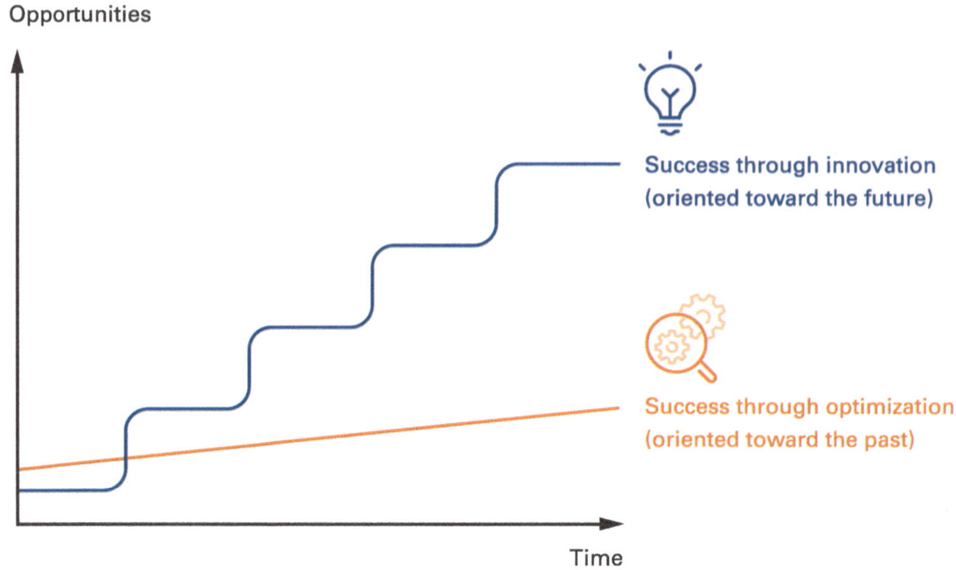

Fig. 3.20 Increasing levels of success: oriented toward the future vs. oriented toward the past. (Source: H&F Solutions GmbH/www.hf-solutions.co)

buy in an external solution?"), and thus have no focus on the actual desired target state. Without knowing the target state, input factors usually remain ineffective. Such projects are likely to head off in the wrong direction, mostly due to early budget overruns.

It is important to do the right thing rather than wasting time (resources) on the wrong approach. If you use the right abstraction from the target state, the probability of doing the right thing increases significantly (Philipp Futterknecht, 2020).

3.3.1.2 Direction of Thought Is Not the Same as Direction of Work

At this point it is important to understand that the direction of thought is significantly different from the direction of work. As a decision maker, we recommend that you get a feel for the elementary thinking steps shown in Fig. 3.21.

These form the basis for innovation strategy development and, later on, the filter for project participants' input and ideas. Within strategy projects it is important to distinguish whether contributions from project participants are input or output variables. Using the example shown in Fig. 3.21., this could be interpreted as follows:

With money you can buy training or workshops. Knowledge emerges from these trainings, which can lead to new products, innovations, or new behavior and, ideally, ensures increasing returns, a better competitive position, or a new corporate culture. This is

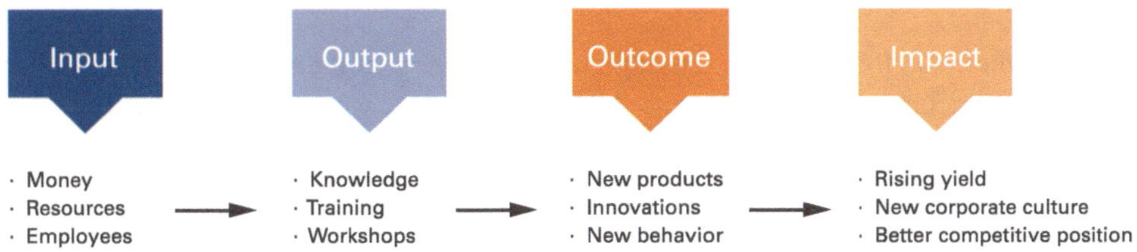

Fig. 3.21 The direction of work. (Source: H&F Solutions GmbH/www.hf-solutions.co)

an example of an input-driven mindset. We would now like to show you how this works in the opposite direction—i.e., thinking backward starting from the goal.

The Goal (Impact)

The goal (or impact) is what you ultimately want to achieve in terms of effects and results, and therefore represents the changed state of a project or undertaking in the future.

Example

Sample goal (impact): **Increase sales.** ◄

Result (Outcome/Key Result)

Planned results define the project scope you are aiming for in order to bring about the desired goal. There has to be a high level of understanding of the results among all participants, so any outcomes must be presented dependent on or connected with the target state. Once these outcomes are achieved, your plan should approach the desired target state.

Example

Sample result (key result/outcome): **Reduce delivery times.** ◄

► **Caution**

As mentioned in the paragraph above, we deliberately talk about "effects" or "probabilities", since no one can guarantee that you will actually reach your goal simply by fulfilling the expected results.

Here are some examples: competing projects, non-compliance with project rules, overall company strategy collides with project focus, etc.

The market situation may change during the project in such a way that any previously developed results lose their effect and the entire process must be rethought.

► To make this process more stable, our customers create clear goals at the beginning of each project. These then allow precise control of the common thread at any point in the project.

Output

Output is the basis for achieving the desired result—i.e., it is the result with which I can achieve the outcome. With reference to the example above, we need to ask the following question: "What needs to be different in the company afterwards so that **delivery times are shortened**"?

Example

An example of output: **Through ERP training employees we will, in the future, be able to derive and implement processes that will ensure the desired shortened delivery times.** ◄

Input

The input is a classic, familiar 'how' question: How do I bring about the result? (i.e., the output). However, you should never start thinking about the 'how' before you have thought through the other three steps. In complex projects, this mindset is key to rapid project success. Try it out on an example of your own devising.

Example

An example of input: **Introduction of an ERP system and employee training.** ◄

3.3.1.3 Your Most Important Project Participants Are Always Humans

Eighty per cent of all projects fail not because of technical issues, but due to communication issues. In agile projects, it is therefore all the more important to have leaders on board. In addition to all the recommendations for action and behaviors we describe, never forget that your daily work still involves dealing with people. In order to make sure you have the right people on board for successful project implementation, you ultimately have three choices:

1. You train internal company staff specifically for this purpose
2. You hire people who already have the required skills
3. You hire outside help specifically for this project

Regardless of which path you choose, it is important to note that the right speed will be decisive for the success of the project. Compare a project with your body: If you have set yourself a goal that requires muscle building, you can't reach your goal in a hurry. Very few people know that muscles actually only develop during resting phases. During a sports session, muscles are stretched (see Fig. 3.22), the fibers form micro-tears and these are then filled by new muscle fibers during rest. This overall process slowly builds muscle. You should take the same approach with your project team members. Anything that needs to be

Fig. 3.22 Muscles only grow during rest. (Source: H&F Solutions GmbH/www.hf-solutions.co)

built up needs to be done either slowly and sustainably or bought in from outside. Never forget the human element in this process.

Example

One of our employees from the software team approached the project team in a weekly meeting. He complained that, due to the project speed, parts of the code he had worked hard to create had once again been thrown overboard. He communicated his displeasure at this situation to the team.

So what happened? We had set a goal for the software teams that had to be achieved by a certain deadline. Due to a lack of communication and control, some functions were programmed by two people at the same time. However, the two people involved didn't manage to coordinate and define whose area of responsibility this functionality was. As the project progressed, it became clear that the functions in question had been programmed twice and one instance had to be trashed. One of our two colleagues was able to celebrate a success (a successfully implemented function), while the other suffered a setback (trashed code). ◄

Referring to the example above, it obviously makes no sense for someone to waste their time on duplicate coding. Communication is therefore enormously important in order to keep everyone informed.

We expect every employee to speak out, not just on technical issues. Only through comprehensive communication is it possible to correctly clarify and assess the situation via understanding of the underlying values. Regardless of what tasks your employees have to deal with within a project or during their daily work, never forget that they also have personal issues that can have an impact on the project. These can be events such as death, divorce, or illness. If such issues aren't discussed, they will have a direct impact on your professional life, and any misjudgments will have a negative impact on your project. However, this doesn't have to be the case, as everyone benefits when a project succeeds.

We have often found that managers want to push their projects through at any price, even at a risk of losing staff loyalty. In the majority of these cases, it was clear from the beginning that the chance of achieving the planned goal was very low, but the decision-maker wasn't aware of this. If the managers concerned are able to perform self-reflection with a member of staff at the same level, these kinds of failures can usually be prevented, especially in long-term projects such as ERP implementations. Long-term projects require staff to achieve big things. In many cases, such projects last 1–2 years, so you can imagine what can happen to your team over the course of a two-year project cycle. If the software manufacturer then has the next release ready and management has scheduled this as the next project without any breathing space, your staff will be correspondingly demotivated. If you then neglect to apply the right management techniques to keep your staff motivated (see Sect. 3.2.2.6), it will be difficult to push your employees further. Even if you don't make it a rule, there is no harm in occasionally celebrating a success after a period of stress, and showing that you appreciate the work that has been done.

3.3.2 Soft Factors That Can Kill an Innovation Strategy Project

Soft factors are those which cannot be objectively quantified, but which have an influence on the success of a company. "We could actually implement the project on our own. We don't need outside help." In our view, this approach is just as wrong as outsourcing a large part of the work. However, external partners are still very important in strategy projects. The intensity of cooperation is less decisive than the output generated together by the internal and external staff. And output can be derived logically.

Why do companies organize their storage spaces, perform warehouse management, and create business structures? So that they can find things more quickly and easily, and to prevent chaos. If you haven't yet implemented a product classification system in your company, your products and services are still floating around in a diffuse cloud. As soon as you try to find a product and distinguish it from another, you will have trouble defining the distinction. However, if you use a product classification or inventory management concept, there is a high probability that you will somehow nail it. What is the probability that you will manage to do the same for a complex innovation strategy or ERP topic? From our point of view, almost zero, simply because these kinds of dynamic projects are virtually impossible to recreate. Things will always turn out differently than planned. For this reason, you should proceed with caution and compensate for all strategically decisive weaknesses and, if these positions can't be filled internally, you will need to fill them using outside staff.

3.3.2.1 Use Expert Transparency Capabilities to Read Between the Lines

Basically, every company manages to implement its project independently, true to the motto: "Everyone is replaceable." By hiring an expert, you only buy yourself time and a faster target achievement rate. Ultimately, you save yourself a lot of the amateurish activity that often takes place and that can sometimes stall a project completely.

Example

In a previous project, we found that the production planning manager was having difficulty understanding the ERP system. The difficulty lay in mapping the logic of the BOM structures, MRP data, and basic core data. As a result, all these data types were created autonomously without an overarching concept for almost 80% of the products being manufactured. There were no clear definitions and no clear rules. Manual intervention made it possible to obtain usable working papers, but the knock-on effects were serious. The ERP system no longer enhanced the process flows and instead stretched any remaining trust between the IT system and humans to breaking point. The confusion was so great that not even simple goods bookings ran smoothly, and many things only worked when initiated manually. All this confusion was actually created by humans, even if it was communicated as a weakness in the ERP system. Using an outside expert has already paid for itself if it helps you to avoid this kind of learning experience. ◀

▶ Never use amateurs in highly leveraged situations—burning money is easier!

3.3.2.2 Raising Awareness Through a Lack of Perspective

We are all too familiar with the rat race. Every day we fall back into old habits, and not only in a positive sense. External staff are often useful, mainly because they are not burdened by your daily business routines and often have other, useful habits of their own (see Sect. 3.4.3 on basal ganglia). With the help of these you will manage to escape from your daily routine and raise your awareness so that the project philosophy you have learned here will take effect. Note though, that it takes time and a little practice before it all comes to fruition.

3.3.2.3 There Is More Philosophy Involved in Strategy Topics Than You Think: Efficient Implementation Is Impossible Without the Help of Experts and Sparring Partners

Strategy topics are actually quite easy to manage, especially today where software is the major topic that everyone is busy with, and the one that dictates the shape of the process. After software, there isn't much left that can be freely defined, and structures are therefore largely dictated by the application. This statement is pretty well true except for the word "largely". In our view, a maximum of 5% of software projects are predefined by the application, and the remaining 95% have to be individually managed. These are topics such as competencies, communication, trust, reliability, mutual expectations, and goal orientation. If these topics are clarified in the context of the project, it is easy to make an innovation strategy project successful. Let's use an ERP project as an example: 95% of any ERP project has nothing to do with ERP and everything to do with the topics mentioned in the previous sentence. So how can you hope to implement such a project with an ERP expert alone? It is simply not possible. In practice, however, this is what happens most of the time. The project is managed exclusively by an ERP expert, whereas it would be much better to have a dual leadership consisting of ERP and process experts. The process-oriented party is often the one who then ensures that the concept is accepted and implemented.

3.3.2.4 The Cost-Benefit Factor in External Resources

External resources only help if they move the project in the right direction. And there are two possible directions that external resources can work in: toward the future or toward the past. However, in this case, the question is more one of the inner direction of any external resources than of finding a technocratic solution. Careful selection and the consideration of appropriate soft factors increase the chance of finding a suitable external partner. A suitable proportion of shared values ultimately increases the chances of a successful project and thus the effects of the cost-benefit factor (see Fig. 3.23).

It is important to weigh up whether the external partner really has the required extra knowledge advantage and the right focus. If not, you still have the option of going it alone internally using internal staff and a future-oriented approach. Under no circumstances should you carry the unaltered past forward into the future.

3.3.2.5 Our Goal Is your Goal

New techniques and new applications appear on the market at increasingly short intervals. If you look at this from a 'helicopter' viewpoint, it quickly becomes clear that every new approach is based on a clear goal, and you should never pass over the topic of goal focus unchecked. We are talking here about overarching goals—in other words, the emotional part. You can neglect the technical part because, as described above, it is only responsible for 5% of success. In the past, competitive advantages were based exclusively on technical products and technologies. After a while, these were copied and thus quickly lost any lasting advantage they may have had. It is essential to make sure you are in the same boat

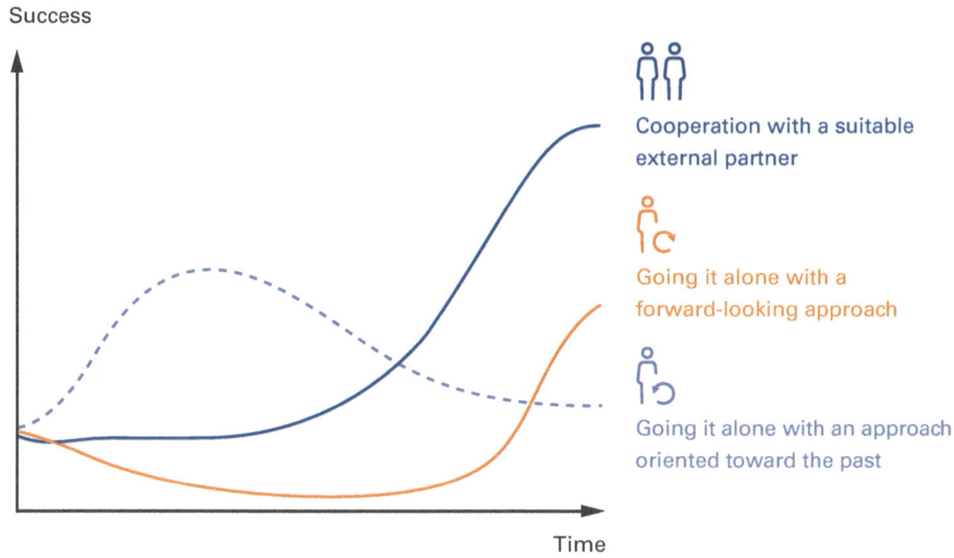

Fig. 3.23 The prospects of success in innovation strategy projects. (Source: H&F Solutions GmbH/www.hf-solutions.co)

with the decision-makers (whether external or internal) from the very beginning (see Fig. 3.24). We never make a project offer to a customer if we identify major differences in strategic focus on our part or that of the customer.

Summary

A future-oriented mode of thinking or a future-oriented process model enables companies to carry out successful strategic project work. This requires a distinction between the direction of thinking and the direction of working. The direction of thinking always starts with the goal, while the direction of working always starts in the here and now. With regard to the direction of thinking, this means defining impact, outcome, output, and input (see table 3.1).

Without external support, however, it won't be possible to achieve an optimal result. Imagine a company is a muscle. If it is too weak, you won't be able to lift certain things and, in this case, time is too tight to train the required muscle mass. This lack of strength can be compensated for using external support. It is important to use this support in a goal-oriented manner, and preferably in the highest available quality. It is important to understand that success always comes in stages and the effect is not immediate. Every time you increase your level of success, there will be different factors that lead to further success. Ultimately, you will only be able to succeed if the external impetus remains small and you work on the same goal as your external partners. ◀

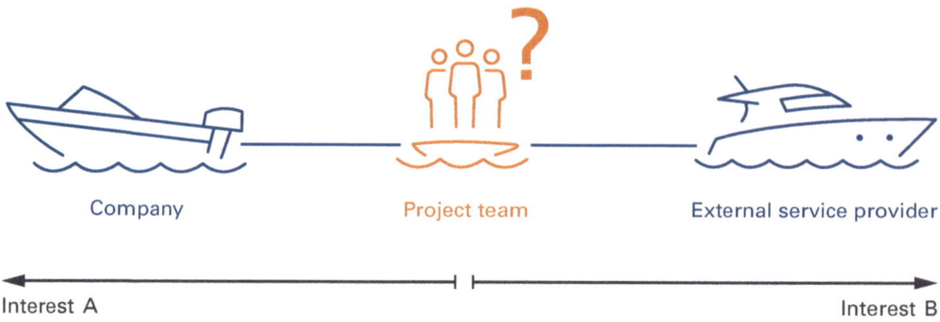

Fig. 3.24 Diverging strategic focus. (Source: H&F Solutions GmbH/www.hf-solutions.co)

Table 3.1 Direction of thinking

Step	Description	Example
Impact (goal)	What do I want to achieve?	Increase sales
Outcome (result)	The scope of what is to be achieved	Reducing delivery times
Output (with what)	What can I use to achieve this?	Staff training
Input (how)	How am I going to achieve this?	Implement a transparent ERP system

Source: H&F Solutions GmbH/www.hf-solutions.co

3.4 Preparing to Implement the H&F High Speed and Efficiency Concept

3.4.1 Shared Values in Companies

What is your company's understanding of values and what values do you stand for as a person? How would you describe the social orientation of your employees? Which values should your project revolve around?

Many people in organizations have a serious lack of understanding for a values-based approach. How can an employee communicate things within the project if there is a different understanding of values throughout the entire project chain and shared values were not defined or established beforehand?

Example

In the course of a project at a well-known mechanical engineering company, we had noticed that the field staff showed strong fluctuations in the quality of the service they provided, with certain employees more demand from customers than others. Analysis showed that different employees conveyed different values to their customers. One was over-eager and allowed himself to be sweet-talked. As a result, he made less sales although he was theoretically the best sales representative for the customer. In contrast, another employee was very goal-oriented and didn't allow himself to be influenced by the customer and thus achieved the desired sales, even though he was less popular with his customers than his colleague. ◀

In the above example, you can see that conveying values that (indirectly) affect employees' inner attitudes is immensely important. How can an employee know that he should appear 'determined' and 'self-confident' to the customer if no-one ever told him?

This understanding of values is enormously important in terms of commitment to achieving a corporate goal. For example, let's look at humility, which is derived from a combination of service and modesty. But how can an employee 'serve' the company if he doesn't know how the project team or the company functions?

► **Important**
By defining values, you empower your employees to adopt appropriate internal and outward-looking attitudes toward the company.

3.4.2 Implementation Strength and Speed

Competition is becoming increasingly fierce and the business world responds increasingly fast. Past business models may still be successful, but will increasingly lose their effectiveness against nimble competitors. You therefore have to learn to act faster and think faster. To achieve this, you have to master the management of business units that operate at very high speed, and to do so without burning out your workforce in the process. The will to succeed alone isn't usually sufficient, so you need a basic set of methods and best practices to stay ahead of the competition in the future. But you will only be able to succeed if your will is strong enough. If you don't make use of these basic techniques, you will most likely fail.

► **Important**
If you are not prepared to alter your behavior, you will not be able to improve your speed or the strength of your implementation.

If you manage to apply specific methods and best practices to your business or project, you will be one of the few who have a realistic chance of reaching the pinnacle of above-average success.

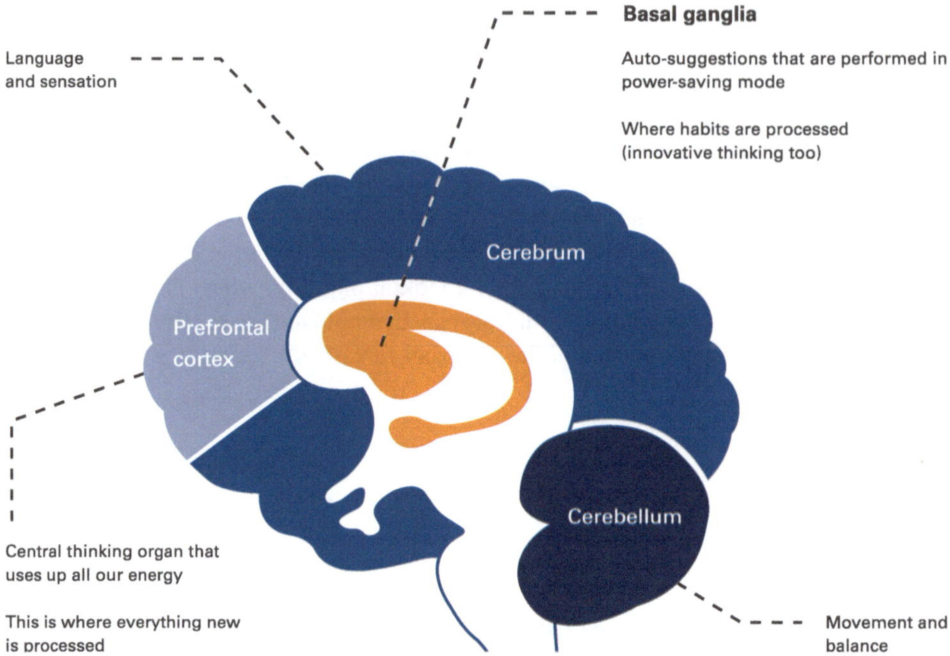

Fig. 3.25 Basal ganglia as drivers of speed and strength of implementation. (Source: H&F Solutions GmbH/www.hf-solutions.co)

3.4.3 No Project Can Succeed Without Auto-Suggestion

In order to be able to apply the *H&F High Speed and Efficiency Concept*, you must be able to apply certain auto-suggestions. These must first be learned and to do this, you need memory space in your basal ganglia (see Fig. 3.25).

> **Caution**
> This description of brain functions is provided solely to improve your understanding. It is not a scientific description of all the underlying physiological interrelationships.

> **Important**
> **Basal ganglia:** This area in the brain where all information, whether new or repeated, is received and sorted. Everything that we consider important or that we already know is passed on to the basal ganglia, the cerebrum, and the cerebellum.
> **Prefrontal cortex:** This is your thinking center, and is where all new input ends up. This information is sorted in a second step. Speech and movement information is passed directly to the cerebrum and cerebellum. Everything that seems to be of

permanent importance is passed on to the basal ganglia and is stored there as an auto-suggestion. This is where new knowledge and auto-suggestions are augmented and processed.

Young people's prefrontal cortex is constantly in operation and is permanently active during the acquisition of knowledge. Knowledge is transferred through repeated training into an auto-suggestion, which is then specifically performed by the basal ganglia. The older you get, the more auto-suggestions you use and the fewer new behaviors are transferred to the basal ganglia. Knowledge transfer also takes longer with increasing age. Anyone who wants to apply our approach must be physiologically able to anchor it in their basal ganglia.

Our *High Speed and Efficiency Concept* aims to counteract 'goal amnesia'. We use clearly defined visions to assign company goals to the individual teams, and then break these down into achievable partial results and partial goals. This way, focus remains on the overall company goal. This works because specialist departments and their staff know best how they can contribute to the success of the company—a manager doesn't have the necessary specialist knowledge and must therefore never specify the path, but instead only the goal.

3.4.4 Added Value: The Benefits

The period of validity of decisions made in the past is becoming shorter and shorter. The COVID pandemic has clearly demonstrated this, and now even the last stalwart non-believers have been convinced that it exists. Once again, it's our basal ganglia that make us cling on to our old beliefs as if our lives depended on it.

In order to achieve the clear goal of progress, we have to generate added value. As Fig. 3.26 shows, decisions that are long in the making no longer help us to achieve this and, nowadays, the effort involved in conventional decision cycles almost always exceeds the benefits they produce. What is required are agile decisions that can be easily adapted to the current situation. Our thesis is that added value can be best achieved through rapid decision-making.

3.4.5 Orientation Within the Diffuse Strategy Cloud

Strategy is a soft and intangible subject that is difficult to depict rationally, and describing a future state is a fairly emotional and visionary matter. It takes practice and clarity of thought to apply the required abstraction and structure to this diffuse cloud. Once you have worked through the following sections, you will find it easier to see and manage strategic matters more clearly. As an initial exercise, we ask you to internalize Fig. 3.27 and draw your own conclusions from it. Then classify your own approach to your previous projects.

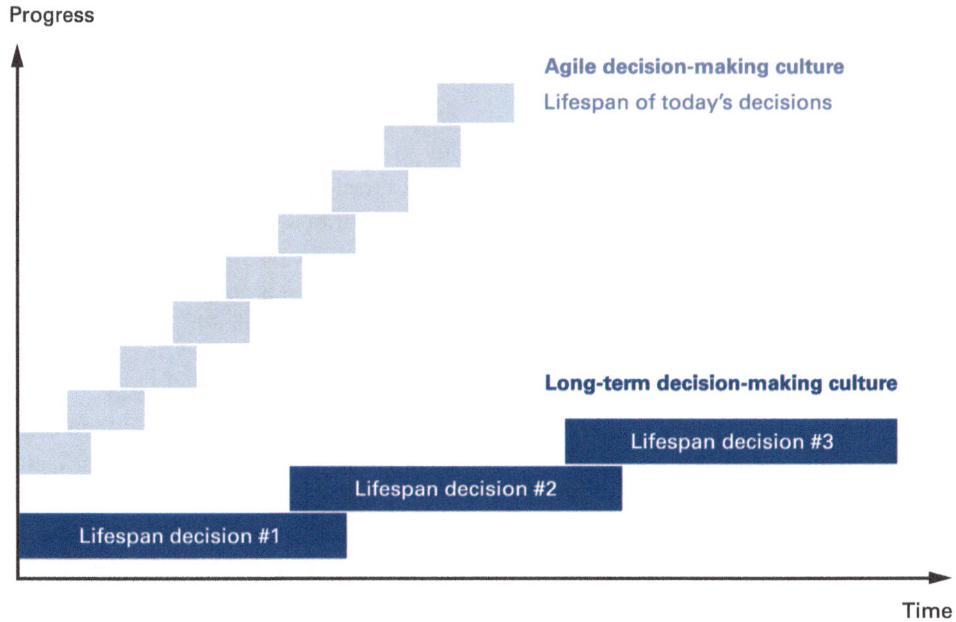

Fig. 3.26 Agile vs. long-term decision-making. (Source: H&F Solutions GmbH/www.hf-solutions.co)

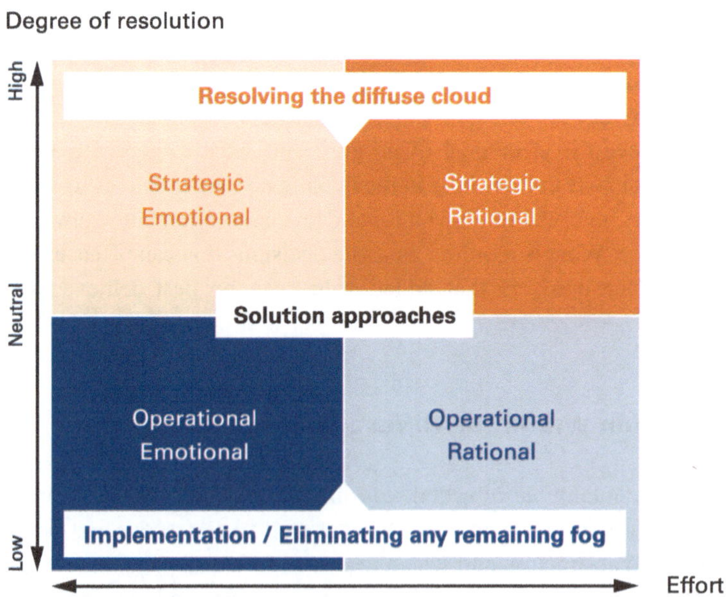

Fig. 3.27 Solution approaches during the orientation phase. (Source: H&F Solutions GmbH/www.hf-solutions.co)

Summary

Good preparation is essential, and this is also true for the *H&F Highs Speed and Efficiency Concept.* Your project can only generate serious speed if your employees adopt the right attitude. To achieve this, it is essential to implement habits and/or auto-suggestions. Habitual actions can always be performed more efficiently. Because decision-making processes are accelerating all the time, without a corporate culture that includes fixed rituals and behaviors, your project will founder. With the help of these rituals you will make enough progress in spite of the state of permanent change that surrounds you. ◀

3.5 The H&F High Speed and Efficiency Concept

Alongside all the human factors and the necessary basic knowledge this section provides you with concrete instructions for action. With their help, you will be able to implement the methodology we describe without our support. After all, you are quite capable of successfully managing and/or implementing IT and ERP projects.

3.5.1 The H&F Strategy Approach from a 'Helicopter' Viewpoint

The *H&F Strategy Approach* uses the increasingly well-known OKR (Objectives and Key Results) method. This was developed in the 1970s by Intel co-founder Andrew Grove and has been used intensively by Google since the late 1990s. Much of Google's success is attributed to the OKR method. While the method's inventor explained it in just two pages, today many large books cover the subject. In this book, we want to share only the core idea with you.

The OKR approach combines the goals of an innovation strategy project with the goals of each individual employee, and fundamental issues are addressed that align the focus of these two hierarchical levels. Because it discloses communication and the focus of the goals involved, this method is ideally suited to quickly checking the viability of project participants, measuring the results, and controlling strategy projects.

The OKR method involves assigning a key result to each objective. These metrics are compared with each other at regular intervals and immediately adjusted in the event of changes. All other project management methods are ignored. This reduces the burden on the company's already scarce resources. Bear in mind that only completed tasks provide benefits.

Now let's go directly to the implementation. To do this, you should bear Fig. 3.28 in mind while reading each of the following sections.

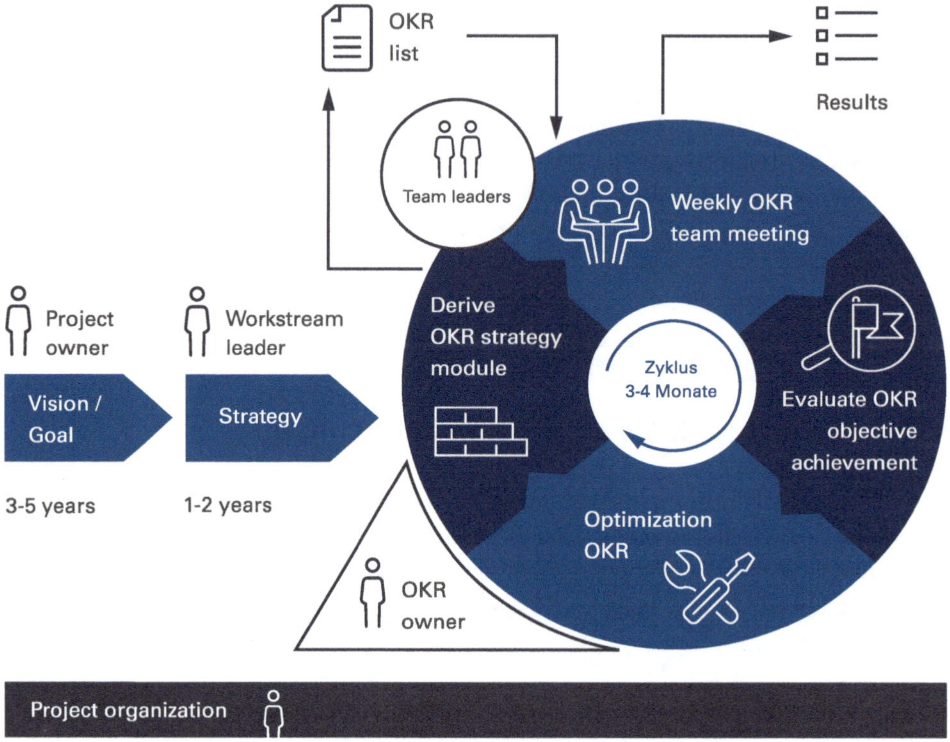

Fig. 3.28 The *H&F Strategy Approach* from a 'helicopter' viewpoint. (Source: H&F Solutions GmbH/www.hf-solutions.co)

3.5.1.1 Vision/Objective and Mission Statement

The vision and the future goal story (3–5 years hence) developed from the goal story (see Sect. 3.5.4.4) provide a mission derived for a shorter (partial) period of 1–2 years.

3.5.1.2 Strategy Modules

Strategy modules are designed for a total lifespan of 1–2 years, although an individual module shouldn't spend more than 3–4 months within the OKR cycle so that achievable objectives are never too far off.

3.5.1.3 Focus and Implementation

Derivation of the Strategy Modules for OKR

The implementation team can now develop key actions and key results from the partial objectives derived for each module. The OKRs are then stored in an OKR overview list.

Team Meeting OKR

Progress and status are reported in a weekly meeting (maximum duration 15 minutes).

Evaluation of OKR Objective Achievement
At the end of a cycle (i.e., after 3–4 months), the degree of achievement of objectives is evaluated in depth across the entire business unit.

OKR Optimization
Following each cycle, regulatory measures are taken to improve the next cycle.

OKR Owner or Strategy Module Owner
The OKR owner's job is to ensures smooth progress.

3.5.2 Clarification of Company Purpose (Every 5–10 Years)

Many companies create products or offer services, but what is the motivation or aspiration behind them? What do these organizations want to achieve in the long term? In the course of many projects, we have found that this mental process rarely takes place at the beginning of a strategy project. People just start working on it. With regard to the products they offer, many companies simply try to cater to every market demand that comes their way and then develop a strategy to fit the product. This often ends up producing unmanageable complexity. Do new products or services even fit the company objectives? And even more interesting is the question of whether the company has mastered the necessary processes at all, or whether it is simply getting itself into trouble.

working for a tractor manufacturer, we were presented with the following mission statement: "We build tractors to help our customers achieve their goals faster and with greater returns."

It can be deduced from the mission statement that the product range doesn't cover other types of vehicles in the same industry—for example, a harvester wouldn't fit the mission statement. The term "faster" implies that the customer should have a competitive advantage through the latest agricultural technologies provided by the manufacturer. The "greater returns" part implies that the cost of a purchase can be recovered by the product within a short time.

These goals were subconsciously followed in the course of every decision made, however small.

▶ **Action #1 (What Actually Has to Be Implemented)** Briefly outline corporate activity. Do this once in relation to your company and once in relation to your personal view. Define a circle of a maximum of five people and share your outlines with them. It is important to clarify where the company or the project team is headed in the future. Don't include any numbers at this stage. At this point, it is all about the tiny dot on the horizon.

Following this meeting, summarize these points and take the summary with you to the next project step. As an example, see the tractor manufacturer's project extract in Fig. 3.29:

Individual definitions

Shareholder #1:	We want to build innovative tractors	Too vague
Shareholder #2:	We want to help customers achieve greater yields	Well-defined
CEO:	Our tractors close the gap caused by the customer's staff shortages	Well-defined
CSO:	We want our customers to be satisfied	Too vague
CTO:	We want to build efficient tractors that protect the environment	Defined

Overall definition

We build environmentally friendly tractors that eliminate our customers' labor shortages and help them achieve greater yields.

Fig. 3.29 An example of defining corporate purpose. (Source: H&F Solutions GmbH/www.hf-solutions.co)

3.5.3 The Emotional Approach (3–5 Year Timeline)

What drives you as a decision-maker or entrepreneur? You are not in your current position due to money alone and, as we all know, money cannot motivate people in the long term. As a role model, you have a great influence on the course of events simply through your behavior. If you have a clear goal, you will be able to motivate your employees too. In the case of the tractor manufacturer illustrated above, the company goals weren't sufficiently clear. In the past, strong growth ensured sufficient sales and returns, and the company was doing well without a vision or a clear goal. When motivation waned in the early 2010s due to a change of generations in many decision-making positions, the company began to experience serious problems. This change was also noticeable within the project. The various decision-makers each had a very different idea of the future company direction. As the project progressed, we noticed that there was no clarity or unity of purpose, and different forces were tugging in different directions. As a result, we took this client on a journey with an overall company goal as its destination. Through a clear goal, you can communicate a future state that you want to achieve over a defined period of time.

> **Overall Mission**
>
> Within the next four years, 50 per cent of our tractors will be autonomous and will be driven by alternative power trains.

Fig. 3.30 Example of an overall company goal. (Source: H&F Solutions GmbH/www.hf-solutions.co)

Emotionally, you now know what the company's purpose is, and you now have to provide definition for this diffuse cloud. This is done by breaking down and defining the overall goal. However, in contrast to clarifying the company's purpose, a goal is specifically attainable. These goals first have to be represented in an abstract form, as shown for our tractor manufacturer in Fig. 3.30.

However, this is only the headline for the company goal. The complete company goal was an emotional two-page story where everyone's innovative thoughts were recorded in concrete terms.

► **Action #2 (What Actually Has to Be Implemented)** To set up your company for an innovative future, you need think freely and playfully according to the guideline: "All thoughts are allowed." This process is all about linking thoughts or ideas that would not have been linked under normal circumstances.

Now you have to put these thoughts down on paper. To do this, you need to fire up your personal time machine and get each member of the previously defined circle of most capable people to journey four years into the future and describe how the project will look when it has been successfully completed. It is important to describe what is specifically different and what has changed in the target state. This future story creates an emotional picture that you should follow emotionally and with enthusiasm during the project that follows.

Each individual participant should describe figuratively what has changed (no numbers allowed). The authors should have already 'seen' these changes, both prospectively and emotionally.

Note that, in the future, the results or changes are already completed. No activities are to be described.

It is important to make sure that you don't pack too much into this image of your goals. Too many variables create a chaos of priorities in the subsequent processes of strategy development and implementation.

This draft is followed by the first face-to-face meeting of the project team. Before the overall goal story can be transformed into an innovation strategy concept, the core team meets for discussion, where they discuss which points the participants find good, what they do not understand, what is still missing, and which points the participants find bad.

Together and critically, they develop an overall story that unites the positive and innovative points so that a common picture of the goal emerges.

► Avoid brainstorming in groups, because this leads not to innovative thinking, but instead to simple adaptation of the associative thinking of the group members. This means that you are operating in familiar territory and are not thinking about anything really new.

In the example of the tractor manufacturer, it could be clearly derived that the future products are to be enhanced using new technology. This also means that the company and its employees should be geared towards developing decisive innovations that are sustainable and profitable, and that provide the customer with a competitive advantage.

3.5.4 Strategy Modules (1–2 Year Timeline)

The future state has now been captured in a defined working paper, so the strategic direction can now be set. To this end, the following steps need to be taken:

1. Development of a 'strategy building'
2. Breakdown of the overall goal vision into individual pillars
3. Creation of a workstream for each pillar
4. Development of detailed goal stories for each pillar

3.5.4.1 The Strategy Building: Goal Pillars and their Strategy Components

On the basis of the overall goal vision, it should now be clear to every participant where the project is headed. For this purpose, the overall objective (output) has to be broken down into its individual components, or puzzle pieces (outcome). These should then be grouped into themes. It is important to allow no more than eight topics. These are then to be grouped together within the thematic areas into individual strategy components.

3.5.4.2 The Structure of the Individual Strategy Pillars

Once the pieces of the puzzle are defined, each pillar must be named, and current and future target states must be defined for each pillar. The difference between the current and the future target state is called the strategic gap.

3.5.4.3 Creating Workstreams

One or two responsible persons must now be assigned to each pillar (workstream). The two assigned persons (workstream leaders) are responsible for the successful fulfilment of this pillar in the future. In turn, they are assigned supporting staff who assist with the implementation. This step finally dissolves the departmental thinking viewpoint and enables a view of the relevant themes that is necessary for successful strategy implementation.

3.5.4.4 Developing Detailed Goal Stories

Each workstream now goes through the same process of creating goal vision stories. During this process, it is once again necessary to define how the individual pieces of the puzzle have to look in order to optimally serve the overall goal. The following example describes the goal story of an employee from an operational change project:

Example

"We record all customer data simply and quickly in a central location. This ensures that there are no duplicates or spelling errors, and that all relationships are correctly assigned (e.g., contact persons for purchasing, technology, shipping, project management, and so on). All data that is entered as part of an order (new business or service) is then directly accessible to the specialist departments. Important information (different payment terms, special shipping methods, different delivery addresses, contact persons for self-collectors, customs requirements such as preferential treatment, and so on) is made available to the departments concerned in such a way that it cannot be overlooked and can be taken into account accordingly. Customer service can see which customers have been supplied with which products in the past so that they can effectively offer targeted services (maintenance, training, and so on). In doing so, a service can easily see when maintenance is due for parts that have a set maintenance interval." ◀

3.5.4.5 Presentation of Workstream Issues in Relation to their Operational and Strategic Components, Based on Impact Assessment

There are now many independent pieces of the puzzle in each workstream, and of course you can't move them all forward at once. So, in keeping with our guideline: "It's important to do the right thing", you need to decide which of these strategic gap puzzle pieces you want to move forward first. A broader view is required to better make and/or support this decision. To do this, clarify the strategic and operational performance components of the puzzle pieces in the form of an impact assessment (see Fig. 3.31).

This exercise will quickly help you see whether the pieces of the puzzle you have defined serve strategic alignment or operational improvement. With the help of the strategy building and impact assessment, you now have a firm basis for prioritizing your individual puzzle pieces in a meaningful way and anchoring this prioritization on a timeline (see Fig. 3.32).

3.5.4.6 Prioritizing the Puzzle Pieces

The existing puzzle pieces must now be classified according to their contribution to overall success. For this purpose, the two puzzle pieces are selected that make the greatest contribution to the success of the project. In addition, two further puzzle pieces are selected

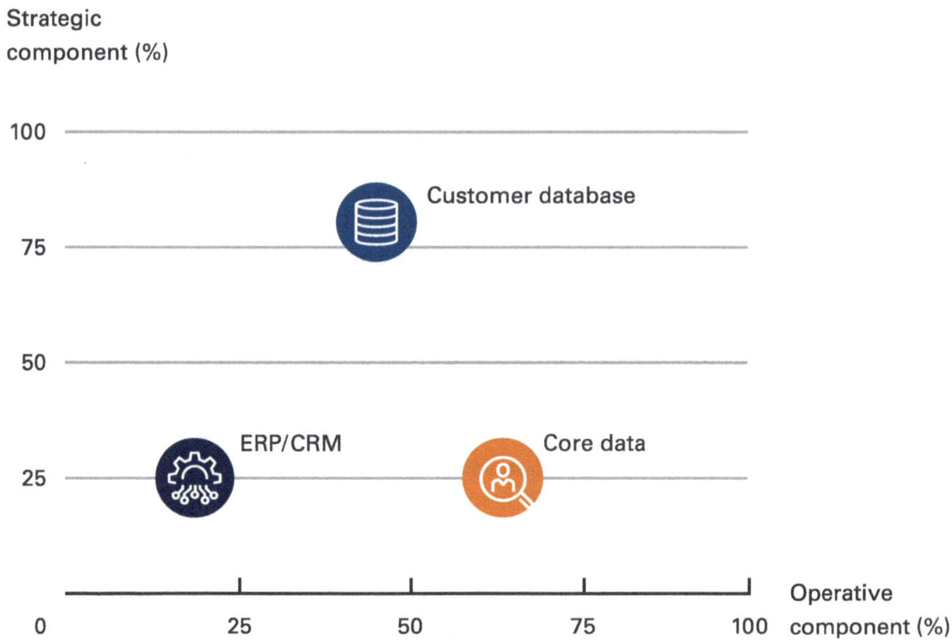

Fig. 3.31 Impact assessment. (Source: H&F Solutions GmbH/www.hf-solutions.co)

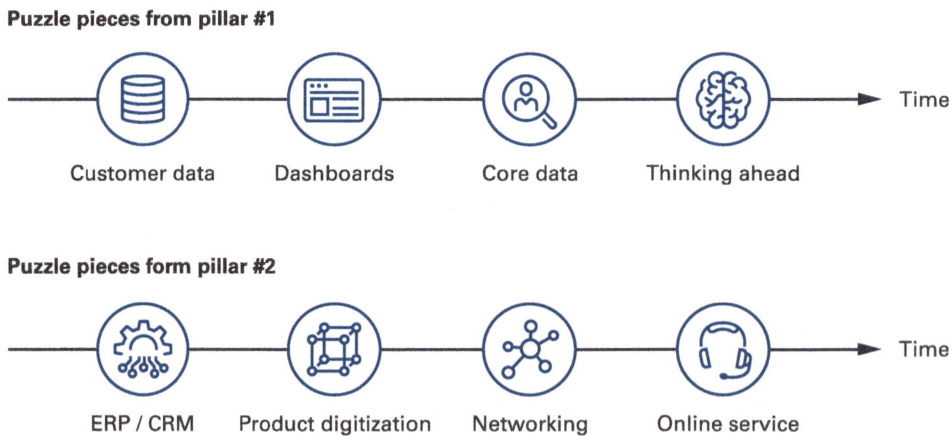

Fig. 3.32 Timeline showing prioritization of puzzle pieces. (Source: H&F Solutions GmbH/www.hf-solutions.co)

to be worked on next. No new work of any sort should be begun before work on these four puzzle pieces has significantly advanced.

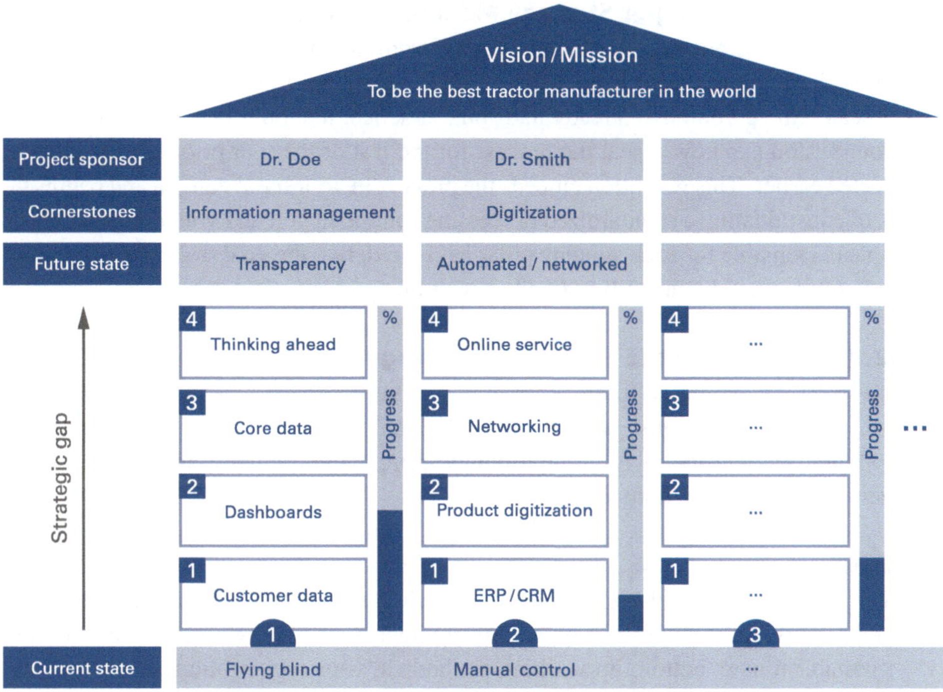

Fig. 3.33 A sample strategy building following derivation of the goal story. (Source: H&F Solutions GmbH/www.hf-solutions.co)

3.5.4.7 The Finished Strategy Building

The strategy building (see Fig. 3.33) provides you with a constant overview of all your topics, and gives all decision-makers and project owners the chance to view project progress at a glance. The project owner receives a compact overview of which changes and progress have been made in which workstream. You will learn more about this in the following sections.

3.5.5 Focus and Implementation: Definition of Detailed Objectives and Key Results (3–12 Month Timeline)

You have now clarified where you are headed (the goal) but not how to get there. You now need an implementation strategy to achieve this project goal. To achieve this, you need to break the topic down further and convert it into small, easily manageable pieces. Here, you need the puzzle pieces that you defined previously.

3.5.5.1 Goal Definition per Strategy Module (i.e., per Puzzle Piece)

For each piece of the puzzle, the strategy process from the future story onward needs to be repeated with the workstream team. This involves repeating a now familiar process on a smaller scale. Since you have already had some practice, it should be easier than the first time around. You can now repeat the process for the rest of the four priority puzzle pieces you selected earlier. This repetition embeds the process in your basal ganglia and begins the process of consolidating a standardized processing routine in you and your company. Now, the people responsible for each strategy pillar begin to derive the goal story with any newly involved colleagues who are still unfamiliar with this process.

3.5.5.2 Key Results for the Predefined Strategy Modules

From this puzzle piece-based future story, it is now necessary to develop the required key results in order to get as close as possible to the goal. A maximum of three or four key results should be developed for each strategy component. If there are more, the less important ones should be omitted or simply ignored.

► **Important**

The key results are always developed by their corresponding implementation teams and are never dictated from a higher hierarchical level. Otherwise, you won't be able to establish new, bottom-up working methods in your organization.

Sample Goal Definition and Key Results

For the strategy pillar "Best employees with the best salary", the situation needs to be transformed from below average (the initial situation) to above average (the target condition). One of the puzzle pieces in this pillar is labeled "Career ladder clarity" (outcome). To achieve this goal, the following key results were defined:

Key result #1:	Clarity regarding remuneration and career steps (clear roadmap)
Key result #2:	Highly efficient work/increased productivity (in order to realize profitability through higher wage levels too)

◄

Measurability, Achievability, and Incentives

It is important not only that the results to be achieved are precisely defined, but also that they are measurable and achievable. Ideally, you should select metrics that enable you to measure progress every week, or at least every month. It is important to define key results that can be realistically achieved. However, there will also be key results that are dependent on other results and therefore cannot be begun immediately. In this case they have to be clearly slated for a later start. In some cases, results will be reached as a series of individual steps rather than continuously. If this is the case, you should try to divide your results into sub-results in order to make your progress visible.

Now that you have worked out your goals, you need to define a metric for each with start and target values. The target value should be defined in such a way that it is realistically achievable. However, it shouldn't be set too low in order to retain its appeal as an incentive. If the target value isn't reached later on, this is a sign that it was set too high. In contrast, if the target value is reached within the initial phase of the project, it was set too low and will have only a small effect on the company's overall success. Ideally, the target values will be set to enable project participants to develop pride in their work. This serves as a motivational aid to overcome further hurdles. Do not forget to celebrate the successes the team achieves. Finding ideal values for your metrics will not be easy at the beginning but, with practice, you will master the art (remember your basal ganglia!). Figure 3.34 shows an example of an H&F OKR overview.

3.5.6 Speed and Progress: Agile Methods (2–4 Week Timeline)

3.5.6.1 Tactics: How Do We Achieve the Desired Result?

You cannot, of course, jump immediately from the start to the finish. Reaching your goals requires a meaningful methodology and appropriate tactics. By tactics we mean all considerations regarding 'how'. How can I bring about a result? How do I get to my next sub-goal? We need to be aware that there are always several ways to solve the same problem. Many roads lead to Rome. Everybody has to be aware that taking one route or another means more or less effort to get the same result. A more elaborate route may, however, be the simplest way to reach 'Rome'. The question now is, which solution path gets us to our goal fastest, depending on its duration and the probability of it leading to the planned goal? To work this out, all members of the workstream have to work together.

In a brainstorming session, the possible solutions are outlined (see Fig. 3.35) and evaluated. This forces us to look at the various possible solutions and stimulates our creative thinking. This is the only way to create views of things that were not apparent to us before. Many employees find this kind of creative thinking for developing innovative approaches or solutions very difficult, and that's why visualizing solution paths is helpful at this point. Remember that this way of working through things still has to be consolidated in our basal ganglia.

▶ Creative thinking can be learned: Try googling this methodology or get inspired by Leonardo da Vinci. He was a master of creative thinking.

Once the team has collected various solutions, one particular path will appear to make the most sense. This solution may well be based on gut feelings without scientific analysis. If this path isn't successful, the team simply switches to one of the previously developed

OKR Workstream 1WS 1C	
Period:	July 2023 - April 2024 (10 months)
OKRs from:	Sample Company
Owner / Sponsor:	Dr. Doe
Main objective:	Transparency in information management
Target OKR:	Quality assurance for core data

Key Results									
#	Result metric	Owner	Parameter	Type of survey	Start value	7/23	8/23	...	Target value
1	Rules for recording core data	Mr. Brown	Rules exist	Input from departments	25%	50%	60%	...	100%
2	Increased efficiency between system interfaces	Ms. Smith	Feedback from departments	Surveys within departments	0%	20%	25%	...	100%
3	Data management and archiving	Mr. Jones	Parameter evaluation	Evaluation	20%	20%	20%	...	100%
4	Automated smart core data creation	Mr. Johnson	Database creation	Development in departments	0%	10%	15%	...	50%

Key Actions #1	Guidelines / Rules			
#	Description	Person responsible	Realizable	Status
1	Entering relevant data from individual departments	Mr. Brown	Yes	Done
2	Grouping feedback and evaluation of the degree of completion	Mr. Rodriguez	Yes	Done
3	Further optimization through H&F project experience	H&F Solutions	Yes	In progress
4	Drafting rules and guidelines	Mr. Rodriguez	Yes	

Key Actions #2	Interfaces Between Systems			
#	Description	Person responsible	Realizable	Status
1	Analysis external to pro ALPHA—how many systems are in operation?	Ms. Smith	Yes	In Progress
2	Setting up system / human interfaces	Ms. Smith	Yes	In Progress

Key Actions #4	Automated Smart Core Data Creation			
#	Description	Person responsible	Realizable	Status
1	Creating the fields to be filled	Mr. Johnson	Yes	Done
2	Analysis of common factors as a basis for links and/or pull-down menus	Mr. Johnson	Yes	In Progress
3	Creation of a database for a pull-down menu	Mr. Johnson	Yes	
4	Creation of rules/logic to extend fields	Mr. Johnson	Yes	
5	Creation of logic that automatically fills other empty fields depending on field input	Mr. Johnson	Yes	
6	Check whether fields need to be filled in a specific order	Mr. Johnson	Yes	
7	Check whether it makes sense to manually confirm automatically filled fields	Mr. Johnson	Yes	

Fig. 3.34 A sample H&F OKR overview. (Source: H&F Solutions GmbH/www.hf-solutions.co)

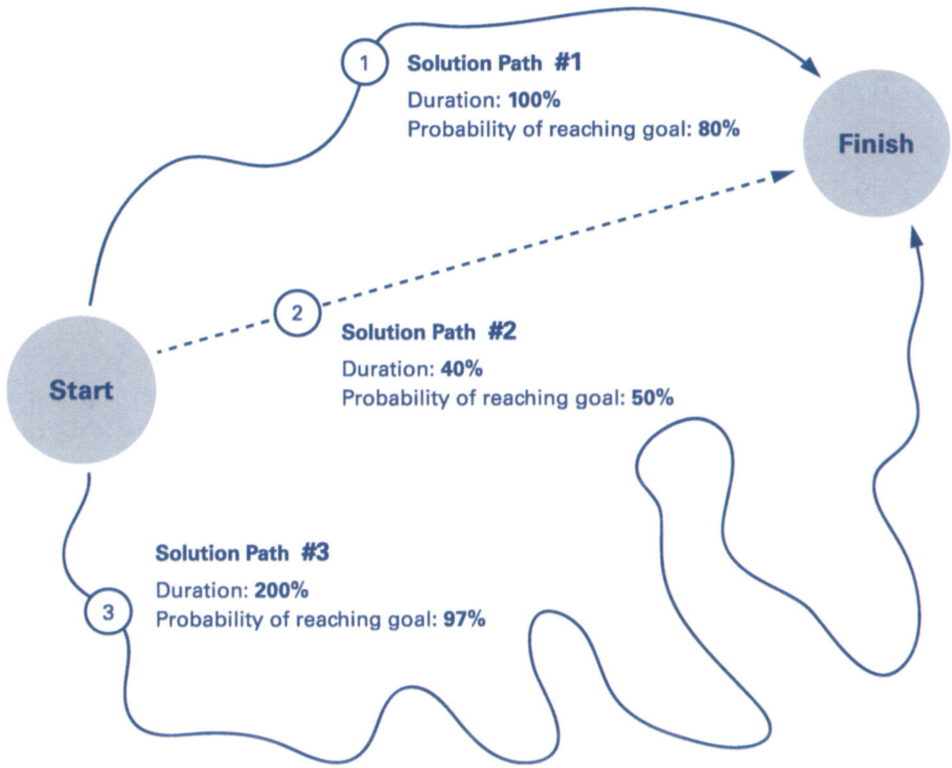

Fig. 3.35 Solution paths for individual decisions. (Source: H&F Solutions GmbH/www.hf-solutions.co)

alternative paths. At this point, you need to stick to your chosen path for a while before considering overturning the selection. There is nothing worse than changing your mind and your priorities every week. Nevertheless, we would like to draw your attention to why many people founder at this point in the process.

Example

We would like to show you why we often fail at the simplest things. This example, related to a strategy project, might seem unrealistic at first, but it is based on the same patterns that influence more complex and far-reaching problems:

All employees are tasked with cleaning the coffee machine once a week in rotation. One day, the coffee machine stopped working and leaked water during cleaning process (problem). Our intern at that time was 16 years old and not yet sufficiently intellectually mature to solve a problem structurally and independently. He was only able to perform tasks that had already been demonstrated to him and couldn't solve a new, unknown situation. We discussed the core of the problem with him so that he could think about how to restore functionality.

Together we worked out the following solutions.

(a) Order a new coffee machine and dispose of the old one
(b) Call the manufacturer's service department to order a repair
(c) Work through the manual, followed by self-study of the coffee machine.

The trainee decided to try variant c. Working on the problem later, he discovered that a loose hose had caused the problem. ◄

What does this example show us about our approach to projects and the development of solutions? Initially, we don't immediately know what to do and may not be able to develop all potential solutions. However, we can still look for solutions, sketch them out, pursue them, and try to achieve a result. We have to learn how to harness our capabilities to get something implemented. We need to shift from talking about doing things to actually doing them.

► People are increasingly forgetting how to apply logical thinking and are thus also losing the ability to see and implement things as a whole. Demotivation of employees reinforces this process.

3.5.6.2 A Board Makes Perfection and Planning Redundant

Since our approach omits most of the planning stages, we now need a tool that helps us to react quickly to new events. A traditional project management approach with corresponding milestones and scheduling devours maintenance resources that could be better used for achieving our goals. Using our project approach, it is simply a matter of assigning the upcoming work packages (key actions) to the corresponding workstreams and completing them as quickly as possible.

Nowadays there are plenty of digital whiteboards that offer these kinds of functions (a quick online search will provide you with plenty of material on this subject). We divide our control and organization board into five sub-areas/pillars, as shown in Fig. 3.36. This way, all the work to be done can be clearly displayed:

1. On Hold
2. To Do
3. In Progress
4. Done
5. Archived

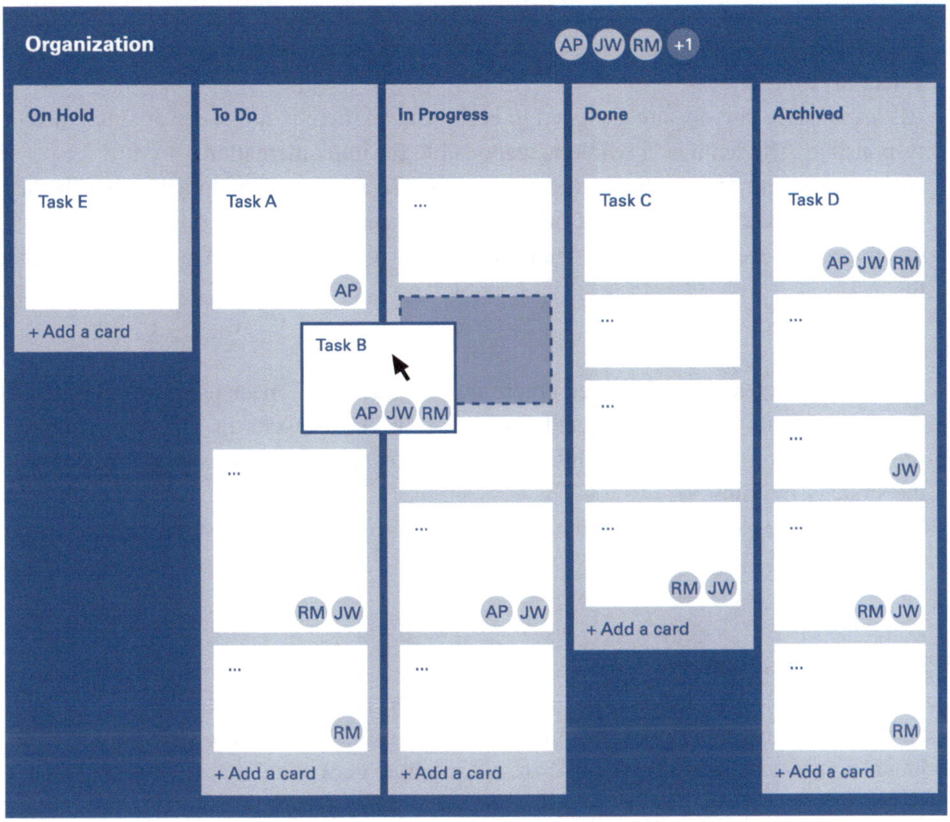

Fig. 3.36 Our control and organization board. (Source: H&F Solutions GmbH/www.hf-solutions.co)

The Procedure:

1. A card is created in the *On Hold* column for each work item.
2. We then discuss which minimum requirements each of these tasks or cards must fulfil by the end of the project. Once the minimum requirements have been successfully defined the card is moved to the *To Do* column.
3. Now select four cards for each project team that are directly driven by the workstream team and move them to the *In Progress* column.
4. These four cards are advanced until the tasks are completed and, following a successful check, are placed in the *Done* column.

The Rules:

- A card/task is not considered complete until it has been jointly signed off by the core team at a weekly meeting.

- A maximum of four cards are advanced in parallel to maintain focus and concentration on specific topics. Too many construction sites make the workstream sluggish and have a demotivating effect.
- All responsible persons are assigned to each task, so there is no leader or single person responsible. The team as a whole is responsible for implementation.
- At the beginning of an activity, the key actions (*To Do*) involved in achieving the task outcome are discussed with the individual task members and a course of action is developed. These activities are then written down in the form of a checklist within the task.

Status:

- A weekly core team meeting then determines for each work package how many points per checklist have been completed for each task. This results in a percentage-based progress metric for the sum of all tasks in workstream. This result is then transferred to the strategy building.
- Each employee can then see who has made what progress until the status changes at the next meeting.

3.5.6.3 Implementation

Our experience shows that most projects fail not because of technical issues, but more because of communication and commitment issues, making these just as important as the technical component. The *To Do* cards are not meant to be worked through mindlessly, but are designed to stimulate thinking and serve as a guide. Nevertheless, each task should cover any technical requirements and come as close as possible to the desired result. At this point, thinking outside the box rounds out a successful project. Overarching considerations should be the basis for achieving the goal so that as many stakeholders as possible within the organization benefit from it. We like to use one-on-one sessions with colleagues from other workstreams or from outside the project team for this purpose. This knowledge transfer and exchange serves our colleagues and enables us to benefit from their wealth of experience. The entire overarching know-how transfer is fed by this networked approach to thinking and working. You will notice that the problem areas are almost never of a technical nature. However, should a technical obstacle arise, you can always bring an external specialist or expert on board.

3.5.7 Role Allocation: The Project Organization

We now need to talk about the specific distribution of roles in your innovation strategy project. A small number of clear communication channels dominate the distribution of roles from the beginning, with a view to implementing this procedure permanently in your

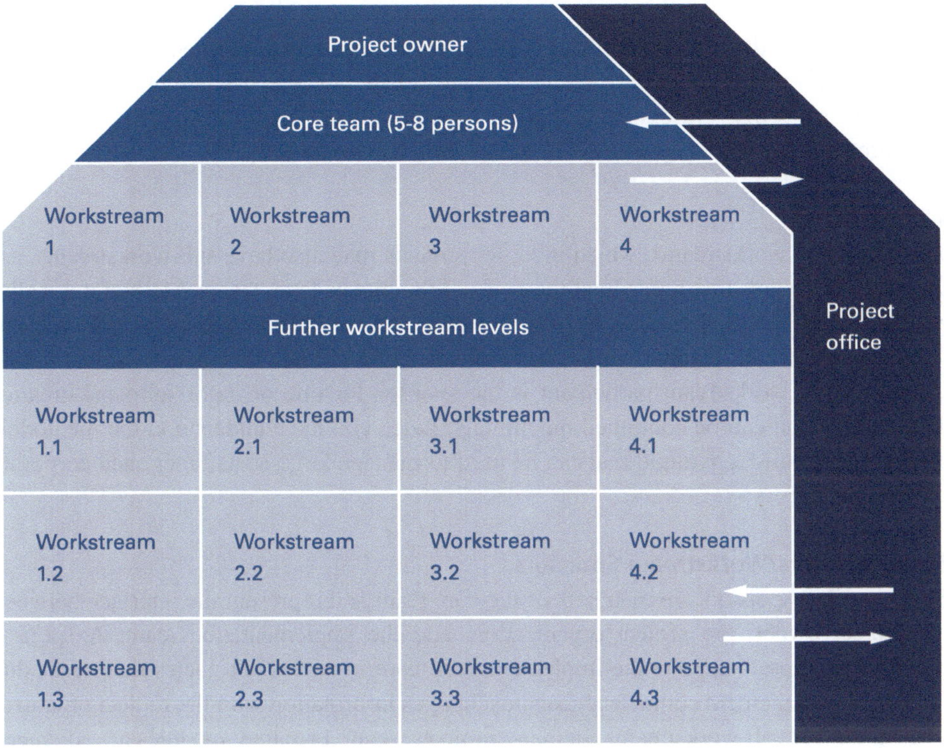

Fig. 3.37 The project organization pyramid. (Source: H&F Solutions GmbH/www.hf-solutions.co)

organization. It is then clear which role has to be filled by whom, and what their contribution to the overall success of the project is.

3.5.7.1 Overview: The Organizational Pyramid

The organizational pyramid shown in Fig. 3.37 is designed to serve as an anchor for organizing your team throughout the project.

Project Owner

The project leader/owner represents the interests of the project. Together with the core team, he develops the target picture and is the interface between the core team, management, and the project organization. As a rule, the project owner is actively informed once a month about the interim status and/or progress in the form of the strategy building (including the individual progress bars). This enables him to get a clear overview of the project in less than an hour.

Core Team

The core team is the extended project steering and management group and gives specialist input (the future stories) on the direction the project should take. The members of the core team are also the professional sparring partners and mentors for the individual workstreams.

Workstreams

The individual workstreams, which in larger projects may also have sub-workstreams, are the execution teams that implement the goals of the higher-level teams. Methodologically, a workstream works the same way as the core team, and this applies to all types of workstreams at all levels within the project. In the case of sub-workstreams, the corresponding workstream participant is the sponsor for one or more sub-workstreams. This subdivision can be continued indefinitely. Once you have understood the methodology, you can build a pyramid that can be used to manage large-scale, integrated corporate projects.

Strategy Pillars/Workstream Sponsors

Strategy pillar sponsors are members of the core team and represent the interface between the project owner, the project organization, and the implementation team. A sponsor monitors progress, supports the implementation team in case of obstacles that occur due to gaps in management competence, and exchanges information with the project organization team across all workstreams. In many projects, several strategy modules are advanced in parallel, making it necessary to have an owner for each strategy module in addition to the workstream leader, who supports the implementation team organizationally and strategically, and assists the workstream sponsor.

The Project Office Is the Key to Success

The project office is the link between all project participants. This can consist of just one, or of several people. All technical and organizational topics converge within this team. It ensures that topics such as scheduling, technical content, or meetings are adhered to and prepared so that the project participants can concentrate on the technical topics. By securing communication and cooperation in this way, the information stream remains intact. Obstacles are immediately addressed in task force meetings or individual sparring sessions, so that progress is made within the weekly coordination meetings without having to address individual issues. Overarching issues are clearly sorted by subject and assigned to the appropriate workstreams, so that they are don't generate duplicate effort. Members of the project office do not necessarily need specialist knowledge, but do need to be able to coordinate and communicate at an above-average level.

► **Important**
The project office is the most important component in the entire project. This is because it ensures structured communication, the lack of which is known to be responsible for more 75% of project failures.

3.5.7.2 Rapid Decisions Are the Basis of all Progress

In order to achieve the desired speed in the project, it is necessary to not just make decisions, but also to make the right decisions. And this has to take place even when you don't know all of the appropriate parameters. Not everyone is predestined for this kind of work. Making decisions is never easy, and is always accompanied by the worry of making the wrong decision, missing an opportunity, or even making a major error. In order to make the best decisions, you should never put them off. First impressions say a lot about how you feel about a particular decision, and the longer you think about a decision, the more things you can think of that will influence it. If you think for too long, you may even lose your overview and reduce the quality of your decisions because you no longer know what is right or wrong. Here is an example:

Example
At this point, we would like to compare two project teams. One team makes quick decisions, but some of them are wrong and the team has to correct the chosen path. The other project team weighs the decisions in the group very carefully and makes almost all of the decisions correctly, but takes much longer to do so. In our example, we assume that a strategy project involves about 1000 decisions (probably quite a small project). As you can see in Fig. 3.38, the group of slow deciders uses many times more effort. If all of a company's projects are handled this way, the company will use much more effort to achieve its goals than a company that reaches project decisions quickly. This is the reason why many projects become time-consuming and expensive. ◄

In our project approach, speed and progress have top priority. Imagine you are a rally driver travelling at high speed and you have a co-driver on board who provides you with all the necessary information that you can no longer acquire yourself at this speed. The communication between you and your co-pilot must be so sophisticated that you only exchange highly relevant information. You won't have time to chat about your latest family vacation at this speed. You are focused on reaching the end of the stage as quickly as possible.

Our approach is almost identical. You should only take time for the essentials and focus exclusively on the project goal. Everything else should be prepared for you at a high level of quality. This behavior leads to permanent progress. Traditional coffee meetings among colleagues become a thing of the past, and you have to build implementation momentum that drives the project along.

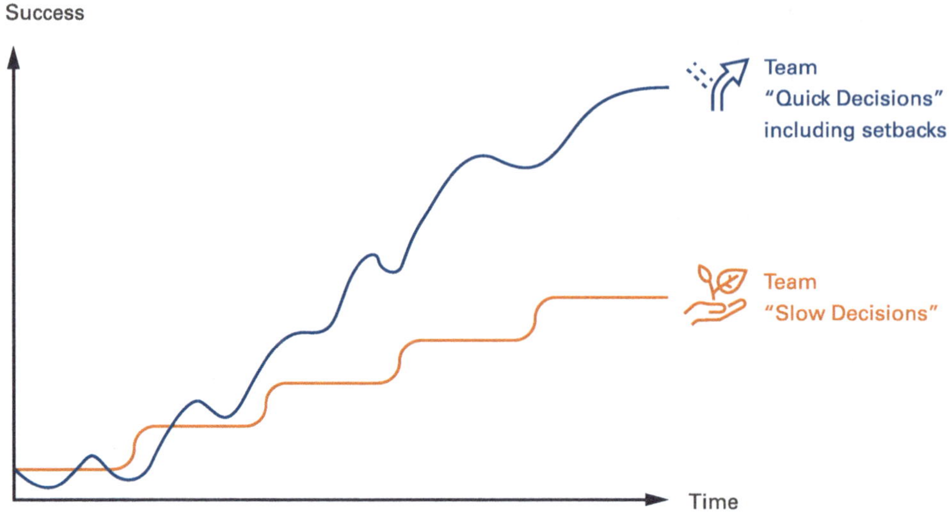

	Team "Quick Decisions"	Team "Slow Decisions"
Number of decisions	1,000	1,000
Time taken for a decision	5 min.	30 min.
Discards due to wrong decisions	20%	3%
Duration of the decision-making process	4,000 min. (approx. 67 hours)	29,100 min. (approx. 485 hours)

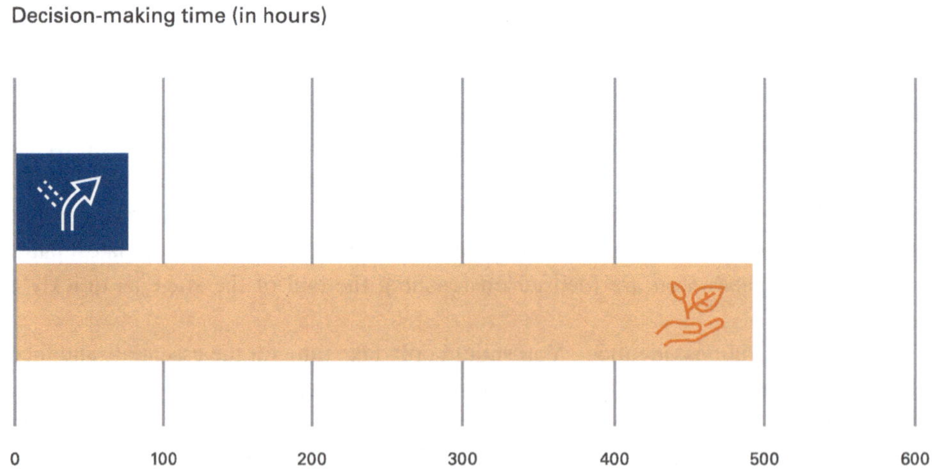

Fig. 3.38 The H&F decision matrix. (Source: H&F Solutions GmbH/www.hf-solutions.co)

Returning briefly to the rally analogy, at the beginning of your project you and your co-driver are sure to drive up a few blind alleys or take some wrong turns before your communication and coordination really start to hum. This will seem chaotic and alienating at first, but later you will generate more progress and, ideally, remain one step ahead of the competition.

3.5.7.3 Key Results Implementation Team

In each workstream, key results are defined for the objectives. For each key result, there is a responsible key result owner and a corresponding implementation team that jointly executes the key actions. The implementation team drives the actual progress.

3.5.7.4 Organizational Units in a Company

The H&F approach operates parallel to your existing organizational structures. Any existing business units can thus remain in place without being touched. You may find that team members from various different areas are involved in a single strategy module. In this case, they organize themselves in the form of agile project teams. If things have to move quickly, independent task forces are formed to quickly and agilely advance their own workstream or OKR goal. Departmental thinking is out of place here.

3.5.8 Rules and Understanding

In order to achieve the greatest possible impact, certain project rules are required. If these are consistently taken on board by the team, this will release a high level of goal-oriented energy. The three associated pillars, each containing one rule, are shown in Fig. 3.39.

3.5.8.1 The Most Important Rule: Permanent Progress!

> **Important**
> The most important rule in any project is to make sure you achieve permanent, consistent progress.

There should never be a week in which no progress is made (at least in terms of metrics). You have to ensure that your metrics change, and that any obstacles are not only reported in the weekly workstream meeting, but are also dealt with in advance and proactively within the implementation team. Ideally, these are then remedied or alternatives are sought.

3.5.8.2 Fast, Proactive Communication

In order to counteract inertia and actively pursue the agile H&F approach, communication has to be proactive and must never break down. Any obstacles, ambiguities, or communication problems that arise are resolved immediately. This ensures that knowledge transfer takes place correctly and that all the project participants involved benefit from it. By

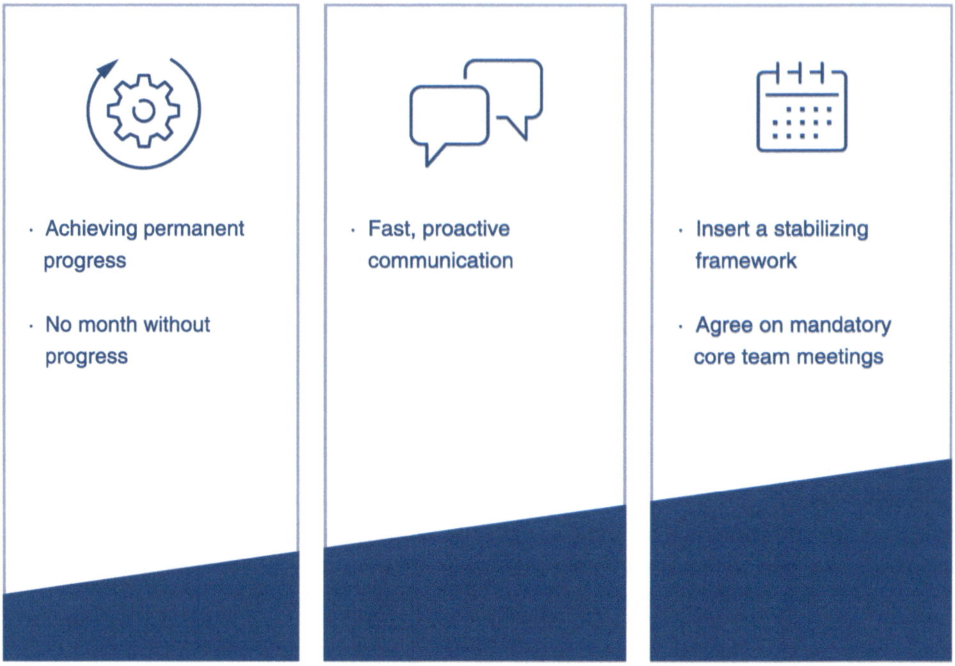

Fig. 3.39 The three pillars of implementation strength and stability. (Source: H&F Solutions GmbH/ www.hf-solutions.co)

communicating this way, you ensure that you are on the right track and moving in the right direction together. Ambiguities are reduced to a minimum or, ideally, are completely eliminated.

Use Mentors and Experts

In many projects, cultural, human, and professional issues lead to obstacles quite early in the project—especially in the areas of innovation strategy development and implementation. Once they appear, such obstacles can rarely be overcome in a goal-oriented manner. As a rule, some initial losers are identified fairly early in the project 'game'. However, this doesn't have to be the case. To counteract such processes, we recommend involving an expert or a mentor at regular intervals. This person can give you valuable support in many situations by providing an outside view. As a result, the essentials snap back into focus and the project implementation loses less impetus than it would without mentor support.

3.5.8.3 Stabilize the Project Framework and Arrange Mandatory Core Team Meetings

To ensure knowledge transfer and monitor it at regular intervals, your need to give your project a fixed schedule. This means that there will be short core team meetings at regular intervals. These meetings provide the various project participants with information on project progress and present the results the team has achieved. This ensures that each core team member is informed accordingly and can contribute his or her view of the results. This 'thinking outside the box' provides a bidirectional exchange of information and again stimulates all participants to embrace new topics.

▶ **Important**

To ensure efficiency, you should never mix organizational, strategic, and technical issues in a single meeting. Core team meetings shouldn't focus on the 'how' but only on the 'what'.

Additionally, it is forbidden to talk about approaches that haven't generated success in these meetings. No-one wants to hear about what didn't work or why. Only progress and new ideas presented.

If new issues come to light that haven't yet been communicated, these should also be presented in core team meetings. However, solution-finding for new issues never takes place in core team meetings, but rather in small, separate task force units that produce quick and proactive results.

Summary

With the help of the *H&F High Speed and Efficiency Concept*, you will be able to define a meaningful strategic direction and implement it step by step. This concept takes into account the future challenges regarding the definition and implementation of innovation strategy projects. For this purpose, the concept uses a variety of digital tools and behaviors. Specifically, these are the *H&F Strategy Approach*, the strategy building, the organizational pyramid, the OKR framework, and the pillars of implementation strength and stability. To this end, it is important to understand that in the future, short decision-making paths and quick decisions will form the path to success. This concept envisages only project phases that generate progress. In the future, permanent progress will be the norm. ◀

4 Practical Examples for the Prevention of Known Stumbling Blocks in OKR Innovation Strategy Projects

It is important to us that you not only learn about innovation strategy projects from a technical viewpoint, but that you also get to look at a basic set of practical examples of how strategy projects do and don't work. To this end, we have examined a project from a variety of angles. We don't aim to provide you with basic work steps to copy, but rather to provide valuable insights into topics that were previously inaccessible to you. Please note that not every practical example will be useful for every application in your own company. Sometimes it helps to recognize early on that a particular approach isn't applicable in your case.

4.1 We've Started, So We're Going to See It Through

"We've started, so we're going to see it through" is a statement we were confronted with early in our consulting careers. The project in question was concerned with implementing a supply chain innovation strategy for overseas customers and suppliers. The original strategy envisaged a tightly scheduled connection of all overseas locations and their suppliers. At the same time, the customer also decided to introduce the headquarter ERP system at all its overseas locations. The strategy was actually fabulous and exploited the company's potential to the full. However, right at the start the company decided that the leap from an Excel-based system to an ERP system with simultaneous connection to all its suppliers was simply too big for the planned timeline. In addition, the ERP manufacturer was not able to provide fully integrated localized versions at that time, and could only supply standalone foreign-language versions. However, management didn't have the slightest intention of changing the existing situation, as in their eyes the goal had been chosen correctly and the budgets were already in place. Revising the budgets would have

P. Futterknecht, T. Hertfelder, *Data, Disruption & Digital Leadership*,
https://doi.org/10.1007/978-3-658-41601-0_4

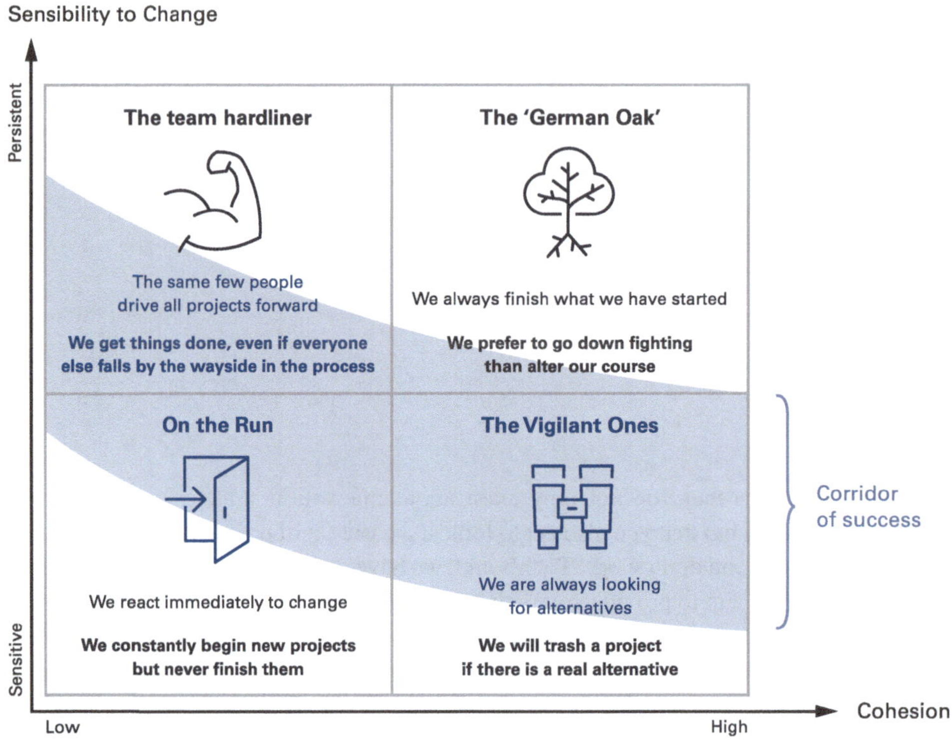

Fig. 4.1 Decision-making sensitivities in strategy projects. (Source: H&F Solutions GmbH/www.hf-solutions.co)

cost an enormous amount of time and effort. So they just went ahead. At the time this book went to press, the overseas locations were still not properly connected and the supply chain wasn't integrated—and this project was already 4 years old back then. The only things that were fully implemented were using up the hardware and software budgets, and staffing the designated ERP and SCM manager roles. At some point, every project reaches the point at which it no longer makes sense to continue. In this example, that point never arrived. In this case, management behavior wasn't wrong, but the decisions made nevertheless had a significant impact on the success of the company. Over the years, we have noticed that these kinds of decisions aren't made arbitrarily, but that there is a methodology behind them. The methodology used varies from company to company, but it is still highly predictable. To find out which category your company belongs to, all you have to do is answer the following two questions and place yourself in one of the categories shown in Fig. 4.1:

1. How sensitive is your company or your project team to change?
2. What is the level of cohesion in crucial situations?

4.1.1 Sensitivity to Change

According to the literature on the subject, sensitive organizations are better suited to exploiting opportunities. However, in the context of innovation strategy work, heightened sensitivity makes for exhausting strategic processes. Exhaustibility and mood swings change behaviors elementally. Persistent organizations produce results not by accident, but because they stay on the ball. Through diligence and discipline, they pursue predefined goals and develop appropriate methods and measures to achieve them.

4.1.2 Cohesion at Crucial Moments

Strong cohesion is found in companies with strong structures and sustainable, professional corporate behavior. There is a great deal of trust in this kind of environment and long-term thinking makes it possible to continuously utilize the existing infrastructures. This stability often feeds the common interests of everyone involved and is usually expressed in the form of a high level of commitment and loyalty to the decision-makers.

4.1.2.1 Team Hardliner

Your company may have many employees, but it is always the same few people who ultimately drive projects forward. This group of people rarely allows itself to be diverted from its goal and has the full backing of management. The fact that many employees are abandoned in the process is irrelevant. These companies sometimes change direction late in strategy projects, but they almost always get their act together before it is too late.

4.1.2.2 The 'German Oak'

This category of company is becoming increasingly rare, but is still widespread. Such companies always stick to decisions that have been made. Unless the project or the management team vanishes into thin air, or entire business units fail, there is no reason to change anything. Most of the time, projects at these companies do not end in a total loss but often remain ineffective. This doesn't bother most of the decision-makers because a lack of success is guaranteed to have been caused by external influences that the company itself cannot control.

4.1.2.3 On the Run

When things get tight, these companies are already working on their next project. In the process, many projects are discarded towards the end of the conception phase, usually because there are always other innovations that are much more attractive to pursue. This behavior ensures that themes are implemented in a large number of small-scale projects or in solo efforts by individuals. This kind of behavior is particularly dangerous in strategy projects, as the company will sooner or later lose the thread of the originally defined strategy.

4.1.2.4 The Vigilant Ones

This category most clearly represents optimal current and future company behavior. This behavior involves a great deal of examination and questioning, but changes are only ever made when there are alternatives that represent a clear improvement. In the process, many individuals gather input, which is then evaluated in short, in-depth sessions.

In our opinion, companies located in the blue corridor have the best chance of successfully completing their projects. Companies outside the corridor generally fail in 80% of their projects. We consider failure to mean that not even 30% of the originally planned results were achieved against the original costing estimates. If you take this categorization into account when setting up your strategy, you will definitely be able to avoid this pitfall, as companies rarely fundamentally change their behavior.

4.2 Do Not Follow Blindly!

Experts naturally feel honored when people or companies utilize their knowledge and experience. Experts of course want to spread their knowledge among companies and industries on a daily basis, and always with a focus on the latest technological means available. Actually, there is no need for further specialist consultation at this point, and what the expert says will be done. This may be technically correct, but it is nevertheless a questionable approach. If it were the right approach to take, you could sit in the passenger seat with your expert and head off to your destination without a care in the world. However, that is not how innovation strategy work functions. In the course of every third strategy project, the customer follows us blindly. This is illustrated by the following case, where we were invited to support a client in the development of a digitization strategy.

With the desire to achieve the highest possible level of digitization, the client wanted to hand over all the necessary information to us in a one-day workshop and we, as the service provider, were then to lead the internal team to success. After all, we were the experts. The responsible division manager made it clear to his team that we (the experts) were to be followed. Project teams are often grateful that the arrival of external experts means that from now on the burden and pressure to perform is no longer borne by the team, but rather by the experts. As the workshop progressed, we asked the team and their management to contribute their expertise and ideas and, from this point on, a solid working foundation was formed. By enriching our expert knowledge with the client's technical and cultural knowledge (see Fig. 4.2), a solid foundation was laid for the rest of the project. If the project had been based solely on our specialist knowledge and experience, the project would not have been nearly so successful.

You should never blindly follow anyone, no matter how successful and knowledgeable they are. You always have to adapt the available resources to your situation, as only then will you succeed in your strategy and implementation work. If you don't manage to transfer your own knowledge to the specific situation, you run the risk of making errors of judgement. That can end up costing a lot of time and money.

Fig. 4.2 Uniting expert and company knowledge. (Source: H&F Solutions GmbH/www.hf-solutions.co)

When we trust someone in the course of our private lives, in most cases this has little or no consequence. If we buy the wrong thing, we simply exchange it. If a partner purchases the wrong ingredient for a cake, we improvise and use this ingredient if possible. However, if you are wrong too often when making strategic decisions, this will have unforeseeable consequences. This is because you mostly won't get to experience what would have happened if you had decided differently. By following experts alongside your own experience and expertise, this uncertainty can be kept to a minimum. Listen carefully to your experts, whether internal or external, and make basic decisions together. A single person or a certain group of people never represents a definitive yardstick.

On the subject of 'following blind', the following sections present a number of effects that must be avoided at all costs. These too are one of the minor building blocks that help to maximize the success of the whole puzzle.

4.2.1 The Aura Effect

If we find someone attractive, we attribute them with a certain basic competence and we include them perceptually in our personal category of successful people—at least until proven otherwise. In strategy projects, this moment often crops up quite late in the game. The best-known example of this effect occurs in relation to babies. Everyone finds babies cute and cuddly, and it has been proven that pretty children get better grades in school. Other confirmed effects of perceived beauty are advantages in job interviews and salary negotiations. 'Attractive' people often attract unfair advantages.

4.2.2 The Glue Effect

The glue effect is based on the theory of expectation errors. Based on a certain behavior, a person concludes that this same behavior will always occur in the future. A classic example is the interpretation of a resumé. It is assumed that, if an applicant has changed employers every couple of years in the past, he or she will always do so in the future. The glue effect means that we unconditionally write past history into the future, and in doing so, we don't take the current environment or changing conditions into account. If you, as a decision-maker, adopt this attitude at all costs, you are unlikely to be able to get a weak team to successfully implement any new projects in the future.

4.2.3 The Pygmalion Effect

You always see a person or a team the way you want to see them, and all your decisions and behaviors will usually be geared toward getting your attitude confirmed. If you like a specific attribute of a particular person, you will try to find confirmation for this attribute throughout the conversation. This behavior ensures that people (or groups of people) are often transformed into whatever their immediate environment would like to see.

Example

One of the best-known experiments in this field took place at a US-American management consultancy. Here, psychologists used a lottery to select 30% of the consultants to take part in a performance test. The results of the test were not disclosed to the test subjects, and only the supervisors were given the names of those who turned out to be potentially gifted and showed good career prospects. Following a repeat test 12 months later, it was found that these individuals showed a huge increase in performance. Analysis of the intervening 12 months showed that the supervisors had unconsciously paid much more attention to the group of 'talented' employees and had handled them preferentially. In reality, there was no performance test, and the supervisors unconditionally preferred a group of arbitrarily selected subjects who were supposedly 'better' than their colleagues. ◀

4.2.4 The Similar-to-Me Effect

There are always people who we like from the very first contact. It doesn't matter what they say, and we listen to them eagerly and rarely resent them. This sympathy is based on a similarity to oneself. We simply assume that anyone who is similar to ourselves must be successful, and this assumption somehow feels right. We then pay little attention to whether this behavior actually helps us to achieve our goals.

4.2.5 The Halo Effect

In this context, people infer all subsequent decisions from the experience made at an initial meeting. In other words, if you made a good impression at the first meeting, you are likely to be a high performer. This single outstanding performance outshines everything else. The conclusion reached at the first meeting is thereby only slowly adapted to reality. If you know how the processes of getting to know someone work, you can consciously counteract these kinds of effects. At a first meeting, you usually only have a short time to get an idea of someone you didn't know before. A few impressions form a picture in our mind that takes deep root, and we then base our behavior on this image. Negative initial experiences often take precedence over positive experiences for quite a long time.

4.2.6 The Benjamin Effect

This effect causes people to judge their counterparts on the basis of their age, not their abilities. People also tend to judge the performance of young people more harshly than that of older people. It is somehow clear that a manager or a member of a strategy team needs to have a few grey hairs in order to be successful. After all, young people can't know much (yet). In reality, young people who are well educated can deliver high performance at an early age. Although experience is an indicator of success, it often leads to misjudgment of younger people.

4.2.7 The Hierarchy Effect

The higher a person's rank in society, a company, or another group of people, the better they are rated by others. A common misapprehension is that an employee cannot be evaluated better than their manager. The extent of this effect often depends on the willingness of the assessor to assess fairly and, since people higher up the hierarchy always assess those below them, this effect is widespread.

4.2.8 The Dunning-Kruger Effect

A study made in the 1990s revealed that incompetent people tend to overestimate their own abilities. Furthermore, it is precisely because of their incompetence that they are unable to recognize their own limitations. In fact, they often believe that they are far superior to others. It is enormously difficult to break out of this vicious circle, and only continual education and feedback can ultimately help.

Please don't regard this book as a magic bullet. Our approaches represent only one of many potential solutions. If all companies pursued a single approach, entire markets would collapse if this approach should turn out bad. We recommend that you take our collected knowledge and use it to help you think outside the box. Take a careful look at everything you do and don't adopt any new ideas unchecked. Let us inspire you to achieve your own successes.

4.3 We Want to Be Like Amazon

Back when we were starting out as independent consultants, we were booked by a client who had set the goal of imitating Amazon and delivering all of its standard products to customers within 36 h. The goal was clearly defined and all the means for a successful implementation were available. Unfortunately, after only a short time no-one was working for the goal, but instead against it. All the changes the company needed to make to achieve its goal were being blocked. Furthermore, a multitude of other work was begun and just 4–5 months later, no-one was talking about the original goal any more. The organization and implementation team that was responsible for strategic issues became larger and larger, and the list of tasks to be completed grew longer and longer. None of the project participants was able to fulfill their tasks anymore. This was a clear example of lost focus, and focus is the single characteristic that has distinguished Amazon over many years. In our case, it wasn't the goal that was at fault—the organization ultimately found itself in an implementation dilemma. Too many open issues were destroying the much-needed forward momentum. Amazon excelled in the early years by focusing on a few selected issues and making do without anything else that might have been useful along the way. In the case of our client, it would have been better not to attempt to deliver all standard products within 36 h, but to start with a single, small set of products. This would certainly have made it possible to reach the set target for the reduced product range within 3 months.

If eight product ranges had been adopted, 80% of these products could have been pushed up to speed within 24 months. Since the company wasn't prepared to forego parts of its plan, it was left empty-handed with regard to the project outlined above. Just like the old adage says: "A bird in the hand is worth two in the bush" (see Fig. 4.3).

Fig. 4.3 The "bird in the hand" in a strategy project. (Source: H&F Solutions GmbH/www.hf-solutions.co)

4.4 The Deep Rift Between the Beneficiary and the Implementer

During a particular project, one of our managers reported a deep rift between the company's main site and a subsidiary production plant. In terms of understanding how an ERP project could be realized, there was an unbridgeable gulf between the management team and the implementing team. The ERP team had a completely different understanding of strategy goals than the executive team. Despite a great kick-off meeting with the whole team and loads of colorful presentations, a seemingly insurmountable hurdle remained. Consequently, the implementation team also understood the goals differently than the executive team. Following the kick-off, communication took place exclusively between one senior person from each team. Many implementation efforts from both sides ended quickly and never reached completion. To make sure this doesn't happen to you, pay close attention to what is communicated to whom and how. If there is too much deviation here, you should immediately pull on the brakes and insert a clarification phase. You won't be doing yourself a favor if you simply sit out these kinds of hurdles. Goal-oriented managers see this kind of call for help as an opportunity to react at a sufficiently early stage.

4.5 External Aid = Internal Dilemma

Imagine that a company board member gets wind of an innovative company at a trade fair and discovers various options that could help his own company to advance a specific issue. Contact is quickly established and the executive is sure that he wants to integrate this issue into the company. The entire second-tier management team is invited to the first joint coordination meeting in order to take a closer look at the issue (strategic planning for production automation) and to make a binding decision. In the past, the company had enormous problems implementing innovative new directions, but now this new, innovative partner is ready to help and the board is already eagerly awaiting the results of the workshop. The workshop is going well and everyone agrees that collaboration would be helpful. Following the workshop, the board members once again consulted internally with their colleagues. It turned out that the entire second-tier management team had a bad feeling about this issue. What had happened? The board had passed the decision on to its team. In principle, it is right to involve the team, but this was the team that had already hindered the company's ability to innovate in the past, and it was equally unenthusiastic about the new issue. In the end, the team that would have had to implement the project didn't see itself as the beneficiary of the potential implementation. At the same time, the board (which would have benefited from the implementation) didn't have a team that stood up for its goals. The moral here is that issues that are introduced into projects as a kind of 'Trojan Horse' should always benefit the implementation team. In the end, the group made up of the board and second-tier management was only capable of low-performing outcomes. This is because low-performing issues are usually operational in nature and always pay dividends to lower-level successes. Innovation strategy projects cannot be implemented this way, and you should always check whether you have enough internal allies for your ambitious projects before you look for external help. If you don't, you may not be suited to strategic projects.

4.6 Starting Too Fast or Waiting Too Long

Have you ever looked at what goes into launching a spacecraft? If not, it's worth investing a little time here, and you are sure to find many parallels to the processes within your company. A rocket launch only works within a certain time slot. If the rocket launches too early, the mission will fail just as surely as if the launch takes place too late. Until about 10 years ago, space missions were considered too costly to attempt. However, since Elon Musk entered this business, that idea has been disproved. Musk has managed to offer successful space flights at a manageable cost using conventional means. He doesn't use custom components like NASA, but instead makes use of many existing components and technologies. Until recently this approach seemed impossible, but Musk succeeded in building a rocket with limited means that functioned reliably within these small windows of launch opportunity. He even surpassed his own goal by making his rockets recyclable. Innovation strategy projects work in a similar way. If you, as a company, fail to drive the project or you launch it with too little preparation, the mission will fail. If you involve individuals who have a good sense of the right time frames and project pace, it will help you significantly with your mission. It will be advantageous if these experts have already been on several successful missions but are still receptive to new input. However, Musk's case things have turned out much more complex than they are in your company, simply because he wants to land on Mars in a few years' time. To do this, it is impossible to carry the necessary fuel starting on Earth, so he plans a first big change in space, where the mission can take equipment on board that was previously brought into orbit. But even this isn't sufficient to make Mars reachable, as it is also necessary to use the gravitational pull of other heavenly bodies to provide the necessary acceleration. For this particular project, the individual pieces of the puzzle don't fit together and missing just one of those windows of opportunity means the end of the mission. It's the same with the time slots in an ERP project. You will only be able to keep your team motivated for a certain amount of time without a demonstrable outcome. If this proof isn't achieved, the strategy work will be over faster than it started.

4.7 A Lack of Application at the Beginning of the Project

Things that fail to get going within the first few weeks of a project can be difficult to catch up on. This is exactly what happened to a client's project. In this case, the CIO decided not to bring decision-makers from other departments into the project until later and, as a result, there was little friction at the beginning of the project and everything proceeded nicely. The project just trickled along, and everyone was certain that the CIO had everything under control. With the increasing integration of other departments and other project participants the mood changed and, 4 months in, the project was still in its initial phase. The project start didn't really happen and the impetus necessary to get things off the ground was missing. Since we only played a small supporting role in this project, we couldn't intervene decisively. One of the most important aspects of an innovation strategy project is to make it important right from the start, and to make sure that everyone involved recognizes this and is ready to actively participate and contribute. If the stakeholders see that there is a group of active project participants who are giving their all for the project, they will be willing to provide active support. If you want to be the first to reach a particular goal, the only way is to start running and pick up speed quickly, and to achieve this, you need any kind of support you can get.

4.8 Dealing with Skeptics

You will always run into skeptics at the start of a new project. Skeptics are different to critics, and it is important to know they often distrust not only you, but also themselves. Too little trust will bring your project team down faster than you can imagine. Once you have identified the skeptics, the key is to deal with them in a way that is conducive to project success—i.e., you have to build up trust. And this means doing some serious persuading, which is one of the main components of any strategy project. Always face skeptics with an open mind, and ask them where their doubts come from and how the missing trust can be built up. Even skeptics are usually receptive to constructive strategy work.

4.8.1 Don't Give Way to Skeptics Who Generalize

Skeptics who never get to the heart of their doubts and don't discuss them in concrete terms are often not serious about their skepsis and usually have personal goals that they would rather pursue than support the project. When these people rebel, the strategy project pays too little attention to these personal goals, and that is exactly what they are fighting for—at least until something better turns up. Many critics like to participate in strategy debates without considering the implications of what they say, which is usually emotional rather than logical. Furthermore, they often overshoot the mark and make only generalized statements that don't contribute to the project. Those who often make sweeping statements tend not to have done their homework thoroughly and make themselves vulnerable on the factual level. We recommend that you always base discussions with critics on facts and scientific certainties, and that you remain specific. If you don't, the critic will often win!

4.9 Copying Too Much from Others

During a strategy meeting with a sales team, the client explained how sales in his industry work. The sales manager made it clear to us that it would be OK if we oriented ourselves toward the market leader and simply did things the same way. The assumption was that the market leader sets the current benchmark, and there was therefore no need for further discussion on this topic. And what happened? In fact, the sales manager was right. If you would behave like the industry leader in the important areas, success would almost certainly increase. However, this is only looking at the output, and successful output requires the right input, which is different from company to company. In order to make this highly complex topic tangible, we would like to illustrate it using a comparable scenario.

4.9.1 Copying Makes Sense

In principle, imitating and copying industry leaders makes sense. Science has proven that companies that imitate other companies are more popular and more successful. There are many companies that are market leaders in certain areas, even though they are never the first to innovate and always copy in some way. If your company wants to copy someone or something, there are a few things you should keep in mind. Completely copying others is the worst possible alternative, and it is always better to copy only what helps your particular business. Figure 4.4 shows how this idea can be successfully incorporated into innovation strategy work.

In order to successfully imitate benchmarks, you need to understand that almost all benchmarks represent only quantitative characteristics. The percentage of what can be copied that makes the imitating company successful is estimated to be just 20%. 80% of these attributes will not lead to success if copied directly. The deeper you dive into the potential implementation and your own fundamentals or prerequisites, the less they contribute to the approximation of the benchmark. You therefore need to pay close attention to whether the pursuit of the desired benchmark is actually worthwhile.

4.9.2 Benchmarking

As mentioned above, benchmarks are very good points of reference or indicators for making your own company successful. However, to successfully adopt a benchmark, you have to understand how leading companies set these benchmarks (or how the benchmarks themselves can be achieved). Our experience has shown that almost all benchmarks can be achieved by any company if the company has the will to allow change. The right approach is crucial because every company needs different things to achieve the same benchmark. One company may only need to adjust a few small things to achieve a

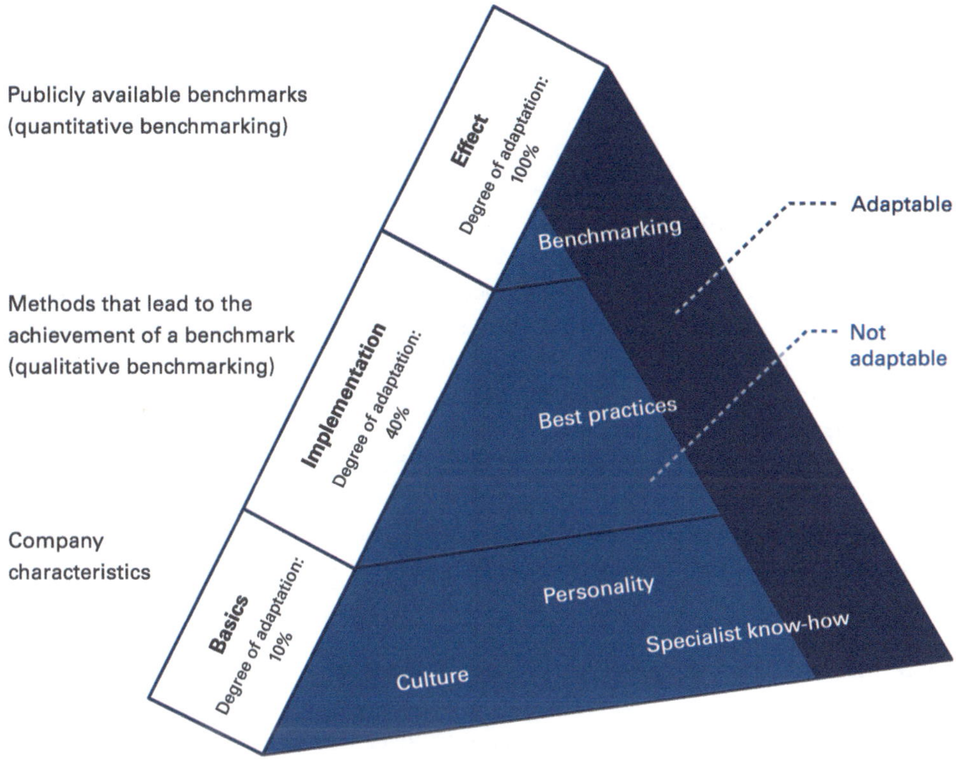

Fig. 4.4 Successful copying in innovation strategy work. (Source: H&F Solutions GmbH/www.hf-solutions.co)

benchmark, while another may have to restructure entire production processes. Once a benchmark has been targeted, it is important to match it with the capabilities and attributes of the company concerned, as well as with the available best practices. Only a complete package that combines these three areas will provide you with the desired success when copying others.

4.9.3 Best Practices

When we talk about best practices in this context, we are talking about the best practices that have helped companies achieve exceptional benchmarks. Because best practices that work well for one company embody behaviors and processes that aren't guaranteed to work in your company, copying best practices is much riskier than copying benchmarks. Experience shows that only 40% of best practices can be adopted directly from one company to another. The remaining 60% are processes that would probably not bring any improvement in your particular case. It is important to take a close look at what is adaptable and what isn't. This is the necessary step the sales manager in our example should have taken. In this case, he copied the processes in the company setting the benchmark almost completely. As an insider tip, we recommend copying from other industries—this approach produces significantly higher success rates.

4.9.4 Company Characteristics

In order to successfully implement best practices, in most cases you need a team that pushes this topic forward. For example, if you want to do this in a company whose managers still haven't made friends with the digital age, it will be difficult to implement a benchmark with fully digitized processes using the existing team. If management doesn't set an example, there will be no lobby for it, and it will probably fail due to basic things like the use of today‘s interactive tools. Companies that set today's benchmarks are all highly digitized, in their daily business and in their strategic activities. Innovative companies rely increasingly on the use of data to build their strategies. For this reason many companies can copy a maximum of just 10% of the available resources to achieve a benchmark.

4.9.5 If You Are Going to Copy, Do It Properly

In summary, copying things properly requires practice. Therefore, start by copying just a few things ("less is more") but copy them with full force. Ninety per cent of all benchmark drivers are to be found in the heads and hearts of the employees and are thus deeply anchored in the company's organization.

4.10 Ignoring New Market Factors

The development of new strategies has come to resemble an oxymoron (i.e., a contradiction in terms). Examples of oxymorons are phrases such as "open secret" or "silent scream". It is the same in innovation strategy work. Strategies are designed for the long term, but continually accelerating change in economic rules forces companies to adapt increasingly fast. An inquiry from a potential customer in the automation sector confronted us with the following situation:

A managing director and his executives had come to the decision to digitize the company, but only in areas where data could remain within the company. All interfaces to the outside had to be approved on a case-by-case basis. At the time, the company was the clear market leader for quality products in its field, and a loyal customer base ensured stable sales. In the early 2010s, when this case happened, increasing numbers of networking products were becoming acceptable in companies. However, the big deals were still being made at trade shows and through long-time business relationships. Only a few smaller customers had turned their backs on the company due to long delivery times.

What happened in this case? Two years prior to this time, the company adopted a growth strategy that was also designed to provide maximum security for the company's knowledge base, and this strategy was adopted in line with the previously defined strategy. At this time, new digital products provided an increase in transparency for industry customers, while modern product configurators and freely accessible product information caused many customers to change their thinking. All of a sudden, many components became standardized and interchangeable. Spare parts that were previously only available from dedicated dealers were now easily and quickly available from a range of suppliers. This transfer of knowledge, or rather the opening up of knowledge to customers, brought about a decisive change in the market, and also a shift in the relationships between customers and their suppliers. The client in question wasn't happy with our completely goal-oriented attitude, and decided to go with a well-established consulting firm that was happy to implement the client's wishes. A few years later, our contact at the client told us that the company then went through a serious crisis that took a while to overcome. The company then caught up with the competition and now offers its customers all the information they need, including a modern product configurator for ordering individual products. In this case, we are not talking about an unavoidable strategic error, but rather about changing market conditions that simply unraveled the previously developed strategy, where a change in strategy would probably have sufficed. It is of elementary importance to continuously work on your strategy and to observe the market. It is only by continuous study of this subject that you will gain an increasing understanding of what might work and what results may develop from different decisions.

4.10.1 The Hockey Stick Curve

No, we are not heading off into the world of sports, we just want to show you an approach that is designed to support you in making courageous decisions. Imagine the side view of a hockey stick held by a player. It forms a long downward slope and, where it reaches the ground, it bounces sharply back up. For this approach, we ask you to mentally trace this curve in the opposite direction. This curve follows closely what often happens in corporate development once strategic changes have been implemented. At first, it appears that the chosen change will never be successful but, after a short period, the strategies start to show results. A famous and publicly much discussed example of this approach is a corporate decision made by Amazon founder Jeff Bezos. In the summer of 2019, he informed the shareholders that the company would withhold the dividend to invest the additional capital in reducing the average delivery times from 3 days to 1 day. In the fall of the year in question, this reduction showed no effect but, when the holiday shopping season began, Amazon was ready. Where other retailers were still making their customers wait up to 14 days due to prepayment issues and the like, Amazon was able to deliver. In order to be able to implement a delivery within 24 h, the entire logistics and warehouse processes had to be redesigned, which was the cause of the poor fall numbers and a lack of immediate success. By the by: amongst its competitors, Amazon was able to achieve by far the greatest market growth in that year's Christmas business.

4.11 If It Hurts, I'll Turn Back ...

You are watching a documentary about the ascent of Mount Everest on your TV or mobile phone. How much will and courage do these mountaineers have to apply to reach their goal? Countless crevasses have to be crossed, the entire route is threatened by icefall and avalanches, but the majority of climbers who dare to make the ascent also reach the summit. Only a few suffer setbacks that force them to turn back. In other words, those who make it to the mountain have a good chance of reaching the summit. Note that, by the time they reach base camp, they have already covered 90% of the total distance. At this point, the climbers already have years of training and preparation in their bones. Many would-be Everest climbers fail in their quest due to the exertions of preparation, but the group of people who fail is hardly ever mentioned in reports on Everest. Think for a moment about how many hours, days, or years these people put into achieving their goal. At some point, the moment came when they abandoned their Everest endeavor. Innovation strategy projects are fundamentally very similar to this: a lot of effort is invested, only to give up or turn back at the first sign of serious difficulties. This 'idle power' component is sometimes so large that it can turn into a real business killer. It is common for individuals and companies who behave this way to blame others for their woes. There are always plenty of reasons why things didn't progress. In recent years, we have noticed that companies that fail tend to focus on the failure itself, and that these companies are often not going through the process for the first time, but fail regularly. In other words, this is a kind of systemic failure based on the mantra: If it hurts, I'll just turn around. People are simply too quick to give up. Figure 4.5 illustrates why this is so.

In order to achieve the desired impact, the input must of course be correctly selected. This means thinking through the project properly and mastering the complexity involved. And remember, your project will almost certainly develop differently than you imagined. If the decision-makers in your strategy project are not in a position to master these challenges, the complexity threshold will drop and force your project team to give up. As the decision-maker you are mostly powerless, as you will not be able to reach the strategy summit or the project goal without the help of your team.

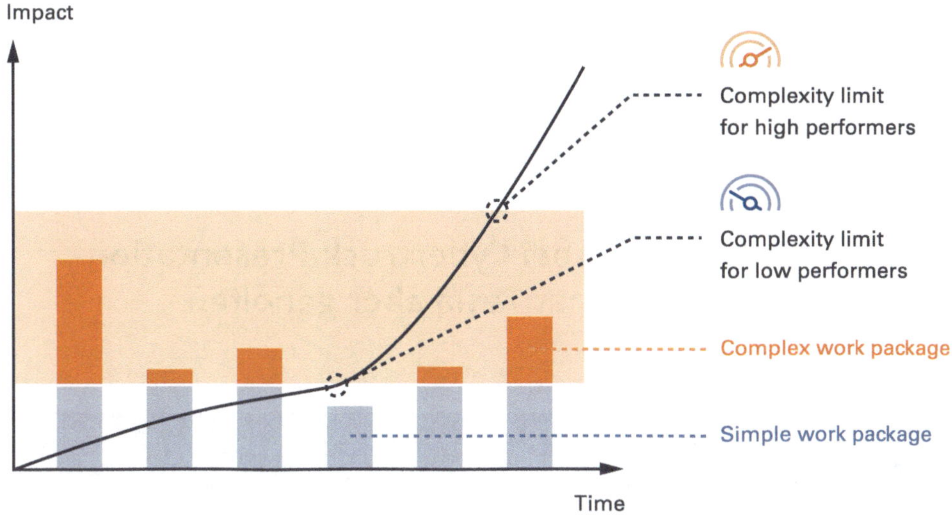

Fig. 4.5 Complexity limits in strategy projects. (Source: H&F Solutions GmbH/www.hf-solutions.co)

4.12 Missing the Upward Spiral Due to Failed Adaptation

Many still remember Elon Musk's 2020 cyber truck presentation. A lot of viewers were amused to find that the truck looked as if it had been created in Microsoft Paint (see Fig. 4.6). Regardless of how it came about, there are a lot of insights in this story about knowledge transfer in innovation strategy projects. The prototype cyber truck looks strikingly similar to a Paint model, which could have been intended as an illustration to be used to design a marketable product.

It is not uncommon for the same to happen in innovation strategy projects, and the effects can affect you here and now in the course of your strategy work. Once you have read this section you will assume that you have thoroughly learned this topic, but you nevertheless can't transfer what you have learned into your organization. You should definitely not fall into this trap.

However, it is undisputed that strategy processes rarely end in the form of a real breakthrough or a sustainable upward spiral. The next two sections illustrate how an innovation strategy project can develop in a positive or a negative way, so that you can find the ideal path between the two extremes.

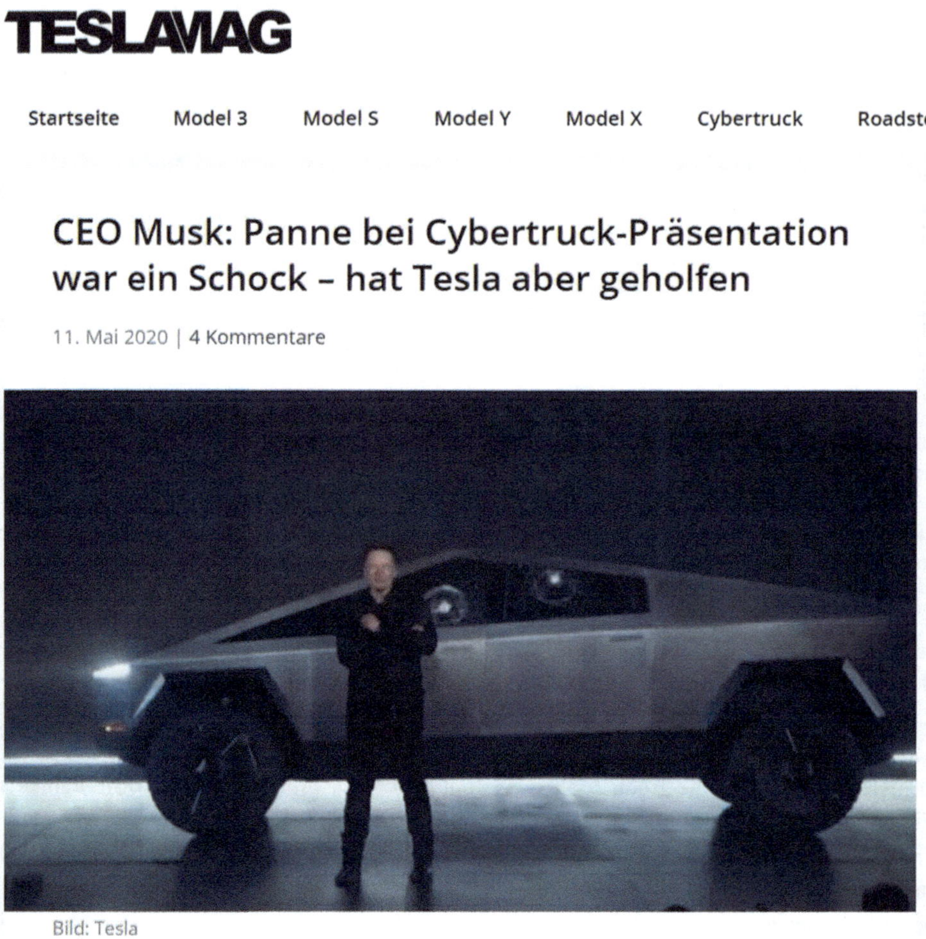
TESLAMAG

Startseite Model 3 Model S Model Y Model X Cybertruck Roadste

CEO Musk: Panne bei Cybertruck-Präsentation war ein Schock – hat Tesla aber geholfen

11. Mai 2020 | 4 Kommentare

Bild: Tesla

Fig. 4.6 Failed adaptation in strategy projects. (Source: H&F Solutions GmbH/www.hf-solutions.co & https://teslamag.de/news/ceo-musk-panne-cybertruck-praesentation-schock-hat-tesla-geholfen-28361, retrieved on 01/29/21)

4.12.1 Adaptation into a Downward Spiral

Project participants are informed of the planned direction and the project goal at the latest at a kick-off meeting. This is where managers (perhaps unintentionally) provide goals with predetermined paths and sample achievements. In weak project teams, this usually leads to a direct adoption of what the managers say. If, for example, Elon Musk had presented his development team with a hand-drawn sketch showing his cyber truck with two splintered windows and the prototype had subsequently exhibited exactly this damage, this would have represented a direct, one-to-one implementation of the sketch. However, the sketch was only intended to serve as an indicator of the desired uniqueness of the vehicle using a minimalist approach. Therefore, you need to know just how adaptable your team is before your present them with a target sketch. Bear in mind that the project participants are the ones who have the potential to adapt your sketch incorrectly, and the downward spiral starts right there with your presentation to the project team. Too many clearly stated management constraints combined with a less adaptive team will most likely end up not achieving your planned targets. You can prevent this from happening if you check the situation beforehand.

4.12.2 Adaptation into an Upward Spiral

Your team treats your draft goal as a template for building an improved market-ready product. This product contains the original goal concept and is implemented using attributes that are compliant with company policy. The management team is proud that the project team has succeeded in adapting the template and turning it into a successful product. This is how things could look if you manage to adapt your way into an upward spiral. The project team merely takes your outline as a starting point and develops it further under their own steam. Close coordination between the project team and project management ensures the desired thrust in the project.

Summary

Innovation strategy work and project implementation do not only depend on theory, but also on the many topics that surround them. In the process, you will repeatedly encounter certain topics that appear to be relevant to at least every second project, and that pose similar challenges to the project participants. This chapter presented practical examples of the following topics:

- We've started, so we'll finish
- Don't follow anyone blindly!
- We want to be like Amazon
- The deep rift between the beneficiary and the implementer
- External help = internal dilemma
- Starting too fast or waiting too long
- A lack of application at the beginning of the project
- Dealing with skeptics
- Copying too much from others
- Ignoring new market factors
- If it hurts, I'll turn around ...
- Missing the upward spiral due to incorrect adaptation

Contrast your project with all these topics and adopt one sentence from each. This will significantly sharpen your viewpoint and contribute to the success of your project. ◀

5 Deep Diving into Innovation Strategy Development

This chapter serves to illustrate the practicability of our approach and to maintain the text flow in this book. It is important to us that every company, manager, project team, or individual decision-maker can understand the *H&F High Speed and Efficiency Concept* introduced in Chap. 3, in order to make faster and more successful progress in innovation strategy development and implementation. This chapter details further important topics that will help you to advance your strategy project even faster, secure it even better, and increase your personal strategy performance even further. If we were to integrate these topics into Chap. 3, we are certain that this would lead to a weakening of our overall approach, as including too many new approaches and topics would take focus off the core topics. We have therefore bundled these additional topics under the title *Deep Diving*. In keeping with the spirit of diving, you should first master the basics (see Chap. 3) in order to benefit even more from the *Deep Diving* topics described here. These topics will provide you with more clarity and understanding of the various process steps and views. Feel free to skip this chapter as you work through the book for the first time and schedule it for a date 6–9 months in the future. You can then start rebuilding momentum using the approaches described in it. At this point, humility will probably get you closer to your goal than too much exuberance.

5.1 Strategy Project Input Factors: Best Practices, Innovation, and Methodology

Sayings such as "You are what you eat" or "Garbage in, garbage out" may be a little old-hat, but they do still provide some insight about yourself and your company when it comes to innovation strategy. If the mixture of basic ingredients isn't right, you should

P. Futterknecht, T. Hertfelder, *Data, Disruption & Digital Leadership*,
https://doi.org/10.1007/978-3-658-41601-0_5

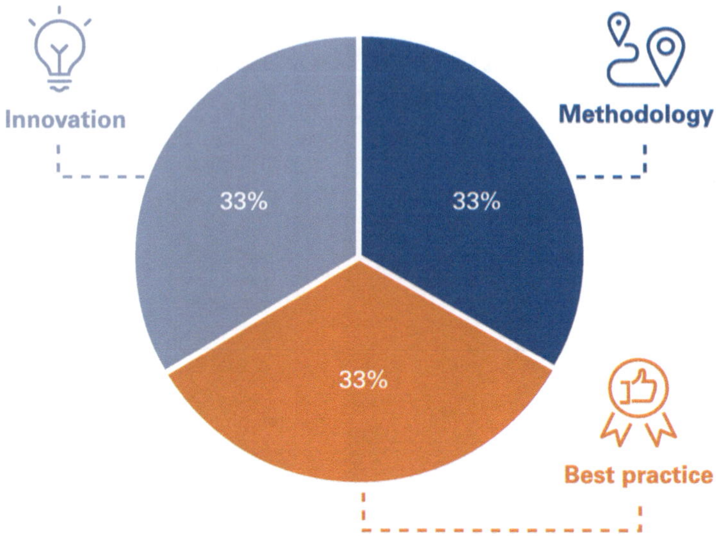

Fig. 5.1 Best practices in strategy projects. (Source: H&F Solutions GmbH/www.hf-solutions.co)

never be surprised if the result turns out wrong. It is often said: "It's the quantity that counts", and your strategy project, too, should have a fairly balanced set of basic ingredients. We have seen many companies where a one-sided ratio of ingredients has led to a lot of input and simultaneously too little output.

We therefore recommend that you create a balance of innovation, methodology, and best practices (see Fig. 5.1). Think of your project as a truck to be loaded in a balanced way that enables you to get safely to your destination. Lots of horsepower, loads of fasteners, or experienced drivers won't help you here, and you will only reach your destination if you use a healthy mixture of all three ingredients.

5.1.1 Best Practices

If you run your project based exclusively on best practices, you shouldn't be surprised if your company doesn't stand out from the market. Best practice approaches don't always yield the best results. This is because the main driver of best practice approaches is usually uncertainty, which leads to project teams deriving certain configurations and scenarios simply by trial and error. If these project teams were driven by certainty, they would avoid the risk of trial and error. You can assume that when you choose a best practice approach, there is nothing in it that will make you stand out in the market. After all, everything you identify as best practice already exists somewhere. And the point of innovation strategy work is usually a different one. Or is it? In our view, no more than one-third of your strategy development work should be based on best practices.

5.1.2 Innovation

The term 'innovation' is nothing other than planned and controlled change using new ideas and techniques. In other words, exactly the opposite of best practices. In the context of strategy work, innovation has nothing to do with technical product innovation, but rather with the creation of a vision that represents the desired target state. Of course, the target vision still has to include a rough sketch of the path to the goal—and anyone who manages to control this is a true strategy innovator. In this context, it is important to implement enough new ideas in the project to expand the planned best-practice approaches even more successfully. At this point, we thoroughly recommend that you read Leonardo da Vinci's biography as it describes the balance of the three themes of this section very nicely. All masters of their craft copied for many years at the start of their careers (i.e., best practices), and only later improved and perfected what they had copied (i.e., innovation).

5.1.3 Methodology

The third component is methodology. This is extremely important, especially in OKR projects. Here we would like to take up the topic of OKR introduced in Sect. 3.5.1. In our opinion, this is currently the most suitable methodology for strategy projects with high IT relevance. In other words, it is just right for the age of digitization. Since this approach is still relatively young, there is only a limited amount of usable literature on the subject. The OKR approach is basically a methodology-driven innovation (i.e., a mixture of methodology and innovation). With its help, you are sure to introduce the right balance into your innovation strategy project.

Side Note

Here is an example from our own innovation strategy development. With the development of our first H&F apps, we were able to reduce the time from purchase to use of the apps from about 8 weeks to 4 h compared to conventional software products. Our product was extremely innovative (i.e., something new). We managed our app project using OKR methodology (i.e., a sufficiently large methodology component). We initially had significant issues selling our apps, as they unsettled the market and were initially not very popular. The reason for this was a lack of best-practice content (see Fig. 5.2). The radical reduction of availability time from 8 weeks to 4 h simply confused our customers, who ended up looking for the catch, even though there wasn't one. Our strategy was highly forward-looking with an innovation component that was simply too great, combined with a deliberate avoidance of a significant best-practices component. ◀

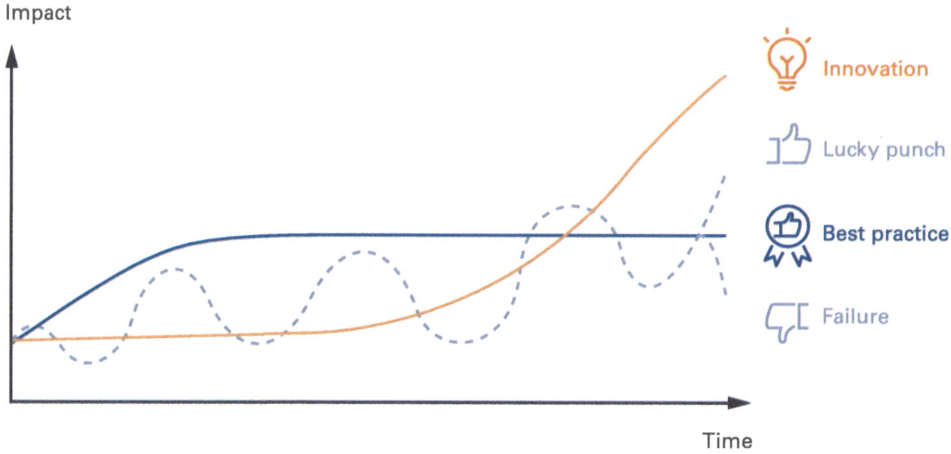

Fig. 5.2 The proportions of input factors in strategy projects. (Source: H&F Solutions GmbH/www.hf-solutions.co)

5.2 Too Many Decision-Makers: Group Decisions Paralyze the Process

How would WhatsApp look today if every user had been able to contribute his or her individual wishes? It is the same with innovation strategy projects. In many of our projects, certain topics are declared as 'must-haves' that are essential to project implementation. In principle, it is right to address important topics at an early stage, while later, once new insights have been gained, other topics may displace or replace them. This process can then be continued ad infinitum. Groups often can (and should) provide input for decision-making, but the ultimate decision should always rest with one person or just a few individuals. At the end of the day, any subsequent success or failure is someone's responsibility, and it is difficult to single out a whole team or a whole business unit to apportion blame. We are not at all concerned with trimming each case down to a single decision, but rather with keeping the focused process going and not losing too much decision-making speed. You will have to revise more than a third of your decisions anyway due to new insights, so here too, you need to pay close attention to efficiency and the cost-benefit balance while keeping your eye on the project goal. Figure 5.3 illustrates the decision-making dynamics that occur in group processes.

Summary

The selected input factors determine the implementation success of every strategy project, so you need to regularly check the balance among the three factors innovation, methodology, and best practices. Disparate distribution should serve as a warning sign

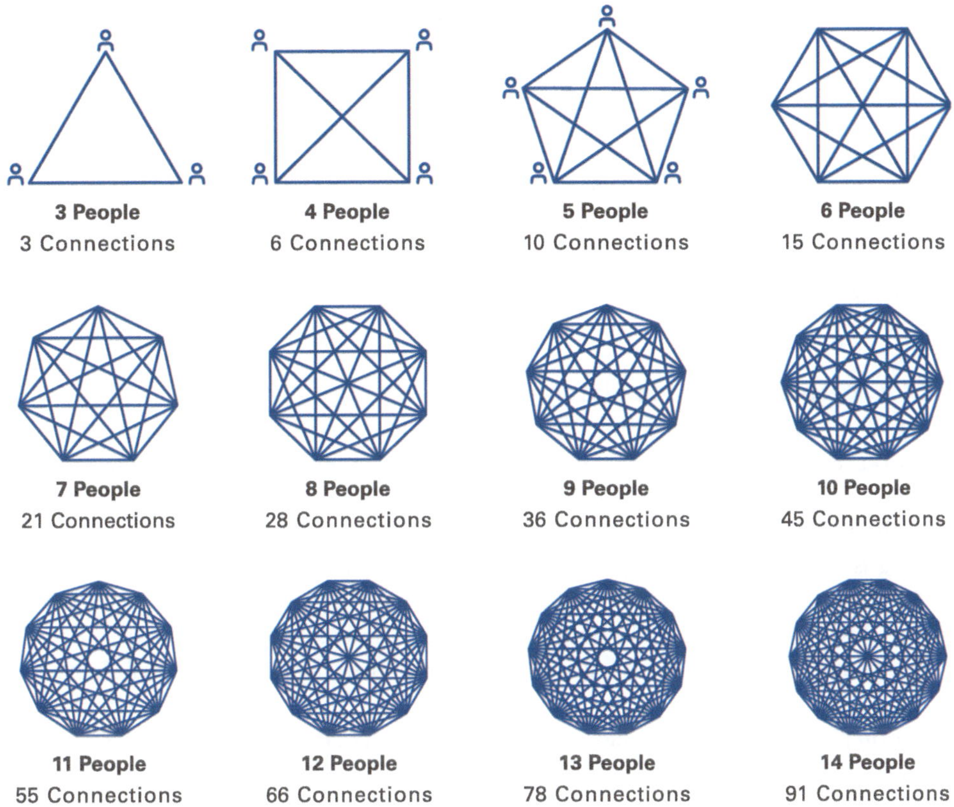

Fig. 5.3 Decision-making dynamics in group processes. (Source: H&F Solutions GmbH/www.hf-solutions.co)

that stability may be lacking. Only a homogeneous distribution of these three factors results in a high cost/benefit factor. In addition, you should always make sure that there is a healthy portion of innovation in your project and/or that things are done differently than in the past. Furthermore, the group that makes the decisions must be limited in its size. A goal-oriented process always comes to a standstill if the group of decision-makers exceeds a headcount of six to eight people. Too many decision-makers are simply counterproductive when it comes to implementation. In contrast, you can invite as many participants as you like to a brainstorming session on strategic alignment. ◄

5.3 Optimizing Project Team Membership

You will probably not have as much choice of potential members for your project team as you would like. However, if you observe certain rules, you will be able to avoid producing too much 'idle power'. In our view, the following points are the most crucial when it comes to staffing your team for innovation strategy projects.

5.3.1 Better No Team Than the Wrong Team

According to many studies, you can only ever change people to a small extent. In other words, it would require a lot of effort and years of training to turn a reserved analyst into an extroverted leader. Exceptions prove the rule, but nevertheless, adapting people's behavior to fit your needs is usually a poor investment. Where possible, you should avoid filling certain project positions at all if the alternative is to assign them to the wrong person. If there is only limited suitable personnel available for your project, you should tend towards increasing its duration and taking smaller sub-steps. This will save you a lot of trouble in the end.

5.3.1.1 People's Ability to Change

People don't change for no reason. Every person has a certain basic set of enduring values, behaviors, and personality. However, the time it takes for others to recognize this varies. It may take just weeks or perhaps years, and is therefore a matter that always affects both sides. In a business relationship, it is very difficult to change this basic set-up. Elaborate training is possible, but is rarely successful. This is because the key to successful change hardly ever lies in the technical requirements, but rather in the ability of those involved to change. Figure 5.4 illustrates the ability to change in different 'types' of people.

If you still want to invest in transforming people, there are two levers that deliver the most effect, namely: pain and the resulting learning effect. Please note that this kind of transformation involves both sides, and the key to success doesn't lie in unilateral change applied only to the person taking orders.

Pain

The output of pain is often suffering. In order to change a person, they must experience suffering in whatever form it takes. This may sound harsh, but you are probably reading this book because you want to make your projects more successful—hence the

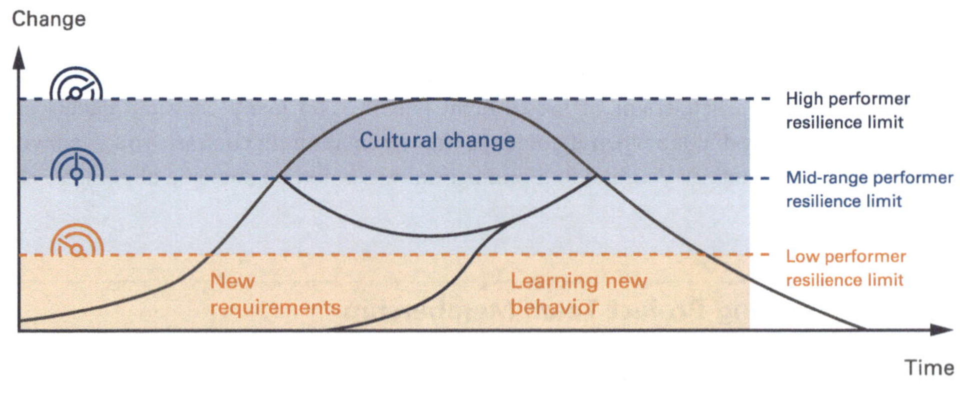

Fig. 5.4 The ability of individuals to change. (Source: H&F Solutions GmbH/www.hf-solutions.co)

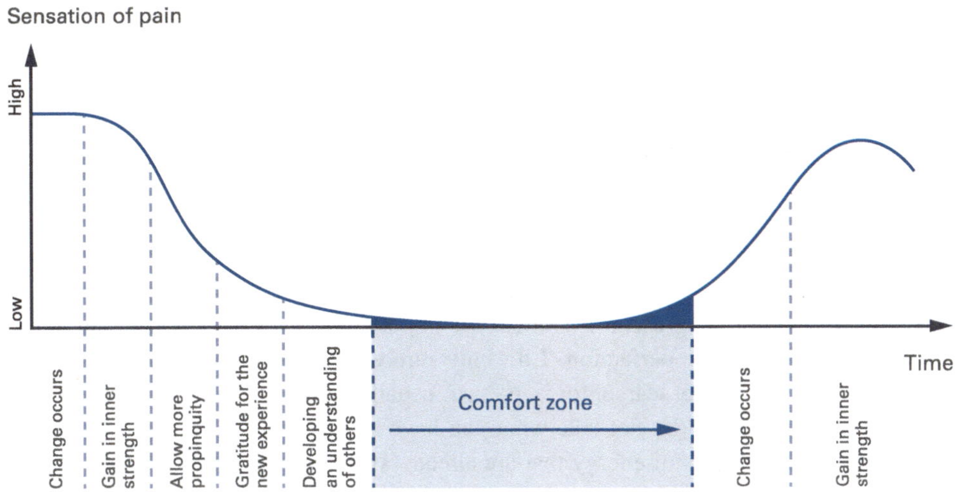

Fig. 5.5 The pain of change. (Source: H&F Solutions GmbH/www.hf-solutions.co)

uncomfortable answer to this question at this point. Suffering doesn't always have to be a negative thing. For example, you may suffer in the course of an athletic challenge, but you can just as well experience pride once the competition is over. In cases like this, we go through a recurring process (see Fig. 5.5).

This process is nothing out of the ordinary and isn't artificially created by managers or companies. It is a continuous loop that runs through our professional and private lives. You can slow this process down or deliberately avoid it, but the result will mean giving up progress and advancement. It is therefore difficult to develop and gain strength without facing critical life situations. We can see this process taking place figuratively in a 35-year-old colleague who we still know from school. On the one hand, we see a person who still displays the same behaviors as back then and has developed very little or, on the other hand, we see a 35-year-old family man who is hardly recognizable due to his development compared to his school days and who has made enormous progress.

The Learning Effect

Through an initiated process of change you can reap what you sowed earlier. It is important to process new experiences in a way that links them to your existing knowledge. All knowledge that is absorbed but not linked is lost in the long term, as if you had never learned it in the first place. People are usually unwilling to repeat earlier experiences of pain, which usually sets an upward spiral of success in motion. The output this delivers is either an improvement or a failure. Anyone who repeatedly misses these kinds of opportunities will never become a pillar of a project team. It is important not to place people with weak development capabilities in important positions within a strategy project. If you don't have suitable staff, you should either fill these positions externally or not at all.

5.3.2 Love What You Do

In recent years, it seems to have become highly fashionable to do only what we like to do. After all, life is too short to waste on things we don't like, and many people are in the process of searching for the perfect job. Strategy issues are, per se, future-oriented but have to be implemented in the present. It is therefore important to love what we do and not be constantly on a quest for perfection. Life only rarely rewards this kind of search, and private obligations or the search for a partner usually make it impossible to reinvent yourself professionally. Why not take what you have and make the best of it? It is better to look for hidden sources of energy that are already available and set them free—even if you are perhaps not happy right now, but would like to be in the future.

5.3.3 Find People Who Are Prepared to Take a Plunge

Some people think they know what is wrong with other project participants, and appear to have a talent for recognizing other people's deficits at a glance. Such people also usually have a solution at hand. Unfortunately, these people often forget the most important point, namely: if you want to change the world, you have to start with yourself. This insight is so sobering for many people that they quickly suppress it. Who wants to identify themselves as the driver of a problem? In order to realize this for yourself, you have to dare to take a plunge. Those who do will begin to influence their environment more positively and help to create improvements. Along the way, you'll lose the overrated trait of staying true to yourself and only wanting to improve others. Start improving yourself and set the other project participants free to improve themselves too. There is no danger of too many people wanting to change at once. You can therefore look with a clear conscience for people who want to jump in at the deep end with you and work relentlessly towards the project goals. Sustaining motivation during this process can be exhausting, so you have to tackle any problems that occur head-on rather than skirting around them. After all, the project participants' goals should be just as important as management goals.

5.3.4 Mix Visionaries with Movers and Shakers

Visionaries

A visionary's strengths lie in his ability to adopt multiple viewpoints. They anticipate or recognize trends at an early stage, and can estimate the likelihood of their success. You need this kind of forward thinkers in every project. They question everything and everyone, and try to identify all existing and missing building blocks that contribute to theirs vision. However, visionaries tend to 'lose touch' and may need to be brought back to reality. Visionaries may also lose sight of the concrete project goals during implementation.

Movers and Shakers (or "Doers")

Doers live very much in the present, analyze issues at high speed, and usually find appropriate solutions. They are enormously effective and goal-oriented. They are always able to make appropriate decisions that contribute to the overall success of the project. Complex situations aren't a problem, but don't always expect loyalty toward other project participants. The success of the project is always more important to doers than a balanced team environment. Doers concentrate on ensuring that the project team functions professionally.

As with a good cake recipe, you have to choose the ingredients so that in the end you get the best possible result. Small deviations are permissible but shouldn't be detectable in the result. Likewise, your team should comprise a suitable mixture of doers and visionaries. This is primarily about the characteristics and behaviors of these two groups of people, and projects only work if not everyone wants to be the boss (i.e., there are enough 'worker bees' who surround the 'queen bee'). Every member of the project team needs to find their role in this context, as it doesn't really match common project methodology. People are used to subordinates obeying bosses and are unfamiliar with the concept of doers following visionaries. It is less important who gives the decisive instructions—the main thing is that they are given in the first place.

5.3.5 Transforming Criticism into Progress

There is nothing more unpleasant than a supposedly fact-based appraisal, mainly because criticism is actually always tainted with emotions and is never purely factual, even if the person exercising the criticism thinks otherwise. Because we all work with other people on a daily basis, disagreements are inevitable, and these often lead to negative or dismissive attitudes. These attitudes then engender a feeling of rejection that builds until the tension makes one (or both) of the people involved feel like a loser. What started out as a minor issue turns into a serious confrontation whereby the parties involved may not even remember how it started in the first place. That said, there is a realistic chance that criticism can be transformed into motivation, and some controversial issues can turn into something quite wonderful. Whether your critic wants to help or harm you, the result of the dialog lies in your hands. If he wants to harm you, but you transform the criticism into something positive, your critic has no way to exert negative influence. Figure 5.6 demonstrates how to turn criticism into progress.

Fig. 5.6 Transforming criticism into progress. (Source: H&F Solutions GmbH/www.hf-solutions.co)

Simply Don't Accept It

You are by no means obliged to simply accept the feedback from someone else and to work through it as presented. You also don't have to agree completely with your counterpart. If you disagree, then say so and stick to your position! The important thing is that there are no losers in situations like this, and it is more important to take what you are given on board and draw the right conclusions from it. On a factual level, it is always possible to find a solution that is helpful to both sides in some way.

Ask Specific Questions

When you receive criticism, it is important to always ask targeted questions. Ideally, you should also ask for concrete examples. This gives your counterpart the feeling that you take his criticism seriously and that you are prepared to deal with it. The goal is to find out what the other person is trying to tell you by expressing criticism. A positive side effect is checking the substance of the criticism. If the other person cannot give you sufficient answers to detailed questions, the criticism is possibly only an emotional cry for help. In this case, you are probably the person who should provide help and support in the spirit of a team project. These kinds of issues occur frequently in strategy projects, and solving them is an important part of achieving the overall goal in the best possible way.

Put Yourself in Their Shoes

Never react emotionally to criticism. Putting yourself in the other person's shoes is crucial to gaining an overall understanding of the situation. Take a moment to understand what the other person's intentions might be and reflect on how you yourself behaved in the situation being addressed. You can make much better decisions based on these thoughts. Think very carefully about how the other person feels. Have you perhaps smothered them with brash behavior? Are you acting on the basis of knowledge that you haven't made available to others? If you manage to put yourself in their position, the result will always be better.

Only Those Who Listen Can Learn

As long as you are the one doing the talking, you won't learn anything from your counterpart. You can only find out what triggered the criticism if you listen carefully, and only then can you judge whether the criticism is justified. If you take up more than 70% of the speaking time in such a conversation, you are already actively defending yourself and are probably not interested in finding a constructive solution. Someone who talks too much is only interested in rejecting criticism or launching a counter-attack. This is simply 'weak thinking'. Always listen carefully to criticism and try to divine the other person's motives. This is the only way both sides can emerge from the situation as winners.

Turn Criticism into Progress

Only pursue ends that move the team forward as a whole. All other concerns should take a back seat. No matter whether criticism is justified or unjustified, you can derive positive things from every situation. You may find that someone brings up a subject that makes you aware of your own errors, or someone may reveal themselves to be a weaker member of the team who contributes little to the project's success, or may even actively hinder project progress. If criticism is inappropriate or can be refuted using factual arguments, this can be viewed as a success.

Finding the Right Moment

Generally speaking, criticism of fresh issues is easier to resolve than issues that have been brewing for a long time. Therefore, when criticizing, choose a moment when the situation is sufficiently clear. The longer an issue builds up, the more we embarrass our counterparts and the more damaging the situation can become. Try to catch your counterpart at a stress-free moment and try to keep everyone else out of the loop for as long as possible. A one-to-one conversation is a must-have at the start of this kind of process.

5.3.6 Questions to Ask Project Stakeholders at the Start

Some companies take the unusual measure of physically bringing participants closer together during strategy projects. This helps to deliberately break down entrenched, everyday habits that build up in a familiar work environment, opens up new communication channels, and provides new impetus for fresh thinking. Some project participants won't know each other at all (or only vaguely) at the beginning of a project but, even without putting them in the same physical space, there are some interesting questions you can ask in order to find out who can make which contribution to achieving the project goal. This approach will give you an excellent overview of the team's potential.

Questions

1. What does 'success' mean for you in the context of this project?
2. How interested are you in achieving or exceeding the project goal?

3. Is everyone willing to accept criticism in order to help achieve the strategy goal?
4. Are you willing to unconditionally support others?
5. Would you actively ask for help in difficult situations?
6. Would you like to take on a pioneering role within the project?

Now use the answers you have received to assemble your virtual project team of pioneers, doers, visionaries, critics, and sloggers (in a positive sense).

5.3.7 Recognition

Not many project teams manage to deliver above-average performance. If they do, the team is usually one that works together for a limited time. At the latest when one of the pillars breaks away due to retirement or job change (or similar) is when such a successful team suffers a bitter loss. We have seen that building and sustaining a successful strategy team is about each individual being willing to take responsibility for what they do, and to do so without reducing their own contribution to minimize their risk. Those who recognize and live for their role will become successful project team members without external help. In this context, taking responsibility means always acting in the spirit of the strategy project. Responsibility only becomes real through positive action.

Summary

Not filling a position is better than filling it badly. People who cannot meet the set expectations don't deserve to be put in such a situation. People's ability to change is crucial in innovation strategy projects. If you combine this with a love for what you do and still manage to jump in at the deep end with this mindset, you will usually end up with a team that is able to deliver above-average performance. At the same time, a balanced ratio of doers and visionaries ensures stability within the project and in the company. This section includes a list of question that will help you to check your team members' required characteristics in advance. ◄

5.4 Finding Alternatives Instead of Persisting

In innovation strategy projects, you will often find yourself heading for a cliff or ending up in a dead end. This cannot be avoided when you are working with a performance culture that is oriented toward above-average speed. This is why you should always have a rough outline of 'Plan B' (or even 'Plan C') in mind for most of your topics. In order to formulate alternative plans, you need to look as far away from 'Plan A' as possible. In order to find high quality alternative approaches, it is helpful to step out of your familiar environment. This approach helps alternative plans to feel like a real alternative instead of just looking like a modified copy of 'Plan A'. The stimuli you need can come from any or all input channels. For example, you may find inspiration when playing with your children or observing a stranger at the supermarket checkout. One of our most valuable observations in recent years was made at a large construction site in Munich.

If you think through the alternatives in good time, you can calmly put them in place when dead ends threaten.

5.5 Characteristics and Behavior of Digital Leaders

At this point, we would like to highlight some of the crucial things that have provided us with clarity in our projects. Over time, we have gained many insights into companies and projects and, in the process, successful strategists, who we would like to refer to as digital leaders, often display the same behaviors. In this section, we highlight what we consider to be the most important points and provide you with an overview in Fig. 5.7.

5.5.1 The Notebook

Surely you know on the one hand about some veteran luminaries who carry all their knowledge around in their heads and hardly ever take notes. On the other hand, there are new approaches that allow all information to be processed digitally. We also have the group of people who neither take notes nor memorize things, and there are all kinds of hybrids in between too.

In addition to all the advantages of a digitized world, many digital leaders use a paper notebook as their core tool for essential tasks, where they record all crucial success factors.

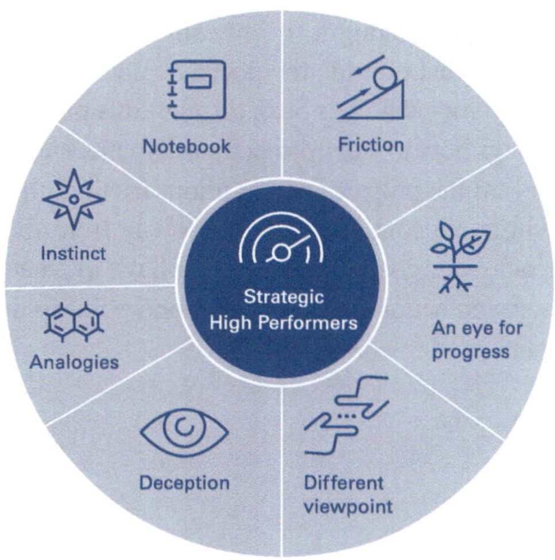

Fig. 5.7 Strategic high performers. (Source: H&F Solutions GmbH/www.hf-solutions.co)

Using this simple aid, important topics can never escape you and all flashes of inspiration are listed in a compact form. Sketch-like notes allow you to immediately reproduce the past few days and weeks on just a few pages. But why are notes like this an important indicator of success?

The main benefit of a notebook is that it activates all the senses. When making notes, you need to hear, see, read, and write. If one of these senses isn't activated, you will have fewer resources to fuel your success, and this is where important details can begin to slip through the net. With the help of a notebook you activate all of your senses and keep all your important topics available at a glance. This effect is reinforced by your own explanations and actions, which then enable you to become a high performer on the output side.

Of course, you can use new media too. We use the Microsoft OneNote tool and an input pen to take digital notes. In terms of haptics, a digital note-taker will never replace a book, but it is the writing habit that really counts. Simply choose the medium that you think you will stick with for longest.

5.5.2 Friction

If you ever attend a meeting where there is no friction, you can assume that it won't deliver any great benefit. Meetings that run smoothly aren't a bad thing as such, but things look a little different in innovation strategy work. Friction indisputably reduces momentum and wastes energy—and, if there is too much friction, progress can stop altogether. However, in terms of achieving your goals, progress is not the only thing that matters, and the direction your project is headed is equally important. Successful strategists always keep these two variables in mind during implementation, and friction ensures that certain things change direction. Think back to the planetary gravitation we mentioned in the introduction. A planet's gravitational force creates a deflecting effect that alters the direction of travel of a body approaching it (if only slightly). Figuratively speaking, successful strategists are the planets that provide the decisive small changes in direction in the course of a project.

Anyone who has been through this process hundreds of times and knows their goal also knows how to steer project participants and use subtle impulses to navigate the entire team toward the project goal. Without friction, these corrections will fail to materialize and you will move continually further away from the project goal. In other words, if you want to reach your goal efficiently, you have to create friction, even if it means treading a fine line between action and caution at one point or another. Digital leaders know how to play this game well.

5.5.3 An Eye for Progress

Many of our projects have a lot to do with ERP. In this context, specialist expertise is required at many junctures. Experts are usually specialists or generalists, and these two extremes send very different messages, but that nevertheless contain certain core messages that are the seeds of any successful project. These core messages help project participants to structure the thoughts that are mainly responsible for the efficiency in project communication. From this point on, a successful project will hopefully grow. Those who flood their project team with general messages but send few core messages tend to perform less efficiently and don't have an eye for the essentials. A digital leader develops an eye for these essentials, which encompass everything that moves the project forward.

Before you start communicating within a project, you have to be aware of the effects of communication. Think carefully about what you want to achieve with your communication and how it effects the recipients. This kind of mental filtering increases the proportion of core statements you produce and helps the team to perceive you as an expert. Furthermore, detailed discussions foster the personal development of all the individuals involved.

To familiarize yourself with this process, apply the following rule to every topic you approach: Describe a clear message in just one sentence.

You can practice by summarizing emails or newspaper articles in as few sentences as possible, but retaining the original structure.

To illustrate what we mean by 'structure', the example below describes the section that follows without structure.

Example

When absorbing unstructured texts or information we have problems to grasp them quickly and without reading them several times if we had the choice we would not process unstructured information at all every text has a structured character in itself because of the capitalization and the punctuation marks you can stop reading at this sentence and look at another document for a minute then return to this place you will notice that this can be quite difficult if we now turn away from the texts and turn to the language then we do not pay so much attention to the topic of structure or we do not notice it so much. The same principle applies here without structure it is difficult to transfer information to the recipient in the case of language it is even more important as you cannot repeat this again as in the case of reading we are of the opinion that we should not expect such unstructured communication from anyone. ◄

Fortunately for you, we will now continue in a structured way. Your task is to send a high proportion of core messages to the other project participants, and this is best done by focusing on the essentials. The clarity you gain from using this approach will automatically transfer to your colleagues and, as a result, they will also be able to follow you better in the future (and you will boost your expert status without any further intervention). People will suddenly understand you better, which will be a benefit for everyone involved and for the progress of the project.

5.5.4 Learn to Observe

Digital leaders have distinct powers of observation, and they can also abstract and implement what they observe. Couple this with sufficient imagination and you have the ideal breeding ground for a strategy project. There is generally nothing wrong with sticking to reality, but strategic topics tend to lie in the future and thus don't actually exist. Let's take a tip from a colleague as an example: He recommends that you think about your project while looking at a white wall. The longer you stare at the wall, the more your thoughts will free themselves from everyday distractions. In other words, let your thoughts run free. We use the wall as an imaginative springboard to help us dive into new thought patterns. All you have to do is break down your thoughts into details and reassemble them according to how they currently feel. In doing so, we are not observing others, but rather ourselves (see Fig. 5.8). The successful strategists mentioned above are among the most disciplined people, partly thanks to behaviors like this. It is essential to learn to self-observe.

5.5.5 Different Viewpoints

Depending on your viewpoint, certain elements of a project may or may not seem sensible. We see boundaries that are constantly shifting, and anything that may be right today can just as easily be wrong tomorrow. Topics that were unimportant in the past suddenly become important, and things that were yesterday's key to success suddenly lose their significance. In innovation strategy projects, this gap between the different ways of looking at things can be extremely wide. There are different ways to successfully deal with differing viewpoints and to use them to drive strategic topics forward.

5.5.5.1 Looking at Things from Your Opposite Number's Viewpoint

This is where most strategy professionals focus on empathizing with others. How does the other person feel about certain decisions? How does he feel about them personally? What could be done better? It is generally assumed that taking the other person's view will show us the results of the decisions we make. It should be sufficient to put yourself in the other person's shoes and derive certain reactions and behaviors from your new insights. However, this approach provides only a 50/50 chance of being correct. This value is not the result of scientific analysis, but rather an empirical value gained from more than 15 years of strategy work. In order to continue developing, we dared to rethink this process and look for alternatives, and in doing so we have come across a simple extension to the idea of adopting someone else's viewpoint. After a short phase of looking at things from our counterpart's viewpoint, we began to question the other person on their view of things. We

Fig. 5.8 Learning self-observation. (Source: H&F Solutions GmbH/www.hf-solutions.co)

discovered that about half of our assumptions were immediately refuted. By combining these two steps we were able to significantly increase the effectiveness of our decisions.

5.5.5.2 Paying Attention as a Change of Perspective

During this process, however, we noticed something else. Following our interviews, our interview partners' perception of us as a person had changed. They suddenly became more attentive and considerate, while the project results remained the same. To start with, we suspected that these people would turn away from us, but the opposite was true—by communicating directly, we were suddenly able to communicate much more efficiently. But even this observation was only part of the success. In fact, a large part of this result didn't come from direct communication, but rather from attentive observation of the other person in situations that included other project participants.

Example

In the course of a particular project, we observed a conversation between two project participants on the subject of project success. One participant took enormous pleasure in immediately reporting achieved results to project management—i.e., providing proof of success. The other participant didn't like this approach because it wasn't yet clear to him whether these results were successes at all, or whether they would turn out to be useless in retrospect. For most of the conversation, both were busy arguing their points of view and defending their positions, and only turned to the topic of success in a small side discussion. The colleague who wanted to present the successes was understandably having less and less fun as the conversation went on. There was no real discussion on the topic of success stories, but both nevertheless wanted to keep the conversation going. In the process, the more active colleague suggested to his counterpart that he should observe the success reporting for a while to see how project management reacted to it. A few days later we had a similar situation with this participant in which he again adopted a rather passive attitude. After a short discussion, we suggested he adopt a more active attitude regarding management reporting for a trial period in order to observe the results in retrospect and decide later on how to proceed.

Through mindfulness and close observation in another case, we were thus able to quickly achieve a usable result. In the end, it took less than 5 min to agree a change in behavior. Practice observing third-party conversations by ignoring the actual content of what's being said and focusing solely on gestures, breathing, posture, and tone. Does the person being observed really care about the outcome or does the person just want recognition? Or is he overwhelmed by the situation and actually needs help? ◀

5.5.6 Deception

Depending on how you have interpreted Sect. 5.5.5, you will now question certain things more strongly in the future and look at them from other angles. It is important not to be fooled by new and unfamiliar perspectives. When you start to think this way, you are sure to encounter plenty of situations in which you have allowed yourself be deceived in the past. We would now like to describe to you how you can reduce their number. Deception is ultimately nothing other than distorted sensory perception. Something appears different to you than it actually is. In terms of innovation strategy work, we would like to take a closer look at the Dunning-Kruger effect mentioned previously. This doesn't directly describe deception, but rather a way to avoid deception in strategy projects or to avoid being overwhelmed by deceptions that have negative consequences. In this context, everything that moves us away from the project goal is to be understood as a deception—after all, nobody wants to deliberately distance themselves from the project goal.

Scientific studies have proved that people who are less competent are most often subject to deception, whether in private or professional situations. This is because those who know least about a subject are often the ones who are convinced that they know better than everyone else. You are sure to have encountered a know-all in a discussion group, who not only knows more about the topic under discussion, but about every other topic too—or at least pretends to due to an abundance of self-confidence. As a rule, the majority of the participants in the group quickly exposes the know-all. So why do know-alls behave the way they do?

There are two reasons for this that we think are worth mentioning in this context:

1. The person concerned is a novice and has rarely received honest feedback on his statements, and therefore believes himself to be competent. If no-one contradicts you, you usually conclude that what you say must be right.
2. The person concerned surrounds himself exclusively with people who are less competent.

Thus, the person concerned cannot be blamed at all, since he cannot see what is going on.

For this reason, only two options remain here:

1. **Get external help to foster self-help**
   This is where you—as a project member or manager—can help. The people surrounding someone with this type of problem are the ones who can best help them gain self-knowledge about their behavior and its effects. Managers can support this kind of help by putting together the right kind of project team. In June 2020, after winning the Champions League and the English League championship, the soccer manager Jürgen Klopp was asked about his skills for success. In response, he cited the ability to assemble a high-performance coaching and support team as his core competency. His own skills are only a small part of the success he achieved. From now on, make sure that none of your project team members are permanently trapped within themselves.
2. **Self-knowledge through personal development**
   People become more self-critical with increasing knowledge. This means that the more you learn, the better you can counteract this effect yourself. The fact that you are reading this book shows that you have already begun to do so, simply by absorbing new knowledge. Once you have finished this book, continuing to absorb knowledge will increase your value as an innovation strategy team member.

The one positive exception to all these deceptions is to consciously ignore a known deception. This makes sense whenever you want to try something new—for example, if you are applying for a new job. Instead of waiting for a job to turn up that matches your qualifications, you can simply apply for a job for which you don't have all the required skills. Maybe the new job will work out and you will become a successful expert in an area that would have been previously unthinkable for you.

> **Important**
> Never let yourself be guided by unchecked deceptions. Instead, do something about it—for the team, not just for yourself.

5.5.7 Analogies: Pattern Recognition

Excellent digital leaders are usually able to behave logically, appropriately, and coherently. To do this, they utilize analogies, often described as pattern recognition, which gives individuals the ability to recognize similarities, regularity, or repetition. Those who wish to explore this topic further can look into the field of cognitive science. If you want to learn more about how computers use analogies and patterns, you can delve deeper into computer science.

Typical examples are speech recognition, face recognition, and text recognition. Humans perform these tasks effortlessly from an early age, and people vary in their ability to process these kinds of information. Almost all information, including most emotions, always follows the same pattern. Good digital leaders are able to recognize these patterns and categorize them based on rules. This ability can be built up in three ways, as shown in Fig. 5.9.

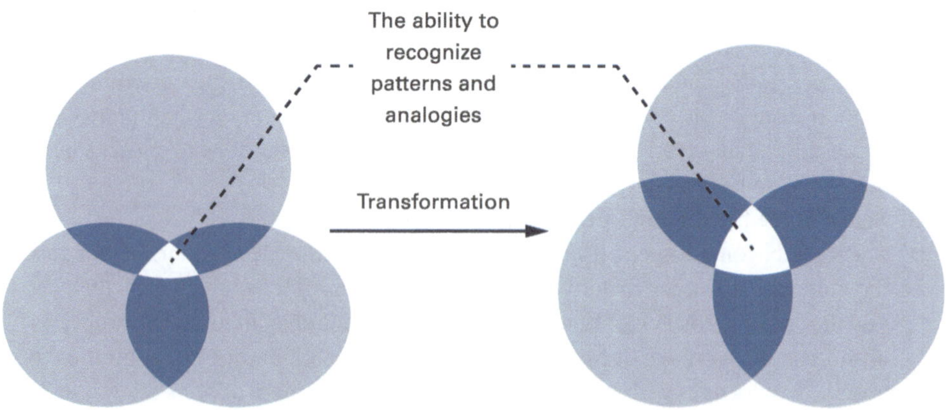

Fig. 5.9 Pattern recognition. (Source: H&F Solutions GmbH/www.hf-solutions.co)

5.5.7.1 Aptitude

This about people's genetic predisposition and how it affects the way their bodies and minds process information, and how it affects their behavior. Some people simply process information faster than others. It has been proven in the past that only very few people have a verifiable genetic predisposition toward pattern recognition.

5.5.7.2 Experience

Experiences fundamentally shape humans. Once these are fixed in our minds, we no longer examine them neutrally in the context of current issues, but accept them as set in stone. This in turn means that we simply no longer perceive a large part of the information that heads our way. This narrows our decision-making field of view enormously.

5.5.7.3 Practice

As far as practicing pattern recognition is concerned, we would like to distinguish between theory and the application of theoretical knowledge.

Pattern Recognition Exercises

The brain behaves like a muscle when learning patterns. With sufficient training, almost anyone is capable of becoming a strategy pattern recognition expert, and taking a course is probably the most effective way to improve your skills. This usually involves applying a wide variety of exercise that train the areas in your brain that are responsible for logic, memory, and language. Through regular exercise, even your IQ can be demonstrably increased. Once you have learned the basics, exercises in the areas of concentration and speed of thought provide a further booster effect. Exercises in this area include Sudoku puzzles or completing sequences of numbers or patterns (see Fig. 5.10).

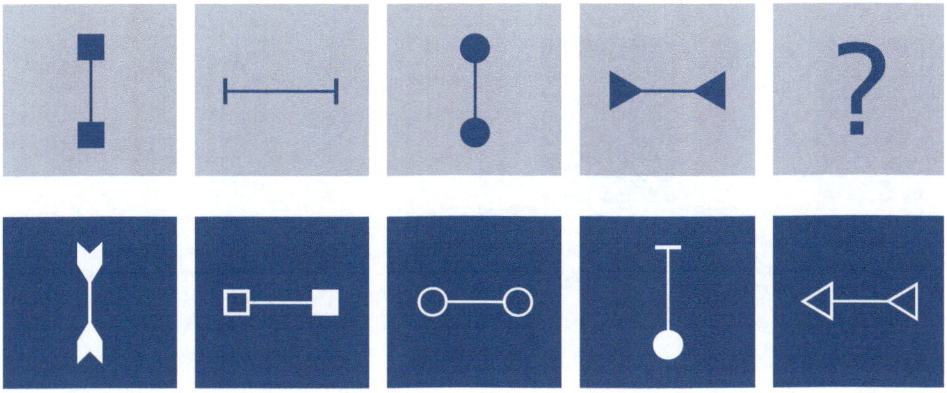

Fig. 5.10 Completing sequences of patterns. (Source: H&F Solutions GmbH/www.hf-solutions.co)

Applying Pattern Recognition Theory

If we possess theoretical knowledge of pattern recognition, we are able to check our experiences against this knowledge, which inevitably leads to different decisions than without this knowledge, it also ensures that we no longer simply accept experiences, but instead constantly re-evaluate them. Combined with a natural predisposition, this in turn ensures a highly efficient ability to recognize patterns and analogies, which for many untrained people is perceived as intelligence. In the context of strategy work, the following pattern types may emerge:

Analogies

Companies in which everything is clearly and cleanly structured almost always operate in highly technological markets (see Fig. 5.11). In this context, market participants are very similar to each other and employees at these companies are usually punctual. We have been able to identify these kinds of analogies in recent years through a combination of experience, predisposition, and practice. If you too have learned to think like this, you will be better able to assess situations and identify deeper-reaching patterns based on these analogies. Using this approach, you can probably implement a quite ambitious strategy. Furthermore, the highly transparent market allows you to combine your strategy with benchmarks.

At this point, please reflect on yourself. Have you tried to recognize patterns in the past, or have you simply succumbed to the wholesale sorting of experiences?

In Fig. 5.12, insights come from the discernible state of the company in terms of many unfinished projects, poor infrastructure, and similar personnel. In addition, competitors also have different product structures. Modest ambitions are probably the order of the day at this company, although it would probably already be a success if the company could get back on track by concentrating on completing (fewer) projects.

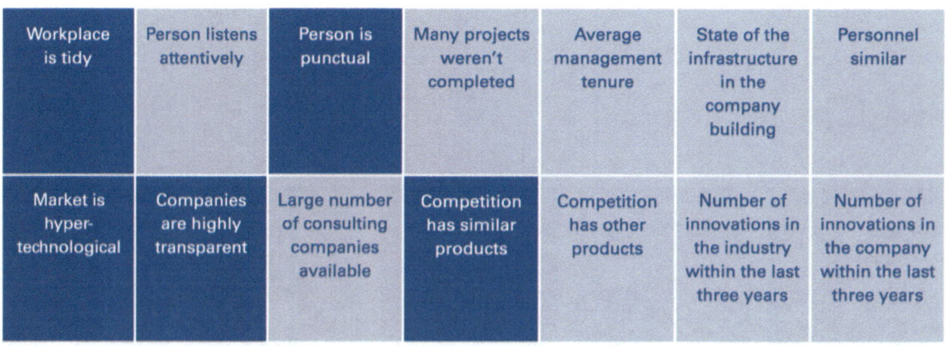

Fig. 5.11 Pattern recognition and analogies in technology markets. (Source: H&F Solutions GmbH/ www.hf-solutions.co)

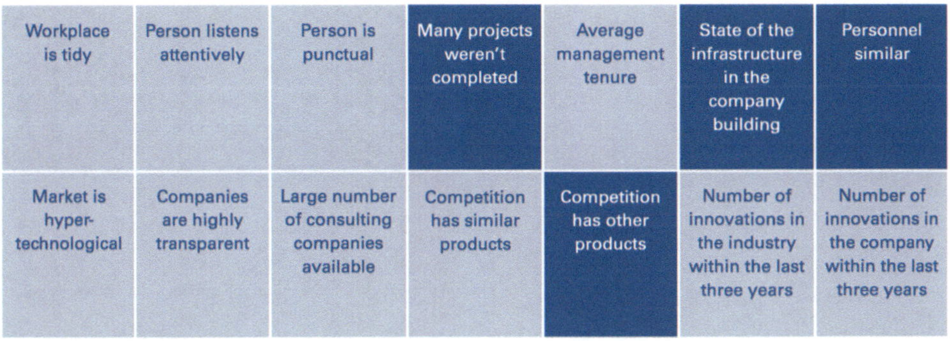

Fig. 5.12 Pattern recognition and analogies in homogeneous markets. (Source: H&F Solutions GmbH/www.hf-solutions.co)

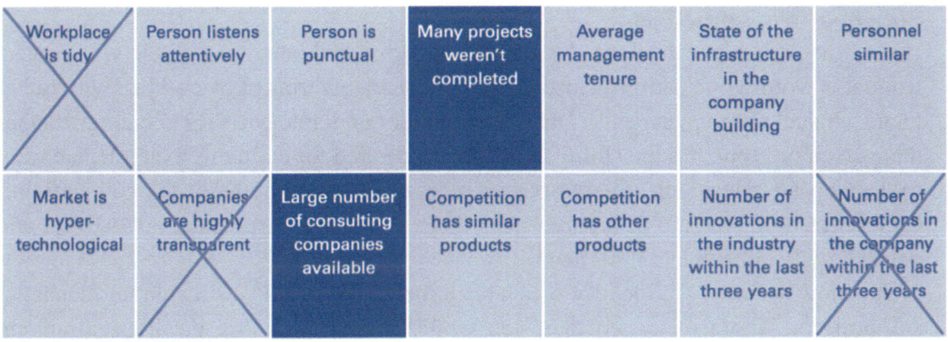

Fig. 5.13 Pattern recognition as related to the ability to innovate. (Source: H&F Solutions GmbH/ www.hf-solutions.co)

Dependency Patterns

Figure 5.13 shows a state of negative dependency. Companies that use a large number of external consultants tend to have many unfinished projects. At the same time, workplaces in these companies are often untidy and there is usually a lack of transparency and innovation. In a case like this, it is virtually impossible to make the strategy dependent on a benchmark. Instead, it would probably make sense to make the processes more transparent in order to be able to make fresh decisions.

Indicators such as long management tenure often speak for extroverted companies, which are also very receptive (see Fig. 5.14). In this case, it is necessary to break open the company's somewhat inflexible shell to make it more networked and give it the ability to react to changing markets in the future. If you extend these kinds of patterns, a clear picture will emerge that will help you evaluate the viability of certain strategic decisions.

At this point we would like to share the following example:

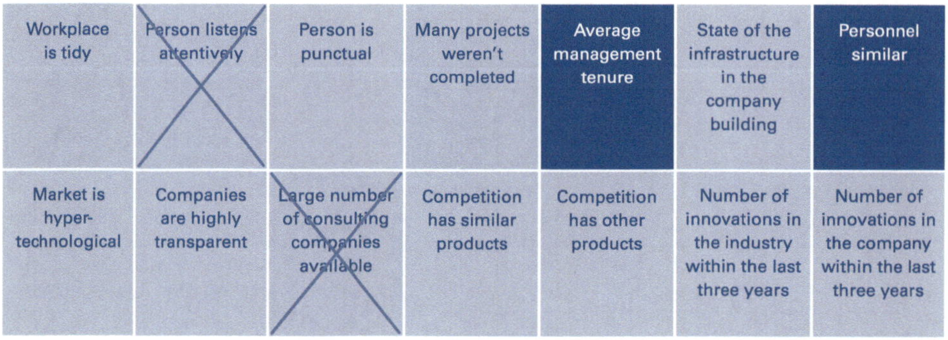

Fig. 5.14 Pattern recognition as related to homogeneity. (Source: H&F Solutions GmbH/www.hf-solutions.co)

Analyzing Your Project Team

If you want to analyze the overall structure and individual behaviors within your project team, it is worthwhile taking a closer look at the team in terms of overall behavior rather than technical pronouncements. This is a much more reliable basis for deciding whether this person or group has the ability to advance a desired topic. In this example, we want to develop a strategy for utilizing our own data. To date, no-one in the company has experience in this area. All that has been done so far is to export data into Excel and painstakingly consolidate it by hand.

It is now necessary to identify which team members would be suitable for managing sub-projects. Based on experience, you would probably choose the highest-ranking person in the project team without thinking twice. If, however, you approach the topic from the point of view of your personal disposition, you would probably choose the person you prefer to work with. If you now use all three areas of pattern recognition and have practiced sufficiently beforehand, you could run a preliminary sub-project and identify the suitable candidate on the basis of the individual participants' behavior. If you have little experience in this area, it is a good idea to undertake some mental training to learn both aspects. Following training, you should be able to identify whole chains of patterns and make better short-term decisions. This will also strengthen your perceived competence and the credibility of your position within the team. Everyone wants to work with experts! ◄

5.5.7.4 Pattern Recognition Still Possible Despite Blur

One challenge of innovation strategy work is that some things remain blurred, although this can be a help and not just a hindrance. For topics where you don't have all the information you need, it is easier to recognize patterns than for topics on which you have full transparency. This phenomenon is comparable with basic human abilities—people who have a broader view and are not specialized in a particular field recognize patterns more easily than people who are experts on a specific topic. The more blurred your view, the more patterns you will see.

5.5.8 Instinct

We have already shown you many rational kinds of support for your work, but now we would like to address the subject of instinct. Time and again we meet people who seem to make excellent decisions instinctively. However, we meet many more people who make predominantly bad intuitive decisions. Especially in situations where things are not going well or a company has its back to the wall, people often rely on their instincts. If you have good instincts, you are quickly able to concentrate on the essentials, make good predictions, and make decisions that are better than most. People with bad instincts tend to devote themselves to time-consuming data analysis during a crisis. In mid-tier companies, instinctive decisions are still predominant, while rational decisions are still quite rare—in corporations, the opposite is true, with decisions much less likely to be made on the basis of gut feelings. Let's take a look at instinct from a technical point of view. Instincts are innate and relatively rigid sequences of behavior that we humans perform subconsciously in certain situations. Instincts react initially to a stimulus and then on a person's readiness to act. This is a 'double quantification' that then generates key stimuli. If we react instinctively, we exceed the quantification threshold and a message is sent to the brain. Crossing this threshold is expressed as 'free will'. In the case of strategy work, the situation we react to could be the economic situation of the industry, where a crisis might cause us to instinctively cut back on our business for a while, even though rational decision-making processes might reveal great market potential for an aggressive investment and growth strategy. Let's take a look back at your life. In childhood, you probably lacked expertise and experience, but you were still able to make decisions. This was possible due to your instinct—i.e., a process that works automatically without you consciously learning it. Instinctive behavior is innate and is characterized by the fact that it works the first time it is used, without being learned beforehand.

It is difficult to fight your instincts, but you can learn to recognize whether people (including yourself) make decisions instinctively or rationally. Instinct is more important for strategy work than it is for operational or structural issues. This is because strategy work lacks rational variables. If you can distinguish between the rational and instinctive aspects of your own behavior, you will be able to add another piece to the strategy puzzle. However, remember that it is impossible to completely and definitively distinguish between rational and instinctive behavior.

Summary

Since the majority of all plans fail, it is important to always have alternatives in mind. Anyone who considers alternatives at an early stage can face changes calmly. In this context there are certain characteristics that repeatedly emerge in innovation strategy projects and that distinguish digital leaders. These are:

1. Friction
2. An eye for progress
3. Viewpoint adaptability
4. Recognition of deception and distortion
5. The ability to adapt on the strength of analogies
6. Instinctive behavior
7. Use of a physical notebook

Those who possess many of these traits or behaviors tend to make digital leaders. And remember that these traits are 90% learned and are not there from the start. Practice makes perfect. ◄

5.6 Efficient Communication

The best innovation strategy and the best technologies won't help you if you don't manage to establish permanently efficient communication. It is simply not sufficient to communicate information once or annually. As the tasks involved become more and more extensive and time is of the essence, you need to apply appropriate methods to communication too. For two of our clients, strategy work in the past consisted of defining these methods, a single PowerPoint presentation, and annual strategy meetings. Outside of this annual rhythm, strategy was mentioned in passing in many meetings, but a consistent alignment of all processes to the overall strategy simply didn't take place. We don't want to rehash the topic of communication per se, but we have noticed an improvement in communication in our projects due to application of the approaches described in the following sections.

5.6.1 Space for Communication

Communication in companies functions best when it is given only limited space and when you try to use it as efficiently as possible. Chap. 3 describes the minimum communication necessary in strategy projects, and this is what you should limit yourself to. Here, regularity is more important than the duration of any communication, and regular meetings are a great place to form opinions as well as exchange information. In terms of the speed of change, these sessions are the appropriate place not just for forming opinions but, more importantly, for correcting them. We are not talking about discussion here, but only about forming opinions.

5.6.2 Using a Moderator

We see great projects fail time and again, and this is nothing out of the ordinary. What is surprising is that communication is often responsible for failed projects. However, good communication is easy to implement if you employ a dedicated assistant to coordinate the required deadlines, maintain communication, and check the content of communication between the project participants. This person does not need to have any specialist expertise, but must have time to spare and a talent for organization. In successful projects, these tasks are often taken on by young people at the start of their professional careers. This task gives them the opportunity to quickly acquire networking knowledge. Let's go through the required processes. Assuming you have all the necessary departments at the table and you want to start implementing the project, simply documenting the content of the meeting, capturing the content that the project participants have written on the whiteboard, and coordinating the follow-up meetings becomes a pitfall for most project teams. This is usually because all the specialists involved are so overloaded with tasks that they don't have time to move the project forward in an orderly fashion. Because of the scheduling problems for follow-up deadlines, a phase begins during which the entire project team will never meet again as a unit. If you have a dedicated project assistant who takes over follow-up scheduling and is also present at every subsequent meeting, your project will run better, if only because your specialists can now concentrate on their 'real' work. What happens now is as follows:

The project assistant is present at all meetings and is the only person who can record the content of all the conversations that take place. She is therefore also the only one will notice if there are gaps in the project logic or if the work starts to head off in conflicting directions. A manager or a technical expert would never take the time to follow all these flows. If there are places where the teams drift apart, the project assistant is there to intervene. In this way, a person who starts as a technical novice becomes a kind of mastermind who contributes significantly to the success of the project. This kind of position is an ideal stepping stone for junior staff. We recommend that you employ freshly trained apprentices for this kind of work.

Summary

Those who succeed in communicating efficiently create a basis on which technical topics can develop at high speed. Short, intense meetings, and the use of an assistant or moderator are the most important aspects of this approach. If you take a closer look at this aspect of a project, you will see that the moderator is often more important than technical input from the individual business units. ◀

6 Technological Catalysts in Innovation Strategy Implementation

In the last 20 years, digitization has become an important part of our everyday and business lives. Nevertheless, we are still only at the beginning of the digitization process. In this period, many new technologies have been developed, implemented, used, refined and, in some cases, discarded. However, what has endured since the end of the 1980s and remains at the heart of every process-related strategy, is the management of knowledge using software tools and databases. The knowledge provided by these tools is the main driver for the success of any holistic innovation strategy project. Without such tools, most companies only make it as far as defining a strategy but run out of steam when it comes to implementation. This is usually because the strategy was defined without taking any data-related insights into account. The following sections introduce the technical catalysts that counteract this effect and that are indispensable for successful strategy work.

In addition to many soft factors, many of today's approaches to strategy implementation use technology to provide basic support. We concentrate on the technologies and approaches which, in our view, make the greatest contribution to the success of innovation strategy implementation—in our view, these are networking and the production of knowledge. If you manage to develop these two areas into supporting pillars for your company, you will be among the top ten technologically innovative companies in terms of digitization. Many readers are sure to feel 'at home' in this chapter, because it's finally about the 'how'— or, more specifically, about which technologies you should use to achieve the desired output. If you still have some catching up to do in the area of digitization, you are probably facing another almost insurmountable hurdle. However, you can overcome this hurdle with the help of this chapter. If you succeed in innovatively implementing networking and knowledge production, the height of the barrier to successful strategy implementation will drop significantly (see Fig. 6.1). Why is this so? Stable networking of systems and the insight production that is possible as a result will enable

P. Futterknecht, T. Hertfelder, *Data, Disruption & Digital Leadership*,
https://doi.org/10.1007/978-3-658-41601-0_6

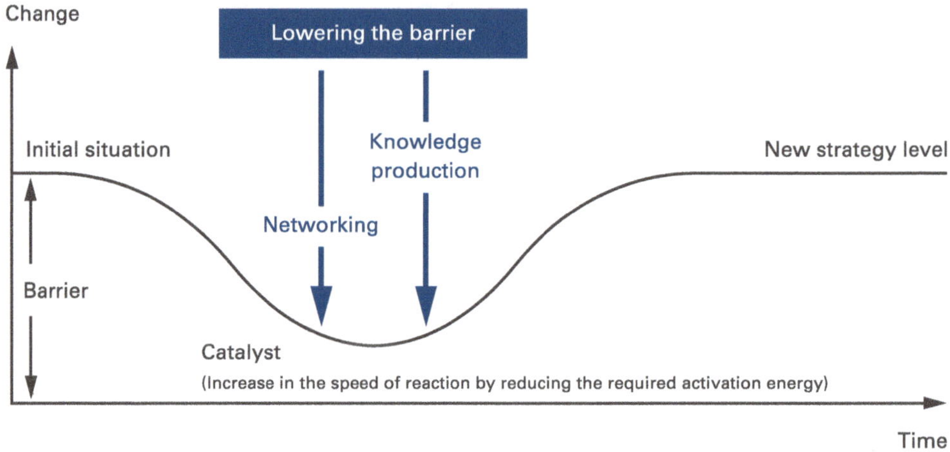

Fig. 6.1 Catalysts for successful innovation strategy development. (Source: H&F Solutions GmbH/ www.hf-solutions.co)

you to see things that you cannot see today without the help of technical tools. By 2030 at the latest, it will be necessary to break this control loop in every company. Once this control loop of gaining knowledge and generating a better basis for decision-making has been triggered, it acts like a catalyst that reduces your reaction times by reducing the amount of activation energy required, just like a catalytic converter in a car.

In Sects. 6.1 and 6.2, we will look at this topic from management and CIO viewpoints. This is intended to present this complex topic concisely in your specialist language. The sections that follow include all the necessary detailed information on the topics of knowledge production and innovative networking.

6.1 Management Level: Summary

The complexity of networking systems in and around companies is increasing at a rapid pace. In order to master this increasing complexity, you require either increasing numbers of administrative tools, or a large number of people who create networks manually. If we take a closer look, it becomes obvious that this degree of networking complexity is extremely difficult to manage manually, especially in view of the necessary scaling.

Today's companies usually operate using individual divisional networks and find their own way through the networking jungle. At the same time, almost all companies require the same kind of output, namely: simple networking. The necessary scaling will become possible for the first time using products that are already being developed today. Based on the idea of community-based solutions, problems will no longer be solved internally, but instead jointly, and the solutions will be available to everyone. The use of state-of-the-art technologies—such as data mining, machine learning (ML), artificial intelligence (AI), big data, and so on—enables you to exchange data fully automatically with just a few clicks.

Example

Let's look at connecting ERP systems as an example. If you want to connect customers today, all the market offers is a technical solution that allows you to apply certain standards. Unfortunately, these don't reflect your individuality at all. In the future, however, you will get community-based solutions will enable you to take your company's individuality into account. This allows you to automatically connect customers within minutes without manual intervention. This will enable you to develop new markets much faster, which of course gives you a competitive advantage. ◄

If you go a step further, you will see that in the future it won't be possible to connect customers manually at all. Let's take a closer look at this concept:

If the number of systems to be networked increases, networking complexity also increases. However, complexity itself can neither be estimated nor controlled. Many CTOs are still of the opinion that IT projects can be planned and controlled, but the future presents a very different picture! IT managers are already finding it difficult to keep track of the increasing dynamics in individual systems, and it is impossible to provide realistic cost estimates for networking projects. The result is time delays and cost overruns. A multitude of individual projects therefore gradually pushes IT departments to their limits, and the maintenance costs, which are not yet foreseeable, will exceed the connection costs many times over. Many companies are unwittingly creating their own 'complexity monster'.

And this is why there is no way around automated networking. The nodes being networked are the source from which knowledge production is fed, and this in turn is the key to the future success of companies. Wouldn't it be nice if, in the future, a digital assistant could automatically tell you with which combination of customer and product groups would generate maximum success?

In our view, a successful networking approach must offer the following crucial cornerstones:

- Extremely simple usage based on central platforms
- Fast, integrated solution for connecting internal and external data systems
- Transformational technology that enables customizable and scalable networking
- No language and communication barriers (data transformers)
- Interactive communication between systems (smart error handling)
- Community-based solutions: standardized instead of individualized networking
- Knowledge and monitoring systems that visualize dynamically changing data (transparency)

6.2 CIO Level: Summary

One of the main strategic tasks of CIOs, IT managers, and IT directors is to master complexity or reduce it within existing IT systems in order to provide management with valuable data for future strategy work. The easiest way to do this is to introduce a small number of software tools and coordinate them holistically. This provides a degree of system stability that companies will be reluctant to relinquish later on. Companies that aim to expand their business by networking with as many other stakeholders as possible but who take a conservative approach to networking, are increasingly running into difficulties. If you choose a path of predominantly manual data and system handling, IT will no longer be able to meet future management demands.

In our view, the following points make an enormous contribution to innovation strategy work in the form of networking and knowledge production:

- Platforms ensure that data from all systems can be networked and easily compacted.
- Parameterizable settings allow systems to define which input and output data are to be processed, and in which file format and data structure they are available.
- The existing platform transformer models transform data between the various defined systems.
- The community approach benefits everyone, as models that have already been created can be used by the other companies.
- Networking no longer takes place one-to-one (from system to system), but instead globally via a single platform (one platform to ***n*** systems).
- The effort required to connect and parameterize new systems must be reduced by 95%.

6.3 Knowledge Production

Let's take a look at a strategy project from the point of view of the goal. We want to gain insights with which we can make better strategic decisions and lead the company into a successful future. Due to the huge increase in the variety of data sources, this gain in knowledge can no longer be achieved without technical assistance. In the future, all data sources must therefore be interconnected. If your company manages to network its data sources and eliminate any standalone systems, you will be able to recognize things that are currently hidden from you and don't contribute to the success of the company. In the future, more than half of all activities will be standardized and automated, whereas today, this figure is only 10%. Networking technologies and software tools that are already available today will ensure this transformation. Let's look at an example:

Example

Demand for a particular component arises in production, and the machine concerned reports the demand to the ERP system, which then determines the optimal combination of quantity, timing, and quality. Next, this demand is automatically transferred to an online purchasing portal, and the ERP system receives all relevant order data. Via the connected shipping service interface, the ERP system knows immediately when and where the goods will arrive. Once delivery receipt is confirmed by the shipping service, the ERP system sends a drone to the incoming goods area to determine where the order was placed and transmits the location with all the relevant data to the incoming goods inspector. Following a successful inspection, the system receives a message that the goods meet all requirements. The subsequent follow-up processes (money transfer, accounting, and so on) are managed by the networked systems. The traditional purchaser/dispatcher role is transformed into a monitoring role. This is roughly what such a process will look like in 2030, when a maximum of just 5% human input is required. Managing this process manually would probably take two people from the purchasing and work scheduling departments several hours. ◀

Ultimately, the process described involves coordinating many tiny cogs in a huge machine. If we now look at the sum of many such coordination processes, we gain astonishing insight into the overall process. In terms of innovation strategy work, this means that complex data management will be indispensable in the future. Your strategy will therefore only be successful if you have this kind of data available and your business is geared towards executing these kinds of processes. A strategy focused on manual processes will fail at the latest when these are replaced by automated processes.

In the future, automated insights will be gained at all nodes between systems. The only real question is the extent to which companies and their data sources are equipped to work this way.

6.3.1 Speed and Forecasting Accuracy as an Outcome of Networking and Knowledge Production

As already described in Sect. 6.3, knowledge production should have a meaningful purpose—in this case, speed (see Fig. 6.2). Your company doesn't profit from the insight itself, but from the resulting speed, and this is what makes the difference. If you are able to connect to five new customers a day, who can then automatically and easily purchase products from you, your chance of enforcing better prices is much greater, and we don't need to explain what that means for your business.

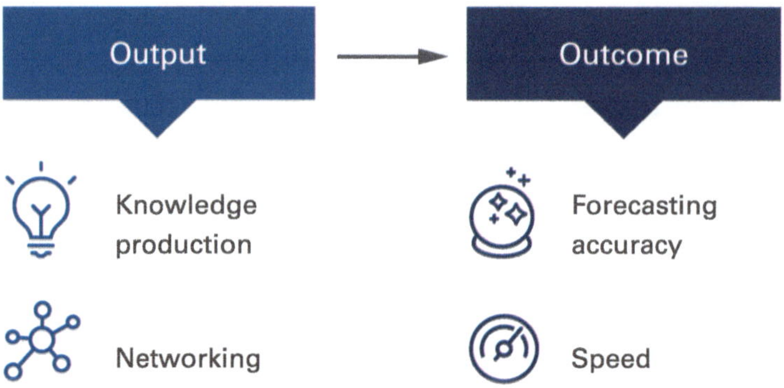

Fig. 6.2 Speed and forecasting accuracy. (Source: H&F Solutions GmbH/www.hf-solutions.co)

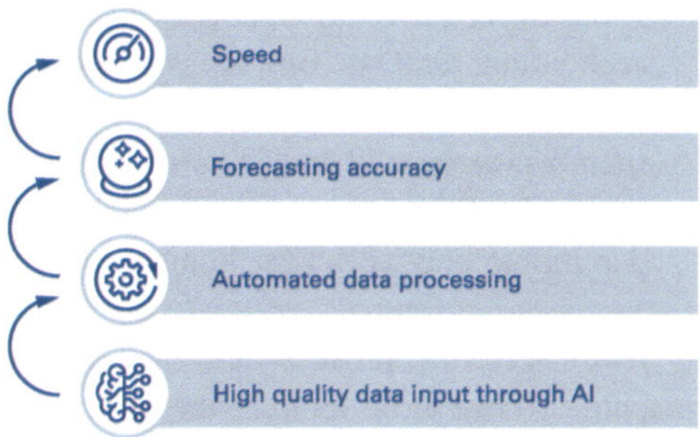

Fig. 6.3 Knowledge production within companies. (Source: H&F Solutions GmbH/www.hf-solutions.co)

Through technical transformation, future systems will enable even greater forecasting accuracy, as well as faster and more efficient process flows (see Fig. 6.3). This can only be achieved on the basis of high-quality data input, the generation of huge amounts of data, and real-time processing. The goal will therefore be to perform administrative and organizational activities at near real-time speeds in order to achieve greater efficiency in almost all processes. This in turn will then produce even greater speed in production, delivery, trade, and financing. Increasing data accuracy thus gradually creates a transparent company with highly transparent processes, based on the networking of data sources and networking with the company environment. The following sections explain how this works in real terms.

Summary

Insight and knowledge production will be the value driver with the greatest growth in companies in the coming years. In the future, these insights can be gathered almost everywhere where the various participants and systems intersect. However, insight production itself serves only as a catalyst to the ability to forecast. Gaining insights without further processing or interpretation will deliver only limited success. However, in the future, software tools will also support the data interpretation process. ◄

6.4 Networking: Tomorrow's Technical Vision

Maximum automation of all recurring activities is what matters when it comes to networking. Today, no innovation strategy should be without this important cornerstone. The following sections detail a concept that you can use to build a stable network.

6.4.1 Today's Technical State of the Art

You are probably wondering why it is not possible, given the current state of technology, to automate dependent processes like those described in the example in the previous section. This is certainly possible, but currently only using custom solutions. A standard that offers a worthwhile cost-benefit ratio has not yet been established. Instead, other internal and external systems and devices are connected via complex processes that include standardized electronic data exchange formats such as EDI. However, this standardization is limited, as additional mappings and format transformations have to be performed. Marginal topics such as connection technology, firewall issues, and increasing data protection are also disregarded. Current *Industry 4.0* solutions usually only consider the technological view, and only within the company—i.e., a machine only communicates with its manufacturer and an ERP system only communicates with other ERP systems (one-to-one connections). The *Industry 4.0* networking concept, whereby a machine can communicate with any external system or end-user device, has not yet been properly thought through. To accelerate the transformation to complete automation, we decided to research this topic more thoroughly. In the context of innovation strategy work, this means automating the knowledge base for use in future strategy implementation processes.

6.4.2 The Requirements of the Future

In the future, digital systems of all kinds should be able to communicate easily with each other. For this to happen, the networking and digitization barriers that still exist today must be eliminated, and this is not a question of 'whether' but rather of 'when'. In detail, the areas illustrated in Fig. 6.4 need to be mastered.

Approaching this topic, we find it to be multi-layered and complex. Or is it just complicated? Obtaining a simple solution to the issues shown in Fig. 6.4 requires sound analysis and an intelligent approach that can only be achieved by mastering complexity. To do this, it is important to understand the difference between complicated and complex. To help make this distinction, Fig. 6.5 shows a graphical representation of the issues identified and listed in Fig. 6.4.

It is clear that most of the important topics will reach such a high level of complexity by 2030 that they will no longer be implementable by individual companies and will become

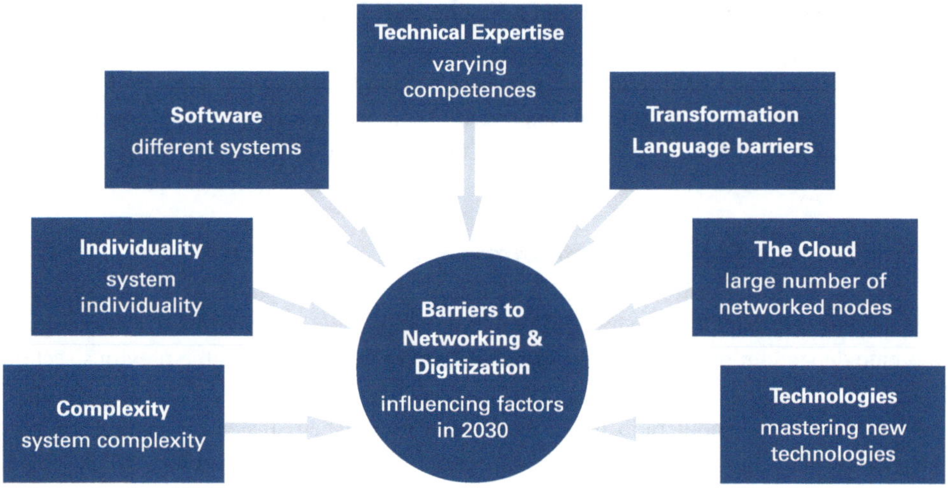

Fig. 6.4 Barriers to networking and digitization in the year 2030, as visualized by H&F. (Source: H&F Solutions GmbH/www.hf-solutions.co)

even more impenetrable than they are today. However, there is still time to manage this issue successfully, so let's dive in and take a closer look.

6.4.2.1 System Complexity

Trends in the world of software are clearly moving toward complex systems. Internal sources at the software manufacturer SAP claim that there are only five people still around who are proficient in the entire SAP core. This means that the background logic, structures, and interrelationships can only be derived through a high level of abstraction, and complexity will increase to such a degree in the coming years that any understanding of complex systems will only be superficial. Consequently, only input and output points will be truly comprehensible. What happens between input and output is only comprehensible to a limited extent.

> **Important**
> Today's systems are complicated and thus derivable. Future systems will be complex and, like a black box, can no longer be explained in depth, but can only be understood superficially or in parts.

6.4.2.2 System Individuality and the Individuality of Data Content

Every software, every ecosystem, and every application has its own individuality that needs to be mastered. Due to the increasing number of connected systems, the effort required to

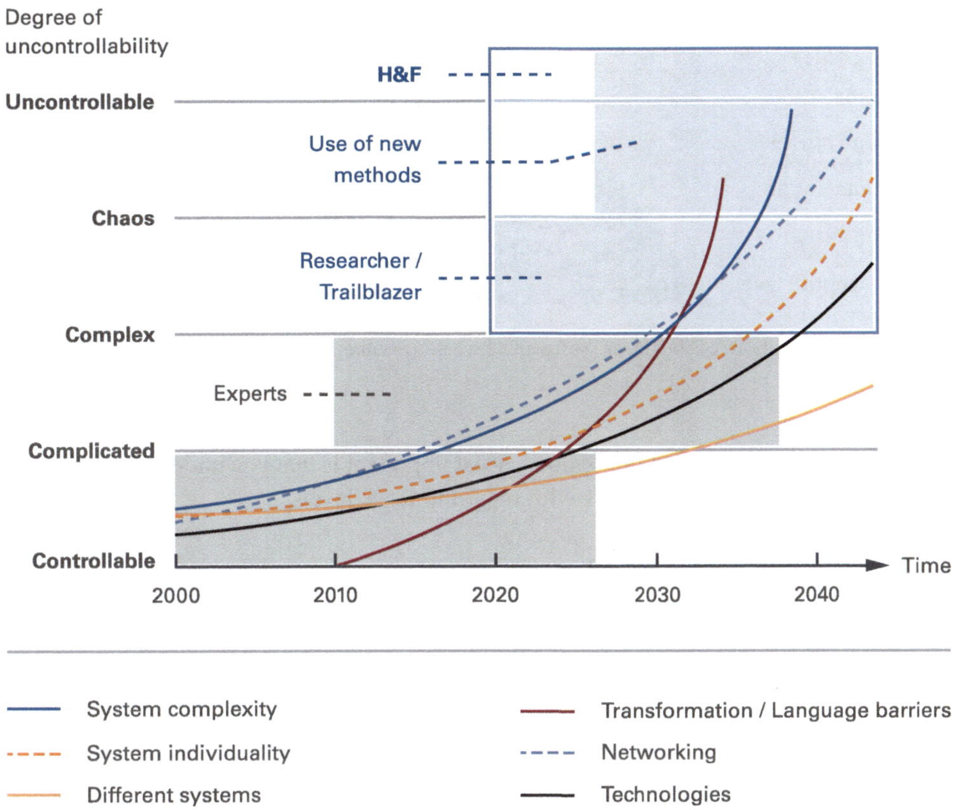

Fig. 6.5 Manageability through logic and structure. (Source: H&F Solutions GmbH/www.hf-solutions.co)

master them also increases. Furthermore, these systems are changing at an ever-increasing rate, which in turn significantly increases the effort required to operate them.

The effort is not only limited to the exchange of data and data exchange interfaces. Constantly changing data content and data structures significantly increase this individuality too.

6.4.2.3 Networking Hierarchies

We classify software on various levels in order to better understand it from the networking perspective. Figure 6.6 illustrates networking hierarchies from a local viewpoint (i.e., the lowest level) through to a fully integrated view (i.e., the highest level where entire ecosystems are networked).

Due to the increasing variety of software and the growing number of tools in use, this pyramid will expand further in the future. However, right now it represents a good view of

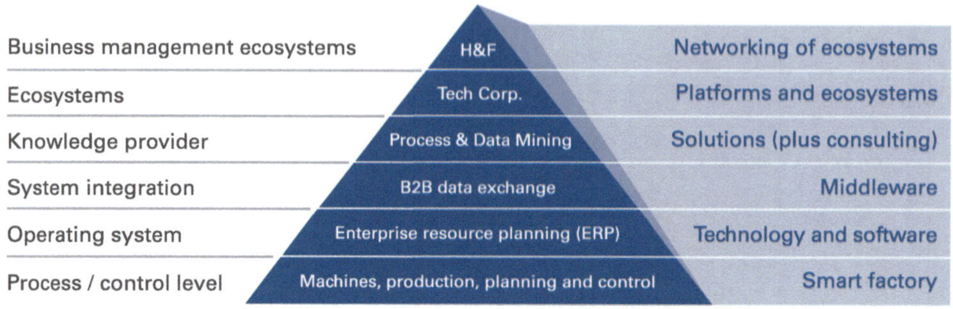

Fig. 6.6 Classification of business software levels. (Source: H&F Solutions GmbH/www.hf-solutions.co)

the different levels of networking options. Most important is that you understand the rough differentiation of software products with regard to these levels.

6.4.2.4 Competence/Expertise

While specialist consultants and experts are still used to implement certain subdomains within ERP systems (such as SAP), in the future complexity will increase to such an extent that these areas will have to be divided into further subdomains, and complexity itself will have to be subdivided too. In most cases, this is done by dividing it into industries and use cases. In the future, there will not only be a 'logistics consultant', but also a 'logistics consultant for the fishing industry as applied to the SAP ERP module Logistics XXX'. In the future there will be new job profiles (such as architects, inspectors, or in-depth project managers) who transform, compensate, organize, and delegate the newly emerging requirements.

In addition, the demand for these specialists will increase in the next few years to such an extent that they will only be available to software manufacturers (see Fig. 6.7). Knowledge will thus be further concentrated and, in the medium term, will migrate from companies to service providers. This situation is not expedient from a business point of view but, since the process is already in full swing, this scenario is very likely to occur. We can thus only decide how long we want to resist it.

6.4.2.5 Transformation/Language Barriers

If several software levels are in use, the number of individual systems will increase and with it, the number of required interfaces too. This also inevitably means an increase in the number of data formats and exchange logics required to connect the various systems. As a result, more and more specialists and/or employees with broad-based knowledge will be needed. Since the capacity of humans to absorb manageable languages and formats is limited, transformation will have to be performed by software components in the future. The only remaining specialists will be the ones who specialize in the transformation of a few niche languages.

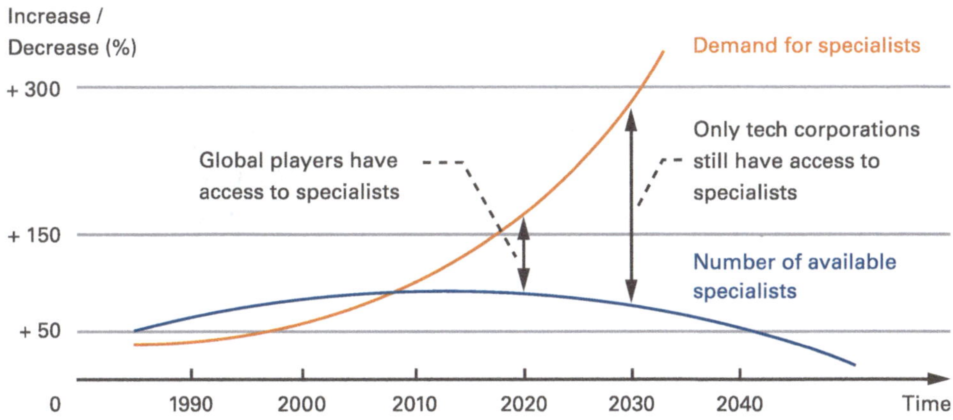

Fig. 6.7 The demand for experts over time. (Source: H&F Solutions GmbH/www.hf-solutions.co)

6.4.2.6 Degree of Interconnectedness

Using Fig. 6.8, you can now categorize yourself according to your current degree of collaboration or your technical level. As described above, long-term success can only be generated by using community applications, and it is impossible to build this kind of network within a company.

The trend will continue to move toward the complete networking of entire ecosystems. In the future, these will already include platforms on which other people and companies can participate, and which actively interact with other systems. Individuality will then also be modeled at platform level. Systems that focus on internal communication will largely disappear.

6.4.2.7 Technological Progress

The IT landscape will continue to change, especially in the areas of networking and security. In contrast, traditional topics such as analytics and ERP will experience lower growth rates compared to other topics (see Fig. 6.9). The reason for this is the exploited (or not yet exploited) potential in these specialist areas. While application software was still installed locally over recent decades, this is now moving to the cloud. This means that it is no longer software alone that is the growth driver, but rather a combined package of software and cloud. Due to today's lack of expertise, AI will lead the way in the future and its use will become ubiquitous. However, its development will be concentrated in a few high-tech companies.

The situation will be similar in other specialist areas: Software will interactively communicate with other software (networking + ecosystem). Power outlets, light switches, and machines will automatically be connected to the internet in order to receive and execute actions (IoT, the Internet of Things). Artificial intelligence will enable learned knowledge to be applied to simple and repetitive tasks, and robots will take over tasks that they can do

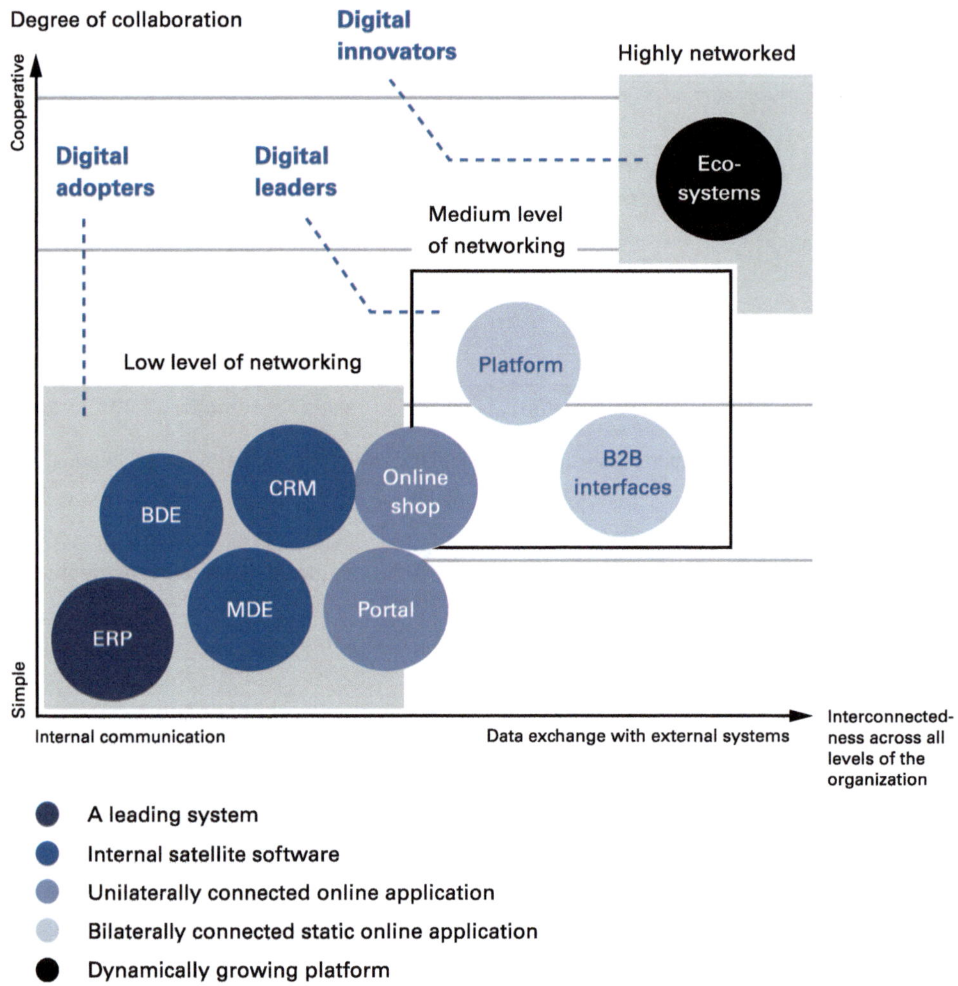

Fig. 6.8 Digital interconnectedness. (Source: H&F Solutions GmbH/www.hf-solutions.co)

faster, more precisely, and with less errors—for example, in order to improve human ergonomics.

6.4.3 Looking Ahead at the Years Between Now and 2030

Networking and digitization have already entered our vernacular, but in terms of implementation we have only just left the starting blocks. We sometimes have the feeling that we have already had enough of these constant innovations, although this topic is only just beginning to really unfold—not just within companies, but globally too, across all levels and stakeholders. Today's systems (B2B, ERP, and so on) and devices (IoT, cars,

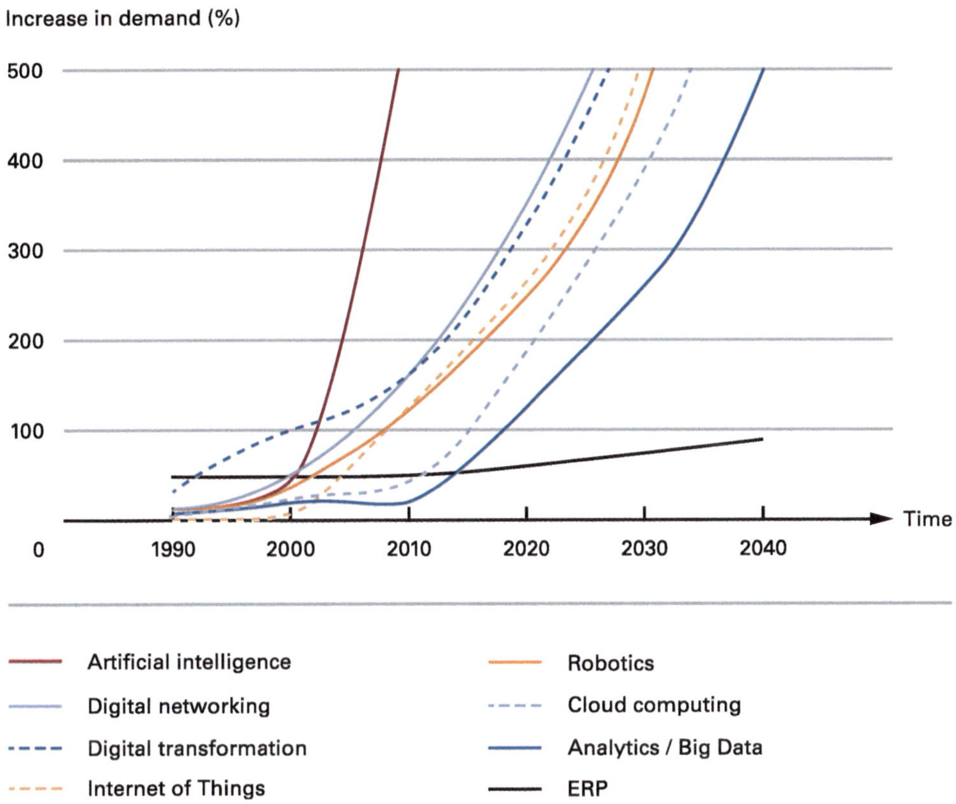

Fig. 6.9 Forecast growth rates for new IT topics. (Source: H&F Solutions GmbH/www.hf-solutions.co)

machines) can already be networked, but they usually speak their own language based on a standard geared towards their own specific usage domain. An overarching standard for data exchange doesn't yet exist. However, this will change in the coming years. The following example illustrates why this will happen:

Reality

Your company requires new consumables, and the purchaser receives an MRP proposal to purchase these from the cheapest supplier. Amazon is chosen as the supplier, and the buyer creates a purchase order manually through Amazon. Amazon confirms the order and the shipping date via e-mail. The shipping service notifies and informs the buyer via e-mail that the goods will arrive at a certain time. The goods are sent to the shipping service, where the goods are handed over and the tracking number is reported. After a while we receive the delivery. Dispatch then performs a visual inspection and books the goods into the system. The Amazon invoice arrives soon after the successful delivery is reported. The invoice can then be manually posted into your ERP system and settled during an automated payment run. This is a (slimmed-down) representation of an order process as it happens millions of times a day in companies everywhere. In this case, we have only mentioned the main steps that take place. In reality, such an order process requires more than 200 individual entries. Assuming that 100 such 200-step order processes happen in a company every day and that (in Germany, for example) we have approx. 400,000 mid-tier companies, this equates to the unbelievable number of eight billion bookings every day. ◀

Given the current state of technology, you are probably wondering why it isn't possible to automate these interdependent processes. It is certainly feasible from today's point of view, but it is currently only possible to handle these kinds of processes via **individual solutions** that are custom tailored to each company and its own individual processes. However, a poor cost-benefit ratio makes such individual solutions unattractive and uninteresting.

Based on today's knowledge, it is already possible to fully automate this kind of process by 2025, and only the physical receipt of goods/quality check will have to be carried out manually in the future. The merchandise management (or ERP) system reports the order to the online purchasing portal fully automatically. Once delivery receipt is confirmed by the shipping service, the ERP system sends a drone to the incoming goods area to determine where the order was placed, and transmits the location with all the relevant data to the incoming goods inspector. Following a successful inspection, the system receives a message that the goods meet all requirements. The subsequent follow-up processes (money transfer, accounting, and so on) are managed by the networked systems.

The traditional purchaser/dispatcher role is transformed into a monitoring role.

6.4.3.1 The State of the Art

Currently, other internal or external systems and devices are connected using complex node-to-node connection processes. Electronic data exchange is based on standardized formats such as EDI. However, on closer inspection, such formats are standardized based on only a small common denominator, and don't include mapping or format transformations. Likewise, other marginal topics such as connection technologies, firewalls, and increasing data protection are not taken into account.

Current *Industry 4.0* solutions focus only on networking subdomains, and usually only within the company or—in the case of cross-company applications—only on a specific process. For example, a machine only communicates with its manufacturer, or an ERP system only communicates with other ERP systems (i.e., one-to-one connections). Today's applications therefore only minimally support the concept of genuine networking.

6.4.4 The Goal

In the future, data networking must take place without technical barriers (transformation, language, technology, interfaces, and so on), and should be as simple as sending an e-mail already is. E-mails are exchanged in a standardized, networked manner without technical barriers. At the push of a button or by selecting the appropriate recipient, the system knows automatically via the selected core data which data transformation processes, language translations, technology connections, and interfaces the recipient system uses, and how the external system is to be controlled in order to transmit data. The goal is to enable fully automated communication from any device/system to any other device/system.

Example

The Internet of Things (IoT): In the future, a working lathe will communicate via a central ERP system with the machine manufacturer and the operator in order to automatically reorder spare parts and to inform the operator of any changes to the processing sequence. These decisions can only be derived with an appropriate quality level if the data sources are networked and can effectively communicate with one another. ◀

Another good example is the Mercedes-Benz *Car-to-X* project:

Mercedes-Benz already envisaged a data exchange platform several years ago in the form of its *Car-to-X* communication project. However, on closer inspection this system is merely sector-oriented, and information can only be exchanged between Mercedes vehicles or via a communication point within a Mercedes vehicle. This system is thus intended purely for networking between cars and traffic devices/systems.

Potentially, the data collected by the system could also be transmitted to other stakeholders, such as shipping services who require data regarding dangers on a planned route. At the same time, the shipping service could send delay information to the recipient via a connected ERP system.

Speed and Forecasting Accuracy Will Be Critical to Success

In the future, control systems (such as ERP) will have to enable increasing forecasting accuracy as well as faster and more efficient process flows. This can only be achieved based on more accurate data input, increasing data volumes, and processing in the form of real-time events. The goal will be to perform administrative and organizational activities in real time to achieve greater efficiency in all processes. In the future, increasing data accuracy will create transparent factories that function based on maximum data transparency.

Summary

In the near future, you will be able to get networking and automation 'out of the box'. This ensures maximum automation of all repeatable and standardized activities within companies and supply chains. At the same time, it will no longer be possible for companies to create custom solutions that remain profitable. This is because the necessary specialists will simply be swept up by large corporations or software companies. Basically, the challenges are so complex that only fully integrated software can meet these complex requirements. Individuality in companies will continue to increase, but individuality will then be available as an automated service in the form of suitable software. ◀

6.5 Added Value to Be Generated by 2030 (Outcome/Result)

With the help of future technologies, companies will be able to participate in the market faster and more easily. However, to achieve this it is not sufficient to think just in terms of products or individual technologies. Instead, a mix of outcomes—as shown in Fig. 6.10—is necessary to provide stakeholders with the information they need.

6.5.1 Scalability

By using manual networking technologies such as IoT, ERP, API, EDI, and so on, you will be able to automate certain things, but you will never be able to achieve exponential growth (see Fig. 6.11). This is because these individual technologies cannot automatically combine to form a whole because they are not directly networked to other systems, and are therefore not directly dependent on each other. While you are technically in the clear, you are once again dependent on a large number of specialists with incomplete knowledge of your particular situation.

It is therefore necessary to think bigger and to create a single, overarching platform (i.e., your own 'ecosystem') from the very beginning. Such a networking ecosystem relieves you of almost all activities except for network monitoring and release management. Technical expertise for connecting and networking with business partners or third-party systems is then no longer necessary, as the appropriate know-how is provided as a service. This significantly reduces complexity for the companies of the future without any loss of scalability. As a side effect, reaching this level of digitization also offers enormous savings potential in terms of the amount of personnel required (see Fig. 6.12).

6.5.2 New Markets and Customers

In the future, today's customers will no longer exist in their current form (see Fig. 6.13). In the future, the customer will in many cases be unknown and will no longer be transparent or committed to its supplier—a scenario that is largely unimaginable today, but that is highly likely to transpire. This means that companies will be permanently occupied with opening up new markets in order to acquire new customers. In order to be able keep up, it is crucial

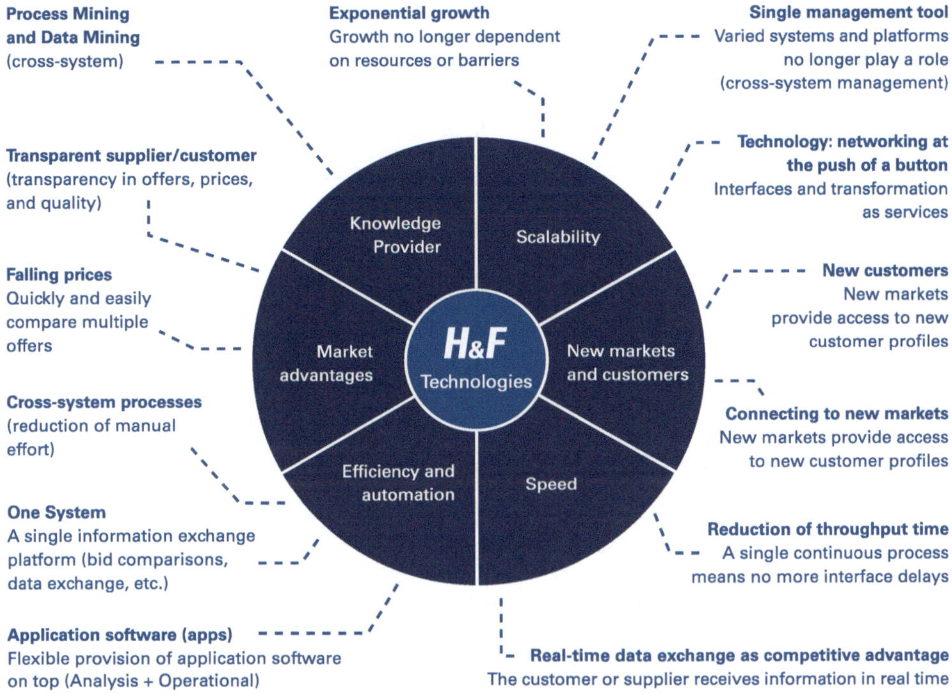

Fig. 6.10 Added values in 2030. (Source: H&F Solutions GmbH/www.hf-solutions.co)

Fig. 6.11 The scalability of manual vs. automated networking. (Source: H&F Solutions GmbH/www.hf-solutions.co)

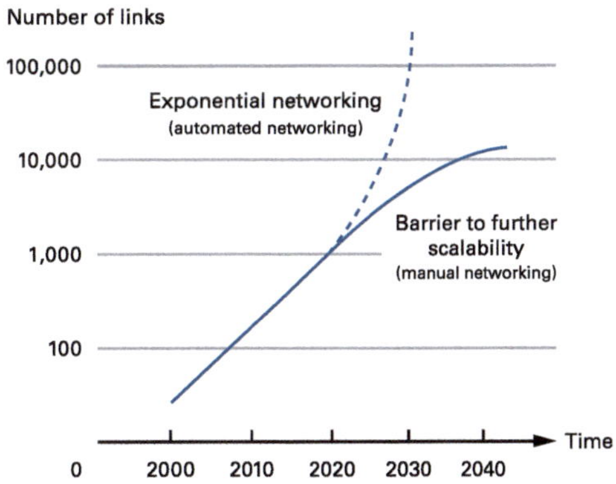

to be able to address and target these new markets quickly and agilely. Today, B2B platforms and similar systems provide some support, but have to be individually accessed by you as the customer. However, in the future you will no longer be able to deal with 10 or 20 individual platforms without involving the market, and you can only exploit a market if you are able to let hundreds of platforms communicate with each other.

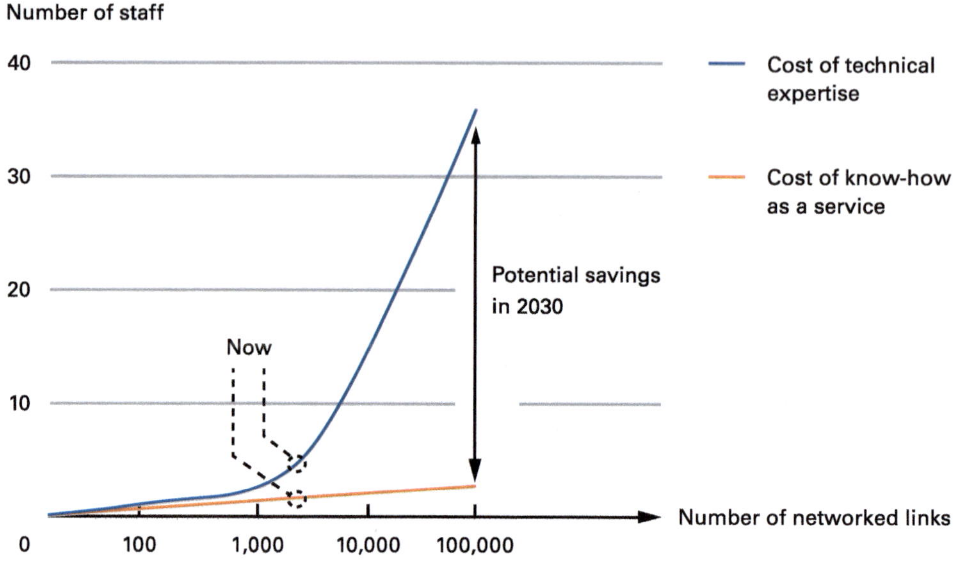

Fig. 6.12 Potential savings in IT personnel. (Source: H&F Solutions GmbH/www.hf-solutions.co)

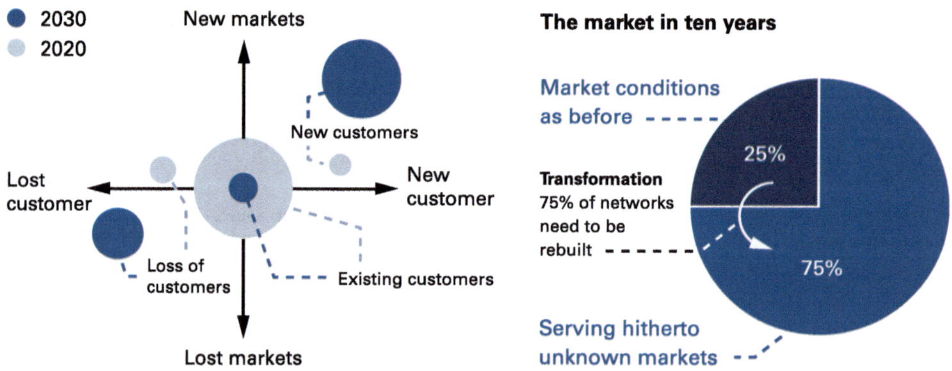

Fig. 6.13 Market changes: customers (left) and future IT transformation effort (right). (Source: H&F Solutions GmbH/www.hf-solutions.co)

6.5.3 Speed

In the future, increasing connection speeds will enable companies to connect stakeholders faster and more stably. The focus here is not on saving human resources within the company (merely a side effect), but rather on reacting more quickly to the market and the speed of change that prevails within it. Today, companies take an average of 12–16 weeks to establish a stable automated connection to customers or suppliers. In the future, this will have to be reduced to a number of hours, or even minutes. Today's analyses

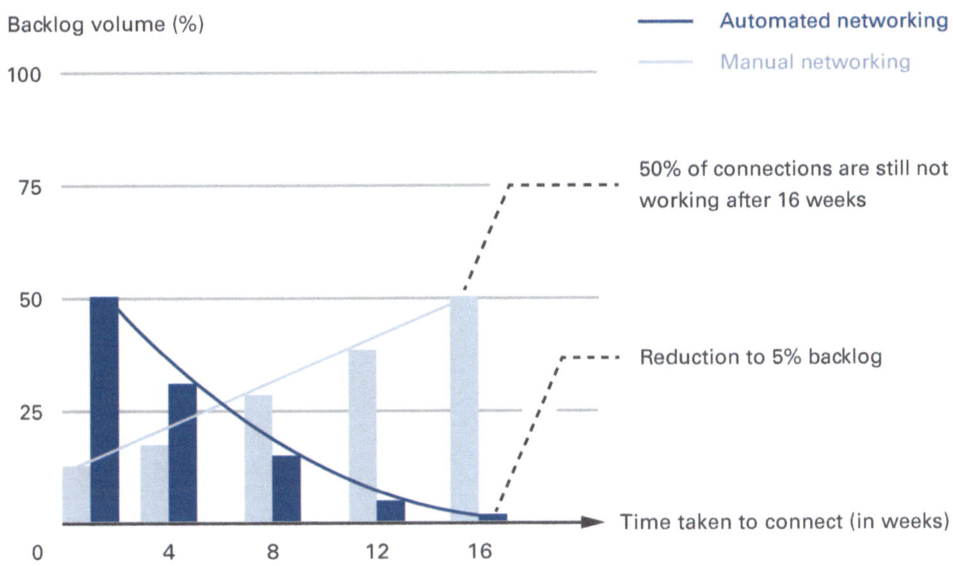

Fig. 6.14 Networking backlog. (Source: H&F Solutions GmbH/www.hf-solutions.co)

show that 50% of the required connections are not yet completed within 16 weeks (see Fig. 6.14).

This development will be unstoppable in terms of speed. By 2030, companies will find few partners willing to wait 2 weeks or longer for a connection. We assume a reduction in process cycle time of more than 90% compared to today's connections. Figure 6.15 illustrates the change to which we will be exposed as a result. Today, approximately 50% of business is still conducted by mail, with the state, government offices, and banks playing a leading role. However, these players are exposed to digitization too, and are thus also participants in the market.

In summary, it is important to reduce the processing time of upcoming networking and networked interaction by a factor of at least 10 (see Fig. 6.16).

6.5.4 Automation Efficiency

Since the previous section at the latest, it should be clear that the networking technology used today has already reached its limits. In recent years we have spoken to many companies who would be happy to increase their degree of networking and automation. The problem is that until now, automation providers haven't been able to offer automation that is genuinely efficient. With the addition of efficient technologies, nothing stands in the way of scalable networking and the enormous potential savings this promises (see Fig. 6.17). Utilizing this type of automated networking will be the only way to maintain or even improve on today's market performance. Neither your current manual networking

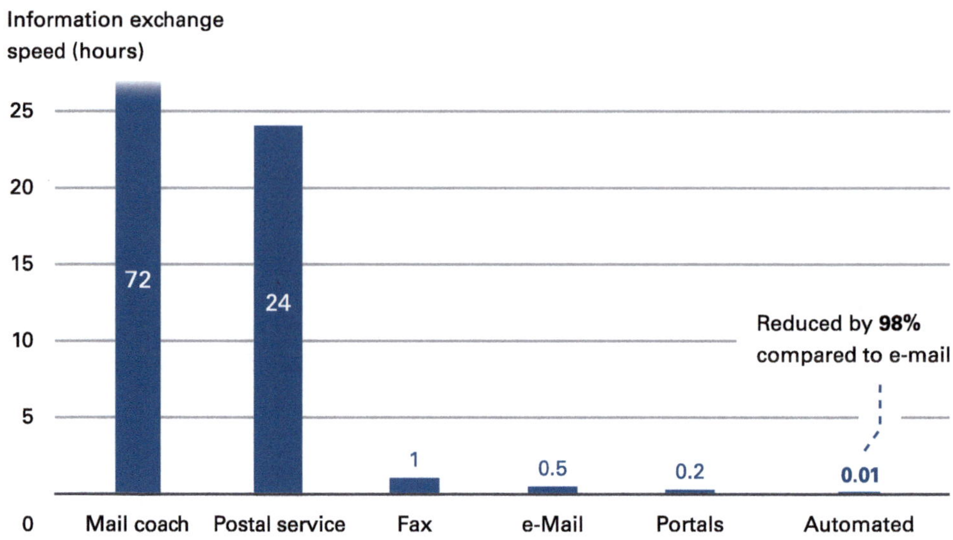

Fig. 6.15 Information and process exchange speed. (Source: H&F Solutions GmbH/www.hf-solutions.co)

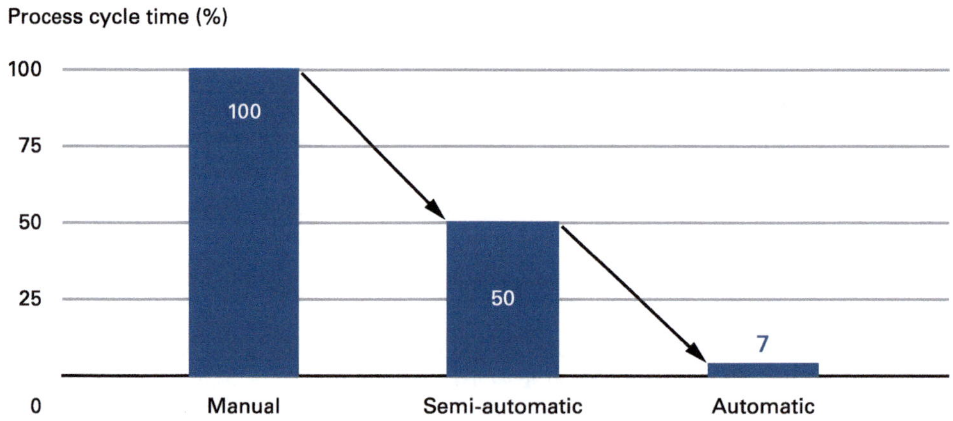

Fig. 6.16 Comparison of process cycle times. (Source: H&F Solutions GmbH/www.hf-solutions.co)

costs nor the degree of digitization at your company are the decisive factor here—the critical factors will be when, and in what form, the switch to fully automated networking takes place.

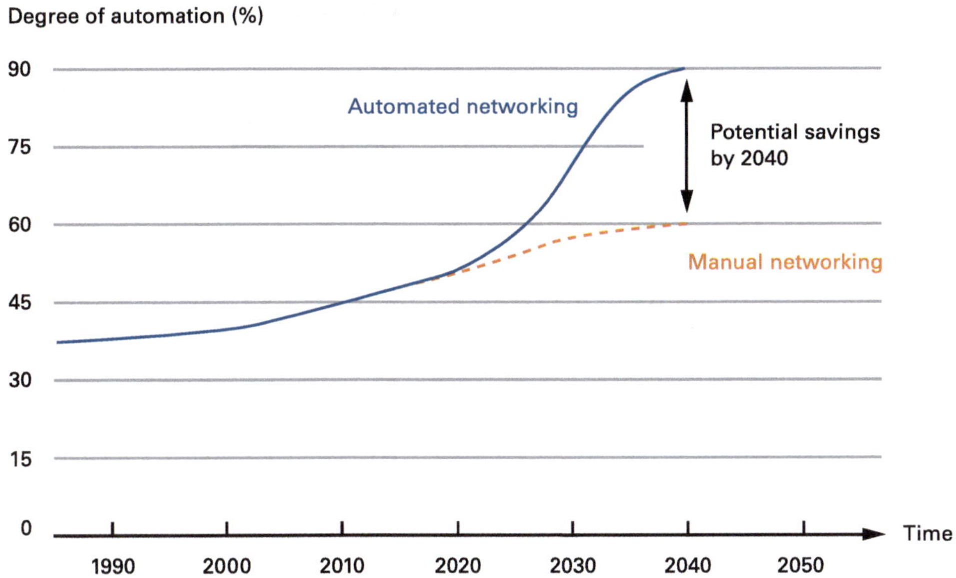

Fig. 6.17 Automated vs. manual networking. (Source: H&F Solutions GmbH/www.hf-solutions.co)

6.5.5 Competitive Advantages

Once new markets are accessible, the implementation speed of internal topics increases, and connection processes are efficiently automated, nothing stands in the way of your company in this respect. Your newly won market power will transform your company from a manufacturer of products into a provider that supplies its markets in a highly transparent manner (see Fig. 6.18). Especially in times when everyone wants everything just in time, this is indispensable for companies who want to be successful. From the moment you reach this stage, you will be perceived within the market as a super-fast operator that can network with its environment quickly and easily at any time, thereby gaining you increasing market power.

6.5.6 Knowledge Provider

Companies that have enormous market advantages usually find it easy to survive in the marketplace. They have everything under control and have done everything right. However, the networking world isn't biding its time, and the market is changing towards companies that recognize events before they come into view (see Fig. 6.19). Those who can see into the crystal ball have already reached their destination when others are just starting out. In this area, many of today's companies still rely on gut feelings or experience, while others are already trying to use smart forecasting tools. In spite of the useful tools

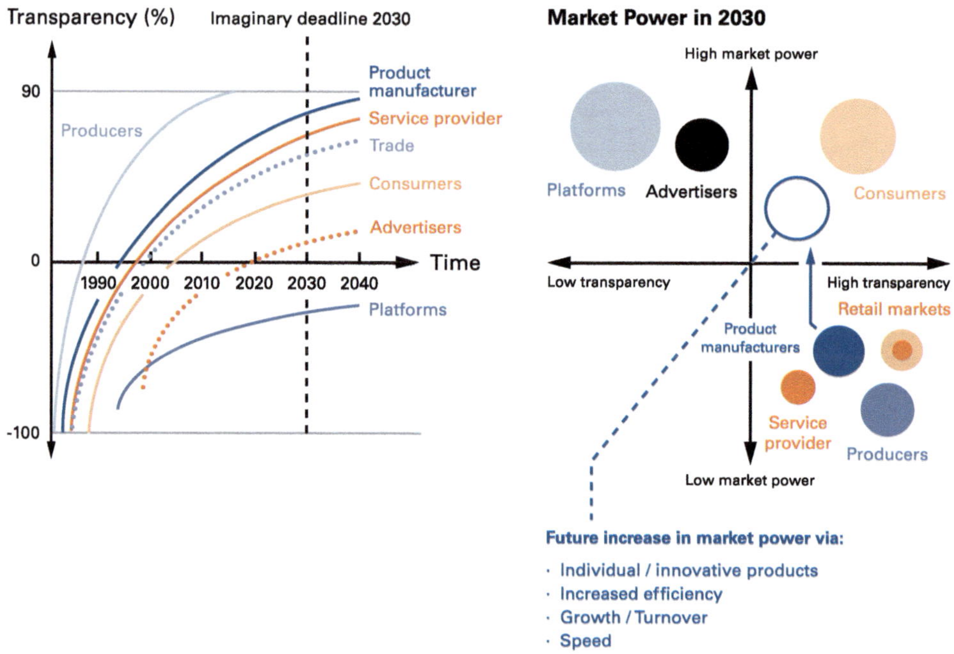

Fig. 6.18 Comparing industry transparency (left) and market power in 2030 (right). (Source: H&F Solutions GmbH/www.hf-solutions.co)

available, there is still not enough data to make accurate forecasts. Once you have overcome the networking hurdle, you also have the opportunity to utilize the networked data that then becomes available and gain insights from it. With the help of data and data analysis tools, the quality of decision-making can be raised to a level that is unimaginable today.

Example

Weather forecasting is a great example for the relevance of data. With the advent of the COVID-19 pandemic, weather forecasts gradually became less accurate. This is because a lot of weather data is transmitted by aircraft in flight, and the number of worldwide flights per day was reduced from 200,000 to about 40,000 by the summer of 2020. This loss of data led to a much lower overall standard of weather forecasting. Today, most companies still forecast weather using a weather station at the company site combined with the view out of the window. This vivid example should be reason enough to get you to take a closer look at this topic. ◄

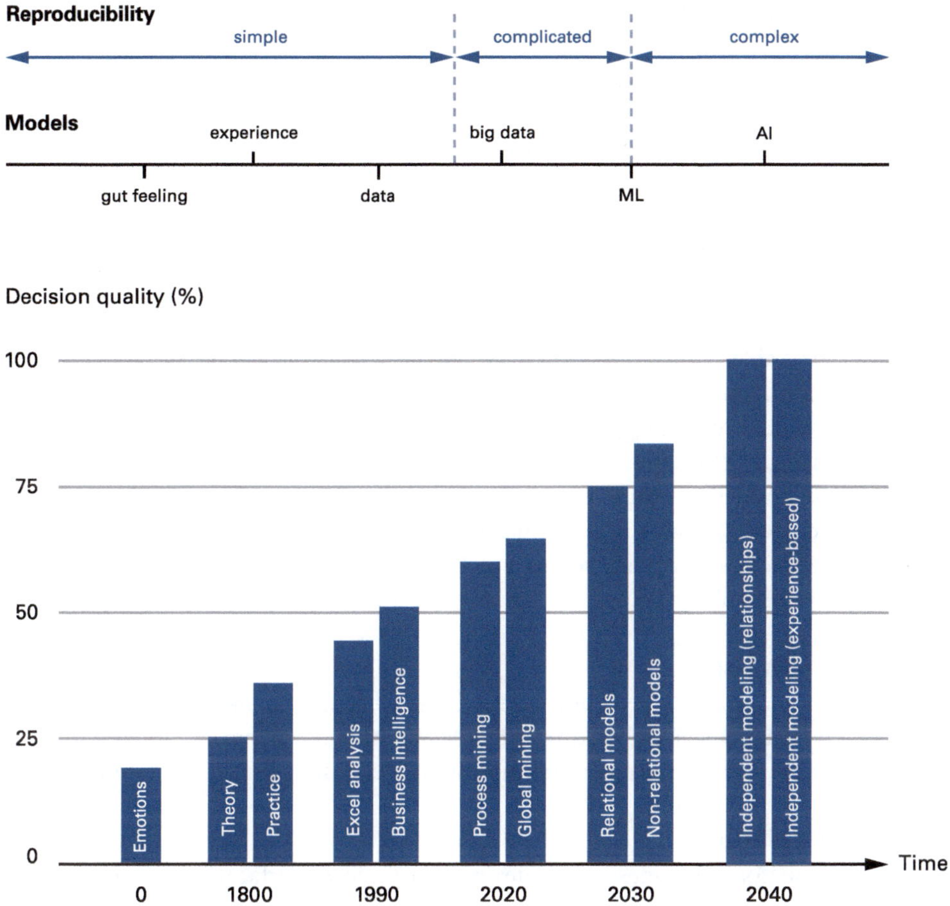

Fig. 6.19 The decision-making quality of various analysis tools. (Source: H&F Solutions GmbH/ www.hf-solutions.co)

Summary

With the help of future technologies, companies will be able to participate in the market faster and more easily. To achieve this, it is not enough to think in terms of products or individual technologies. In order for companies to be technologically competitive by 2030, they will have to deal with the generation of insights, good scalability, swift action in new markets, a high degree of automation, and the generation of market advantages through significant customer benefits. All technologies used in the future must be able to cover all of these topics. ◀

6.6 Products and Solutions (Output)

In this section, we provide you with concrete recommendations for action on how to approach networking as a basis for gaining knowledge. To do this, we have selected platforms as our blueprint, as they represent the core of all networking activities.

6.6.1 The Concept of Platforms

In the future, increasing networking volumes can only be solved by using platforms. No company will be able to operate its own fully integrated solution, and we are convinced that a central platform must be provided that connects devices, systems, and their users. The platform serves as a technology supplier (integration, exchange, and data transformation platform) and as an element that links, controls, and regulates the required networking. This platform should provide a central product portfolio (developer platform, apps, connectors, artificial intelligence, data stream management, transformation models, language translators, data connectivity, and so on) and thus overcome the barriers erected by today's state-of-the-art technology.

6.6.1.1 Today's Issues

The biggest problem with today's interconnections is that they are mostly custom solutions built by individual companies, making scaling and further development virtually impossible. However, complexity increases enormously with each new connection (see Fig. 6.20).

6.6.1.2 The Solution

A networked platform provides companies with just a few interfaces to manage (perhaps even just one), and makes it possible to exchange data centrally with other companies on a 1:n basis, irrespective of the number of connections (see Fig. 6.21). This provides the basis for scalable networking.

6.6.1.3 The Future: One-Click Networking and Implementation

As previously described, in the future new stakeholder groups can be networked automatically. Think back to the first iPhone—it was the first smartphone that was easy to use and at the same time provided simple applications. In other words, it was intuitive to everyone. Similar to this concept, our top priority is to provide networking in the form of processes, software products, developer platforms, and connectivity software in a simple, one-click way.

No Annoying Firewall Issues

In the future, existing connectors will be made available to the platform user fully automatically via a process, and can be installed independently within the end-user's system infrastructure. Special mechanisms then use standardized open HTTPS ports to

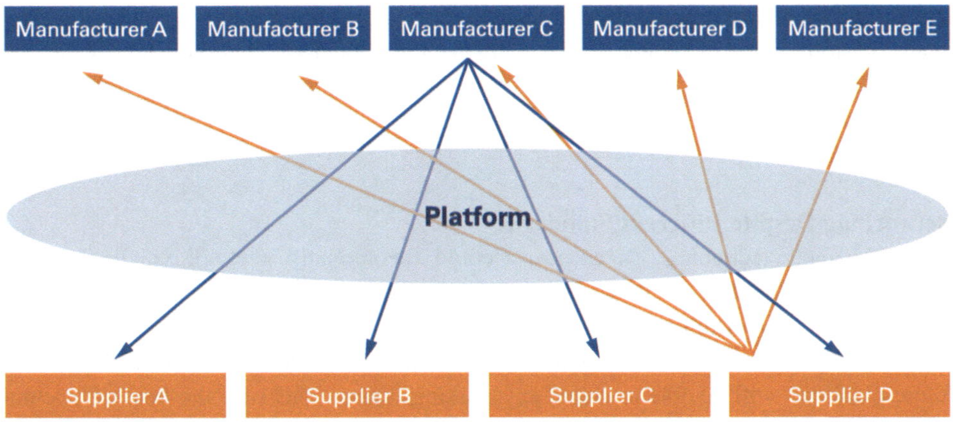

Fig. 6.20 Individual one-to-one networking. (Source: H&F Solutions GmbH/www.hf-solutions.co)

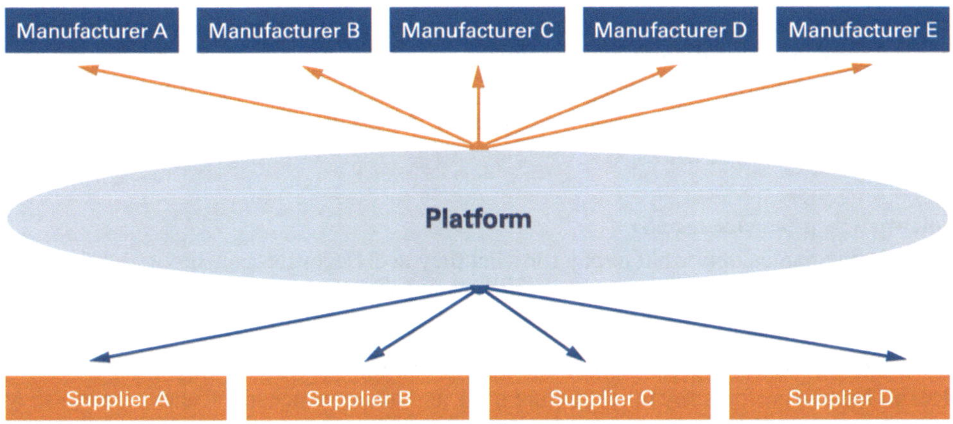

Fig. 6.21 Networking via digital platforms. (Source: H&F Solutions GmbH/www.hf-solutions.co)

transform data into a platform, making firewall issues for port sharing a thing of the past. In the future, administrators and users can start connecting to their database via plug-and-play immediately after download.

Networking at the Push of a Button

Similar to today's social media platforms, in the future every company will have a separate company profile for each platform, which reflects the specified networking technologies within that profile (for example, connectivity options and data transformation technology). At the push of a button you can then make a kind of 'networking request' to another company or another networking node that links the endpoints. Using various settings options, you can then define which data and processes are to be exchanged.

Ordering and Using Applications in Real Time

In an app store, you will get application software at the touch of a button that provides you with evaluations, insights, and data processing based on the data to be exchanged. In doing so, these applications and their various providers make use of a variety of the available technologies.

Networking Despite Different Standards

Using this new technology, a company could theoretically network via five million interfaces (more on this later) without incurring enormous costs. The challenges to maxing out networking opportunities in the future will be very different to those faced by today's networks. New issues that arise will largely be solved by networking technology, and future platforms will be able to create any missing connections with the help of machine learning. To do this, the software will draw on all the logic processed to date, and on custom solutions created by customers. As a result, only a very small amount of manual work remains when networking the systems of the future.

6.6.1.4 Software/Platform as a Service

In the future, platforms will no longer be able to operate independently, making the concept of *Platform as a Service* an important pillar of the digitization process. The following sections explain how it works.

Software as a Service (SaaS)

Today's companies only want to pay for what they use. Software-as-a-service applications can be ordered and used with just a few clicks, and cancelled with a single click when they are no longer needed. If you need an application again, all you have to do is put in a new order. Digitization can be that simple. With this type of software usage, the customer doesn't have to perform any infrastructure or IT and maintenance tasks, and there is also no need to install and manage middleware or hardware. In this case, the company assumes the role of the end-user.

Integration Platform as a Service (iPaaS)

Integration Platform as a Service refers to cloud-based services that can be used to integrate applications and data from different cloud and on-site environments. Data and applications can be connected to form integrated datacubes, regardless of their underlying functional model.

Data Streams as a Service (DSaaS)

In the future, data will be delivered as a service, similar to an e-mail today. Via special data stream services, these will be controlled locally (on-site) by the recipient's platform. Using this kind of data stream management, administration as a service is as good as plug-and-play. Infrastructure and middleware issues will become a thing of the past thanks to the unification and standardization of data connections.

Data Transformation as a Service

This is the core of future platforms. The crucial thing here is enabling the sender-receiver communication links to speak the same language while dealing seamlessly with their individuality. As with an e-mail written in Chinese, the recipient requires a transformer (translator) to decode the data and translate the content. If no transformer is present, the recipient will not be able to render the content. Such transformations currently take place almost exclusively within individual processes as part of an adaptable interface between companies. Today, an order from an ERP system cannot be automatically processed by a supplier without prior clarification of the technology and the processes involved. The reason this is so is the lack of a functioning transformation model.

Future transformers will solve precisely this problem. With the help of artificial intelligence, machine learning, and application models, it will also be possible to have data models communicate with each other. They will also use online communities to accelerate the learning process.

6.6.1.5 "I Can Connect That Myself" Is a Fallacy

In 2019, we had a heated and fruitful discussion with an enterprise-level IT architect from a large corporation about future connectivity between ERP systems, customers, suppliers, and platforms. The manager in question was of the opinion that all these things can be networked using today's resources. He was right, and together we took the trouble to check the maximum number of connections. The results were as follows:

Example

You are the IT manager of a corporate group and support the following infrastructure:

Multi-client systems:	50 (subsidiaries, headquarters, branch offices, and so on)
On-site connectors:	5 (file, API, SOAP, and so on)
Platforms:	20
B2B contacts (customer/supplier) per platform:	1000
Various logics and rule sets, per platform and customer:	1
Direct connections to customers:	1000
Formats:	Idoc, XML, CXML, EDI, EDIFact, and so on. (5)
Average number of different records:	6
Rough calculation of complexity based on platform connections:	**Variability factor** = number of platforms × number of B2B contacts × number of rule sets × number of mappings × number of formats × number of multi-client systems = 20 × 1000 × 1 × 1 × 5 × 50 = **5,000,000 individual connections**

◄

Even if this example wasn't derived in a highly scientific manner, the resulting five million individual connections is a pretty accurate number. In the end, it doesn't matter whether there are 100,000 or five million connections. As soon as you have to manage more than 10,000 connections, it will be extremely difficult for any company to manage such a network manually or semi-automatically. You will now ask yourself why today's platforms or technologies make it necessary to perform individualization that depends on the recipient of the data being transferred. The reason for this is the wide range of settings that these platforms and networking tools offer. For example, a price change may be handled as a field value by one customer, but not by an different customer. This kind of process individuality makes network standardization impossible today.

It is therefore impossible to network these individual systems using one-to-one connections (see Fig. 6.22). Many of today's corporations work with existing platforms and networking products but, due to the complexity involved, they use them to handle only a small portion of their business. The best way to improve things is still to develop the supplier side. However, this won't improve automation, but will instead just shift the networking effort to suppliers and other participants. Due to the lack of other options, each of the five million possible connections is carried out more or less manually, or the effort is simply passed on.

The solution is by no means to simply put a brake on individualization—markets don't work that way. In the future it will be essential to be able to map individuality automatically. If individuality is not served in the marketplace, the market will cease to exist. Future approaches will therefore pursue the automation of individuality and the generation of its associated competitive advantages.

6.6.2 Knowledge Though Data

Once a networked exchange platform has been established, the amount of analyzable data its connections deliver increases exponentially. This data can then be used to identify patterns and repetitions that were previously hidden. Used in conjunction with artificial intelligence, networking models can then be built that allow us to achieve a level of forecasting accuracy that is unthinkable using conventional methods.

Example

Heinrich von Pierer, the former head of electronics and industrial multinational Siemens, once said, "If only Siemens knew what Siemens knows." He was talking about making all company-internal knowledge available to everyone within the company, and about the huge competitive advantage and added value this would create. Wouldn't it be fantastic if you could make all of your company's knowledge accessible in one central location? For example, a future platform will be able to determine that your shipping service providers (package delivery company, freight forwarder, and so on) are late with a delivery. In this case, a data model would be used to determine the delivery date, goods

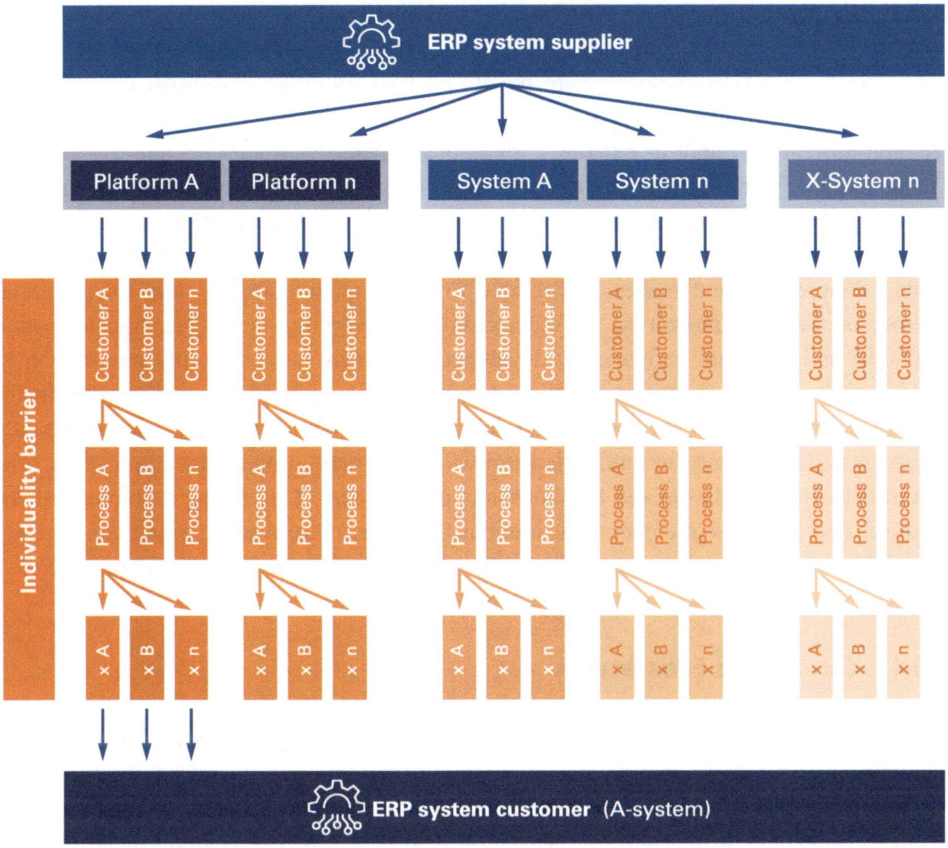

Fig. 6.22 Networking with individuality issues. (Source: H&F Solutions GmbH 7 www.hf-solutions.co)

received data, and shipping date, and to enrich this information with past data in order to identify which delay exists at which supplier, as well as which actions to take and the effects they will have. Using these kinds of methods, production planning will no longer be based solely on in-house data, but will include the entire supply chain. This represents an enormous head start in the knowledge department.

This kind of networked system can also be used to generate insights such as: Did you know that night shift productivity drops every time shift X is on duty?

These insights are only possible using networked systems, advanced data derivation, the generation of a data model, and smart evaluation techniques. ◀

Therefore, the goal must be not only to derive data at the process level, but to do so globally across multiple ecosystems.

6.6.3 Community Spirit (Global, Not Individual)

Up to now, networking solutions are mostly custom solutions developed by individual companies. Although similar requirements exist, most interfaces, data transformations, etc. are built individually and the existing endpoints are then connected on a one-to-one basis. Future platforms answer this challenge by providing for central networking of business logic, and also for the use of other users' recurring, previously established interfaces. This makes it possible to leverage the networking knowledge that companies have built up among themselves, and makes it available to every other company too. Of particular interest is the standardization of connectivity, networking, and data transformation solutions, and these are permanently developed further by all community members (i.e., participating companies and platform developers). These parties constantly work on the benefits of the platform for the community, and this collaborative approach constantly improves and optimizes the future platform while integrating innovative approaches. The platform is thus revolutionized by thousands of members. Due to the scalability of the platform concept, new members can immediately benefit from joining and can actively participate without having to parameterize anything or program a single line of code.

6.6.4 One Single Ecosystem

No company is really interested in setting up and managing a complex IT landscape, although companies of a certain size still have to take this step in order to manage their internal networked structures. If companies could be controlled and managed without using IT, most companies would jump at the chance to work this way. It is therefore worthwhile to pursue the 'One Ecosystem' approach in the future. The aspiration of future ecosystems is to act as a digital networking partner that provides all the necessary exchange formats and corresponding transformation models. Ideally, a customer only has to network with one single ecosystem that performs all tasks and management related to the World Wide Web and its participants. Figure 6.23 illustrates once again the added value of an ecosystem compared to individual platforms and portals.

6.6.5 Data Mining

With the help of data mining, a central ecosystem can analyze and network individual data sets, processes, and structures across divisions without the need to program a separate set of rules. This technology will be expanded step by step toward the year 2030. We distinguish between the development steps shown in Fig. 6.24.

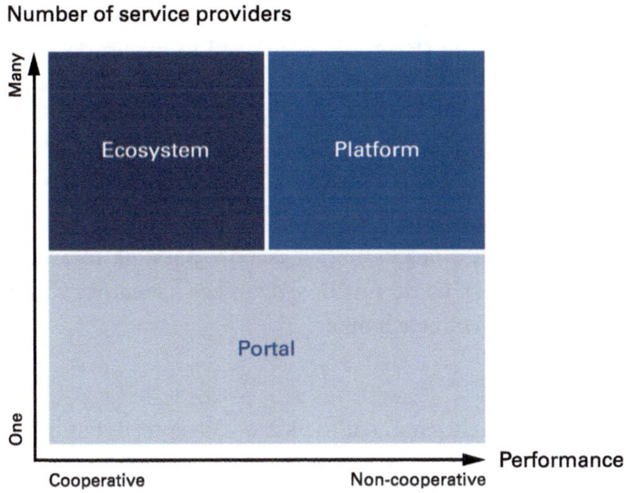

Fig. 6.23 The difference between an ecosystem and platforms/portals. (Source: H&F Solutions GmbH/www.hf-solutions.co)

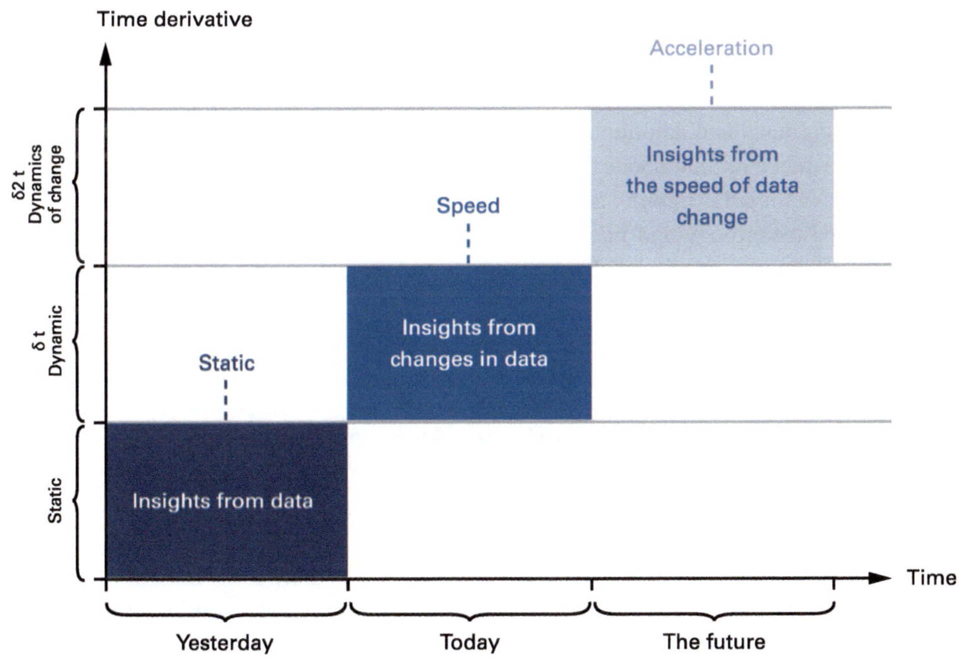

Fig. 6.24 The development of data mining in ecosystems. (Source: H&F Solutions GmbH/www.hf-solutions.co)

6.6.5.1 Static Data Processing

In the past, business intelligence (BI) tools were used to export data and derive insights from them. Such data is static—i.e., it only reflects a snapshot of the exported data and not the actual situation in real time. A change between different data sets is not recognizable, and thus cannot be compared or evaluated.

6.6.5.2 Dynamic Data Processing

With the help of dynamic data processing, it is now possible to analyze the dynamics between varying data statuses. To do this, a system permanently evaluates data sets and compares the different states with each other.

An Event-Based Approach

Today, comparisons between different data sets are widespread, but no longer state of the art. Innovative companies now work with event-based approaches that not only examine the base data, but also records when, how often, how fast, and via which interfaces and subsystems data is processed. This approach exponentially increases the possibilities of data usage and, with the help of machine learning, makes it possible to almost completely automate processes, but only using the appropriate networking technologies.

Summary

To be successful in the future, you need not only a theoretical approach, but also concrete products and solutions. If you consider that companies will need to network with more than a million nodes by 2030, this won't happen if you use technologies from the 1980s. In the future, companies will have to join platforms that provide the necessary networking technology and make it available to each and every node. Once you have read this chapter, it should be clear that going it alone will have little chance of success in the future. ◄

6.7 Community-Capable Software Architecture

6.7.1 Networks

The basis for a strong community is the establishment of networks. In order to enable complete networking, different types of networks are required. The key to success is the creation of various smart gateways.

The key facts here are:

- Each network has its own custom, system-side connection (technical aspects of data, potential barriers to access, and so on).
- Each exchange interface has its own individually standardized data structure, address structure, and logic.
- The different interfaces talk to each other in a standardized way (using the same language, networked by using a central transformer).

6.7.1.1 Enterprise Networks (ERP2ERP, EDI—1:1)

In this context, corporate networks represent traditional networking structures that work either for a single company location or a globally networked company. Today, the core of these networks is usually a conventional ERP system. Although today's data formats are already standardized (for example, using EDI), the exchange interfaces are still not able to automatically correct or prevent the tiniest stumbling blocks (for example, automatically transforming decimal commas into decimal points). There are many service providers who deal exclusively with this type of problem, and the greater the number of documents that are exchanged within the system, the more effort it takes. This challenge could easily be mastered using today's technologies and, since in almost all cases custom solutions are required, these kinds of service providers can earn good money. Smart volume models (based for example on the number of documents or a share of revenue) make this an attractive market and, as a result, the software industry doesn't feel any pressure to change and create better, smarter tools.

6.7.1.2 Platform Networks (B2B or B2C Portals)

B2B or B2C platforms really mushroomed in the years between 2010 and 2020. Due to the pain of interconnecting business networks, these platforms were designed to promote the idea of universal networking and thus save a lot of associated costs. Now, you are probably wondering why we are talking about 'popular' platforms here. These platforms are mostly delivery portals where sellers and buyers can find each other easily and, after a match, can conduct their business in a highly automated way. All documents are exchanged and stored digitally. These systems have simply ended up migrating manual effort from the buyer to the seller. The buyer can set his conditions and demands and the seller has to comply with them unconditionally. Since every buyer now has his own terms and conditions, every transaction through B2B platforms is a veritable job creation scheme for sellers. The added value is only on one side, as purchasing activities have been automatically delegated to the platform so that the vendor now hast to take over these tasks. Attempts to streamline this process for sellers with the help of robotic process automation (RPA) fail because the platform providers actively work against it.

Buyers and sellers also have to pay considerable fees to the platform operator and, since the total added value doesn't increase, but is instead simply redistributed, it appears that additional costs arise within the value creation chain.

6.7.1.3 Portal Networks (API: Amazon, DHL, Etc.)

Networked thinking includes not only portals, ERP systems, and merchandise management systems, but also portal networks. These are large mail-order companies, shipping services, and other providers that are mostly active in the areas of logistics and mobility. They provide their environment with standardized interfaces in the form of APIs that are already very easy to connect to.

► An API (Application Programming Interface) is a programming interface defined by the system via which it is possible to exchange data and processes with other systems. These APIs have individual structures and can therefore differ in how they are called and the transmission format they use.

In most cases, APIs are accessible via the HTTPS protocol and corresponding authentication methods (e.g., tokens).

Example

For example, using the DHL online interface you can retrieve a lot of information about a specific shipment via the API. Amazon has already integrated this API into its own platform and retrieves shipment information for its customers that is then directly available via Amazon's central platform interface. ◄

Today, no supply chain is complete without connecting these kinds of companies. If you want to offer a fully integrated approach, you have to connect thousands of different APIs with each other automatically. In the future, therefore, we require a fully automated process that allows new providers to be added automatically on an ongoing basis.

6.7.1.4 The IoT Network (Devices, Industry 4.0)

Welcome to the world of talking devices and machines! When this idea was first introduced in the early 2000s and we heard that all manner of machines would be connected to the Internet, many were taken aback and wondered what the benefits would be. At that time, the Internet was more of a knowledge platform than a networking platform.

It was not until the late 2010s that it became clear that the Internet would serve not only as a knowledge portal, but in the future also as a networking platform. Machines will then be used for automation and information exchange—for example, by automatically reordering tools and permanently monitoring their own stock. Maintenance intervals and routine services can also be managed remotely by the manufacturer. In the future, this can then be applied not only to manufacturing machines, production robots, or fully automated warehouses, but also to all electronic devices and machines. BMW and Tesla have already installed hardwired SIM cards in some cars, which permanently transmit data to the manufacturer. In the future, Tesla will not only use the data from its car division for maintenance and service, but will transform itself into an advertising platform that has a side job in moving people around. This may be unimaginable today, but is a realistic vision of the future. Imagine you are walking around at work and, based on your various interests (based on personal use of your company data), your augmented reality glasses show you which challenges your current orders are facing and which measures you can apply to remedy things. Just as Tesla will no longer be a car manufacturer in the future, you may no longer be a manufacturer of certain components, but rather a provider of a machine that is a knowledge collector and not just a functional tool. This is like when your refrigerator starts to display advertisements from the supermarket around the corner.

However, all of these things will only work if these devices can be easily networked, if the data streams can be selected and evaluated, and if insights can be gained from the data they provide.

6.7.1.5 Cloud Networks (Azure, Amazon, Google, EU Cloud, and so on)

In this context, "the cloud" is a set of storage locations for files and application software. Some infrastructure is provided by cloud providers as a service, while the actual application, file, database, or service systems are merely hosted within it. Compared to today's practices, "the cloud" means nothing more than moving data from a local hard drive within a company to a physically unknown location on the Internet, where this data can be accessed at any time. This has the advantage that it is detached from your physical infrastructure and is scalable and expandable at the push of a button. The technical connection to the Internet and the constant high-performance infrastructure also offer advantages here, although today's cloud technologies face the same connectivity and data security challenges as local installations, and these have to be addressed directly in a similar way to local systems. The same hurdles (firewall, data protection, and so on) exist as they do for traditional enterprise networks. However, due to its scalability, this technology will continue to expand, as it is more cost-effective and secure compared to local installations. *Cloud 2.0* will therefore function differently than today's cloud, and will be even more secure and easier to network.

> **Our Tip**
>
> In general, many companies assume that data stored locally is more secure than data stored by an external provider in the cloud. However, due to the concentration of processes, the security technologies at public cloud providers can be expanded more easily and updated more regularly than you could ever do at your own company. Cloud vendors don't employ security experts, security concepts, and various layers of security systems for nothing. These all make your data more secure online than it is in-house.
>
> How much did you invest in IT security last year, and can this compete with the IT security investment of a well-known cloud service provider?
>
> In this context, cloud-based data is far better protected than local data stored on a computer that is connected to the Internet.

6.7.2 Data Flows/Networking (Pipelines)

A data stream is the exchange of data that takes place between fixed start and end points. In terms of networking, this requires a permanently accessible connection between these points.

6.7.2.1 The Input/Output Concept (Satellite Systems)

Here, the end points are controlled according to the classic transmitter-receiver model. Similar to a satellite system, the base station (the platform) is the lead system and the satellite (the connected end-point system) is the receiver. As soon as a satellite (the end point) provides new information (input), this is processed by the base station and, if necessary, sent to another satellite.

6.7.3 Connection/Connectors (End Points)

In the future, systems can only be connected via plug-and-play. Similar to today's remote maintenance or video meeting tools, they contain a small installation application that independently installs all necessary applications, and configures them using a helper subsystem. Data and system connections can therefore be made as part of a simple process.

6.7.3.1 Technologies (REST API, File, On-Site Etc.)

In the future, it will require a data exchange technology via REST API, file transfer, on-site tools, and similar, that can be accessed by all other systems. These tools will then be managed centrally, so that participants only need to install the application software in order to access them immediately. If the connection is stable, central synchronization mechanisms and data management technologies take over the data networking and access tasks. In the future, mini-apps will be available to make fast connections between almost all formats.

6.7.4 Transformation Models

By transformation models we mean logic, a set of rules, and a simple intelligence that are adapted to a defined task and that transform input data into output data. The goal is not only to transform different data structures, but also to adapt the data content so that it is usable in the target output format.

Example

In October 2018, Google published the paper *BERT: Pre-training of Deep Bidirectional Transformers for Language Understanding*. The paper described for the first time a model for transforming languages bidirectionally (i.e., English ≫ German ≫ English)

The novelty of the *BERT* model is that the source language and the target language are now directly linked. Until October 2018, translation always involved an intermediate transformation step into English, regardless of which origin or target language you were using. Accordingly, the grammar and sentence structures were quite poor. The new model made it possible for the first time to translate directly from end-point language to end-point language, and the result is significantly improved translations. ◄

In the context of transformation models, the future aim must therefore be to create an architecture model that enables direct transformations based on empirical values. Similar to today's weather forecasting models, future transformation models will allow predictions and, as a result, models will already be available before companies need them.

6.7.4.1 Technologies Used

In the future, self-learning data models generated using machine learning and AI will form the basis of networking. It is important to understand that this type of model generation differs from familiar programming processes. It is not necessary to create structured code, but only to create a certain logic with defined rules upon which the models then build themselves. These models are learned by experience based on existing or custom-generated data sets and, similarly to the image recognition software in driver assistance systems, results can be generated based on the data thus obtained. In the case of a driver assistance system, the result could be recognizing a traffic sign. However, it is not only the traffic sign that is important, but also any influencing factors that need to be correlated too. After all, a sign that says "50" could have different meanings depending on where it is placed—at the roadside it probably represents the speed limit, whereas if it is on a sticker on the rear of a tractor, it defines the maximum speed of the vehicle you are following. Using multiple data sets, the system is thus taught to calculate the probability that a "50" sign defines the speed limit and how often it actually means something else.

The same applies to the learning in networking transformers. Google took an easy route and used 54 million Wikipedia articles as its learning basis. Since translations are available for almost all Wikipedia articles, Google was able to read all this data using a crawler and use it as a giant learning data set.

The amount of data required to learn a system depends on the system to be modelled. A weather model, for example, is so complex and has so many influencing input factors that weather can only be predicted at an accuracy of about 89–95% for tomorrow, about 23–50% for next week, and only about 15–40% for 2 weeks hence.

For stable transformation models (in our example for language translation), the complexity and the influencing parameters are known and predictable. In the case of traffic sign recognition, the complexity is known, but the variable parameters (e.g., rain, poor visibility, sensor failure, and so on) are not predictable.

Thus significant technological advances will be necessary to achieve the desired results.

6.7.4.2 The Transformation Model (Components: Mapping, Splitting Etc.)

Based on the aforementioned technology, it will be necessary to create a large number of transformation models in the future. A transformation model consists of many building blocks or task components that have to be completed. A language transformer (i.e., a translator), for example, has the tasks of translating words, positioning them, checking the grammar, and observing the sentence structure. This means taking all existing restrictions into account.

A data transformation model has the following tasks:

- Mapping the data structure
- Content translation (transform data content, translator-within-a-translator)
- Adjusting formats (decimal points, thousands separators, date formats, address formats, and so on)
- Data splitting and merging
- Handling of structure restrictions (file format schemes)
- Data validation (for example, check that an address exists via Google Maps API)

Without these mapping functions, it will not be possible to automate the required connections in the future.

6.7.5 Cloud and Connector Architecture

6.7.5.1 The Feedback Model

Today, systems act together and exchange data with one another, although sometimes data is invalid and thus cannot be exchanged, or data is simply not accepted by the receiving system for whatever reason.

Most existing systems don't currently provide a feedback loop that informs the sender system when data isn't transmitted correctly during data processing within the target system. The system administrator usually only receives a message along the lines of: "Data could not be processed. Manual intervention is required". Using a utility, manual derivation, or manual data comparison, the IT administrator must find out for himself why the data was not properly delivered and which appropriate corrective actions need to be initiated in the interface.

In the future, a feedback model will cover this process. With the help of a regression loop and a regression model, it is then determined whether a solution already exists within the model for the reported error (for example, "Date format only possible in the format YYYY-MM-DD") and thus whether the existing transformation model can be used as a correction model. The feedback model then independently determines which existing models can be used to correct a particular error. It also determines whether different companies always correct this error in the same way or whether everyone deals with it individually.

6.7.5.2 Functional Overview: Connectors and Cloud Connections

Since most data will no longer be stored locally in the future, trust in the providers who manage data is elementary. The issue of data security will improve over the next few years to such an extent that by 2030 at the latest, it will be the norm for data to be hosted on decentralized virtual servers spread all over the globe. Figure 6.25 shows a general view of the various components and processes that represent one particular option for a future solution path. The key components include a connector, cloud space, and an operating system with an integrated API. These components will ensure the smooth flow of data between different systems in the future.

Connector (Local Application)

The connector will remain the only on-site application—or at least it will until nearly all enterprise data is no longer stored locally. It resides behind a firewall (customer network) and is responsible for mediating data access between the cloud and a database end point (e.g., the database you want to connect). With its help, the cloud can then access the remaining local network. The future cloud architecture can use these connectors to access almost any on-site application by connecting to the cloud via an outbound HTTPS request to the cloud service API. The cloud creates a new data end point and returns this address to the connector. The connector establishes a mutually authenticated, SSL-secured session with the cloud to connect the local database to the application (API or apps) located within the OS.

The connector enables connections to almost all current database technologies via plug-and-play. These include: Salesforce, Oracle, SQL Server, DB2 (IBM), Amazon Redshift, Microsoft Dynamics, Apache, PostgreSQL, MySQL, OpenEdge, Rollbase, Google Analytics, SugarCRM, FinancialForce, ServiceMax, Veeva CRM, Greenplum, Sybase, Informix, JDBC, and many more.

Plug-and-Play

The connector is set up via a standardized installation routine within a very short time (a maximum of 5 min for setup and installation). All that is then required to control the database is a user account with access data. Local driver installation isn't necessary. All these driver technologies are already fully integrated with the connector via suitable mechanisms. By releasing defined ports with firewall policies that connect the customer database to the cloud, data exchange is enabled and explicitly approved for the cloud only. Tapping the data from another IT address range is therefore impossible.

Cloud (Data Storage)

The cloud is the primary service for controlling and managing data connections, data flows, and data exchange to and from the platform. In other words, cloud technology manages

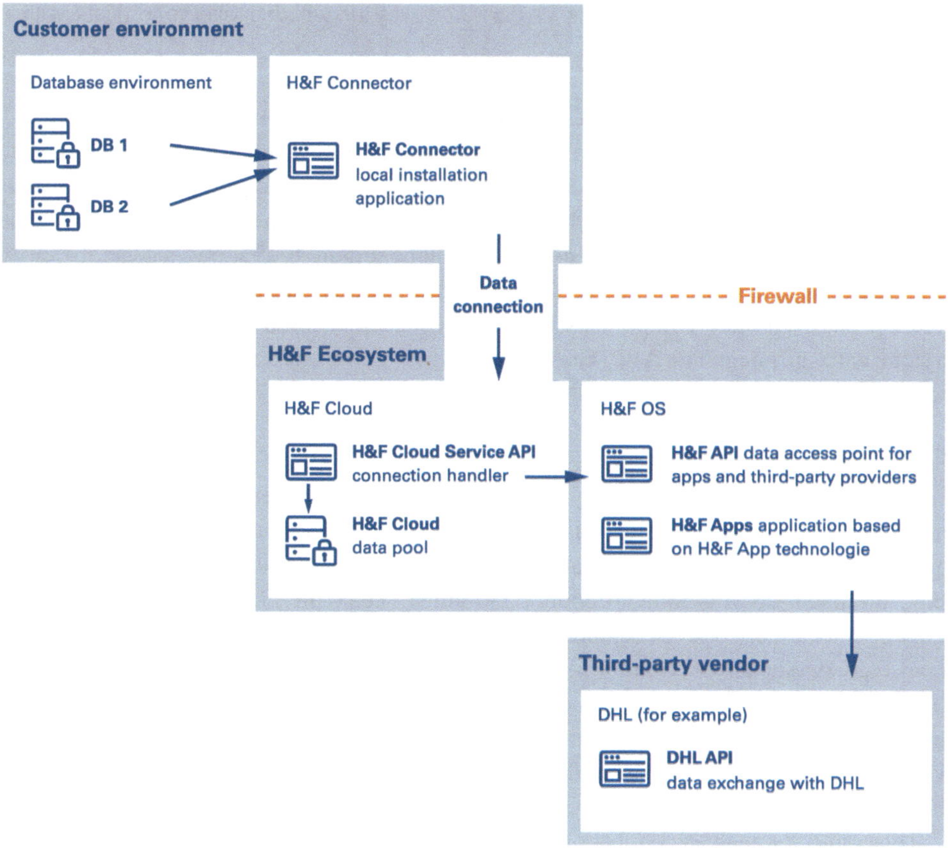

Fig. 6.25 Functional overview: connectors and cloud connections. (Source: H&F Solutions GmbH/ www.hf-solutions.co)

connector communication and thereby enables connector and database scaling. User and service configurations are stored by a connector application that is provided by a networking provider. The database itself is connectable, allowing administrators to use their preferred relational database (typical choices are Oracle, SQL Server, or MySQL). All communication with the plugin database is configured to occur via a channel encrypted using REST technology. Communication with the cloud service takes place using the HTTPS protocol only. For more information on this topic, see Sect. 6.7.8.3.

The cloud uses built-in performance safety mechanisms that control the data connection in such a way that there is no noticeable loss of performance in the Internet link or the database servers. This is controlled by an artificial algorithm and built-in intelligence via the connector and the cloud API.

Future Data Rooms by Industry

In order to utilize information relating to a specific industry, in the future this will be stored in custom data rooms where comprehensive insights can be collated and evaluated. Only data that has been anonymized and approved for release will enter these data rooms. This type of centralized knowledge can lead to a significant increase in knowledge for entire industries. Examples of such industries are automotive, health, agriculture, energy, mobility, or logistics.

Example

A tractor manufacturer could use the vehicles it sells to collect on-site data regarding the amount of pesticide applied to a given area, while a harvester manufacturer contributes data on the quality of the resulting harvests. Correlating these kinds of data could then make it possible to optimize the amount of pesticide used to produce a healthier and/or larger crop yield.

Another example is a manufacturer of computer tomograph machines, who could collect scans of cancer indications and store them in a data room together with knowledge contributed manually by doctors. Artificial intelligence could then be used to develop a data model that draws on the collected data to produce a real-time diagnosis while a patient is being scanned. In such a scenario, doctors would then only be responsible for monitoring the diagnosis made by the computer. ◀

Ecosystems and Services

Using an API, applications (for example, a BI analytics or data management tool) will connect in the future via a standard SQL and REST data access interface (ODBC, JDBC, or OData). Existing applications communicate with the cloud via HTTPS to read and/or write data to a downstream application or database that may reside in the cloud or behind the firewall. In this case, firewall policies only allow communication between the cloud and the OS. External access to the cloud is only possible via an API that must be enabled beforehand.

API

The API is a standardized interface that allows apps to retrieve data via a secure access point using an authentication key. This access point can also be used to provide data to third parties.

Within the OS, apps use this standardized access in the background, and the API app must be approved for use by third parties. Specifically, the API app can be used to define which data can be accessed externally using an authentication code. The API is based on REST technology.

Development Platform/App Technology

The OS is a platform which can be used to program, manage, and apply apps. The OS can also be used to provide developers with a toolbox of standardized functions that can be used to program quickly and efficiently. The standardized data interface API is one of these tools. The OS is designed so that only data that is also logically assigned to the customer can be retrieved.

6.7.6 Research Findings

In the future, enormous resources will be consumed by research work. The focus here is on simplifying existing processes while taking into account the latest and most stable methods. In this chapter, we would like to share some insights and enhance your knowledge with topics related to networking and automation.

6.7.6.1 Why Robots for Process Automation (RPA) Already Work but Struggle to Gain Acceptance

With the help of robot-controlled process automation (i.e., technology that imitates humans), manual processes can today be reproduced automatically. This way, processes are replicated and automated on many platforms and individual applications. Where software manufacturers notice these processes taking place, they prevent automation with the help of detection/interception programs, which in turn means that the RPA application is halted immediately. This results in a tedious cat-and-mouse game that sees RPA vendors try to circumvent and outsmart the software manufacturers' intercept software.

In addition, RPA-supported applications only work for existing assignments. If a field name changes within the app (which happens regularly), the RPA robot can no longer detect it and either stalls or loops indefinitely.

Example

In the past, many companies have tried to use RPA solutions to automate processes that connect SAP and B2B platforms such as ARIBA. Initial tests on the platform delivered useful results after just a few days. However, after a while, increasing numbers of errors appeared. The robot could no longer identify fields (based on the underlying source code, for example: field name changed), or the fields were moved to a different location, or the label was renamed (for example, from "Name" to "Name 1"). For an everyday human colleague, these are the tiny deviations that human intelligence adapts to without thinking about it, whereas for the robot, these are elementary failings that it can no longer comprehend within the process. As a result, it can no longer perform its assigned task and fails to produce usable results. ◄

Software manufacturers therefore fight with everything they have against bot-based solutions that cost them huge amounts of revenue via their self-developed standard interfaces. It is therefore easier for a software manufacturer to use a mechanism that confuses robots by feeding them misinformation so that they can no longer find the information they need. Internally, the machine causing the confusion knows via its built-in logic how to handle the data being processed. In the end, this process is no longer about efficiency, but about the battle for market share, and this fight is ultimately paid for by the consumer—i.e., you. As is plain to see, all this has very little to do with efficiency or savings.

RPA's Raison d'être

In most companies, short-term savings potential is more important than medium- or long-term savings. Profitable business models and scaling for short-term business growth are prioritized over permanently implementing long-term value drivers. Think about why ERP systems (SAP, Oracle, Microsoft Navision) are still running on 1990s database/application software technology rather than using modern web technologies. Facelifts of this old-fashioned technology are all it takes for the manufacturers to continually maximize their profit. Software vendors also argue that security requirements mean that they have to intercept RPA solutions to offer maximum system protection. However, this also means limited networking and savings for their customers. Furthermore, it is actually relatively easy today to provide the market with a secure solution.

Advantages of Vendors' Customer Loyalty Programs

Many software vendors offer standardized interfaces (for example, API, REST API, SOAP) for linking to other systems. However, these are usually volume-based licensing models (number of documents, revenue share, amount of data, etc.), which gradually reduce savings as the company grows. An alternative is to use custom-coded software that generates costs that are independent of data volumes. In many cases, you can register as a manufacturer-certified development partner and develop the application yourself. The resulting applications are then distributed exclusively via the vendor's app store on a commission basis and are available to everyone. This way, you can create precisely the application you need, and the software manufacturer keeps you as a committed customer. This creates advantages on both sides, which can lead to a reduction of the overall effort.

6.7.7 Manual vs. AI-supported Data Standardization

The central building block of any networking technology is data transformation or data normalization. Technically, a transformation must take place from the original input format to the final/target output format. There are two ways of doing this (see Fig. 6.26).

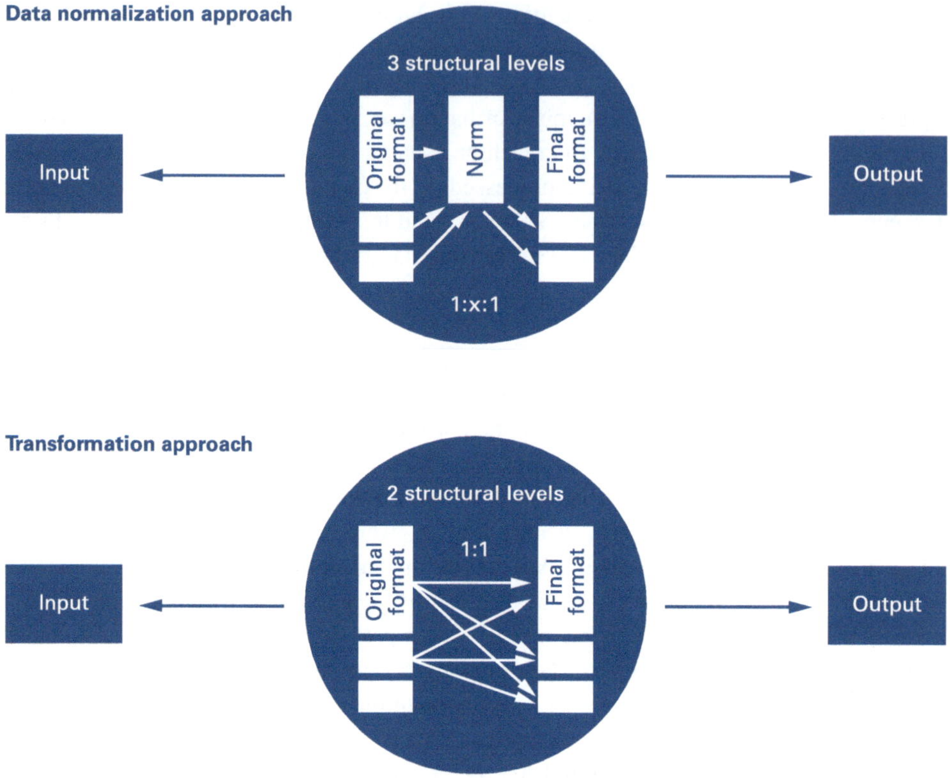

Fig. 6.26 Schematic diagram of data normalization vs. transformation approaches. (Source: H&F Solutions GmbH/www.hf-solutions.co)

1. The data normalization approach converts data to an independent intermediate format (or "norm") and then derives a final format from that.
2. The transformation approach models the final format directly from the original format.

Data Normalization Approach

Advantages:

- Direct transformation to a data format
- Apps, developers, and customers can access standardized data or other formats can be provided at the push of a button
- Final format models always based on the norm
- Low effort (n + n models = 1000 + 1000 = 2000 models)
- Easy to handle

(continued)

Disadvantages:

- Metadata and all other necessary information must be included
- Two transformation steps
- Difficult to find a universal standard norm
- Standard must ***not*** be built ***as a static structure***, but rather as a dynamic object (alternatives: JSON, metadata, etc.)
- Dynamically growing structures (no more 'tables')

Transformation Approach

Advantages:

- All information is available at the time of transformation
- Only one transformation step

Disadvantages:

- Direct transformation
- Output format is a standalone norm
- High effort, since a model must be specified for each input/output structure pair (approx. n^2 models $= 1000^2 = 1{,}000{,}000$)
- Handling complexity too great

The transformation approach is much more complex, but also the much more efficient. It also provides the best results. However, data has to be converted to a universally high quality before it can be transformed. This approach is an important component of future networking products, although the normalization approach can still be used during the learning phase for new models when networking multiple individual systems. If sufficient normalization models are available, the transformer continues to normalize automatically.

6.7.8 Security and Data Protection

The following sections explain how both data protection and data security can be sustainably provided by future technologies. The various products must be developed in such a way that they can guarantee comprehensive data protection across multiple security barriers via a wide range of consistent security mechanisms, security policies, and corresponding configurations—both against physical attacks from outside and against hardware and software errors.

6.7.8.1 Preface to Security and Data Protection

This section describes risk and vulnerability management strategies that apply to the security of the ecosystem, and in particular to future products (cloud, connectors, data streams, and so on). Future products will use robust security mechanisms and, as these are deployed on-site and via a private cloud, it is essential for the customer to ensure that end-to-end security is properly configured and managed. This includes leveraging our deep defense strategy, network security, encryption, access control, and other protections. The security principle of deep defense is a layering of security technologies and protection methods against known and emerging threats. Every entry and exit point from which a protective measure is required is managed, inspected, and validated through routine self- and third-party assessments to prevent, identify, and correct vulnerabilities without compromise. Together with appropriate on-site IT security mechanisms, the connection (between connector and cloud) provides secure data access. For security reasons, this book doesn't specify specific firewall policies (defined ports, IP addresses, cloud addresses, and so on). The policies explained here were developed in 2021 and are subject to permanent technological improvement.

6.7.8.2 Data Differentiation (Independent Customer Database)

The OS manages data in separate logical data containers. When addressing data from the cloud via the API, it is therefore impossible to access another customer's data pool, ensured using logical and securely separated data management.

6.7.8.3 Strategies for Reducing Public Cloud Risks

Identification and Monitoring

End-to-end security is properly configured and managed, and firewall containment, load balancing, real-time application query filtering, and round-the-clock monitoring are performed in the cloud. Cloud and local servers need to be equipped with virus and malware protection. Providers perform maintenance that accounts for known errors and vulnerabilities, while a security assessment (including penetration tests) is performed by a third party.

Compliance

General Data Protection Guidelines: On May 25, 2018, a new data protection law called the General Data Protection Regulation (GDPR) was adopted within the European Union (EU).

The GDPR expands the rights granted to EU individuals and imposes many new obligations on organizations that market to, track, or handle them with respect to EU-based personal data. The GDPR must be complied with by organizations based in the EU or doing business in the EU that collect, store, transfer, or use personal data relating to EU citizens.

Personal data is any information that relates to an identified or identifiable living individual. Information that can be collected and aggregated to identify a specific individual includes personal data such as, last name and/or first name, address data, email address, personal ID number, IP address, or location data.

Storing Personal Data in the Cloud

The cloud server is responsible for managing user and service configurations, handling data exchange between clients (client databases), and communication with local connections (through a connector). Personal or non-personal data transferred from the client through the connector to the cloud does not persist during the transfer process. Data required by apps and APIs is stored in the cloud.

Database user and configuration data storage is handled by the connector app (in the cloud). The user information stored in the configuration app may contain personal data related to usernames, credentials, and IP addresses.

Encryption

Data connections are configured to accept only authorized (cryptographic) communication from known administrative end points.

All client-related data elements (including stored remote credentials/database pairings) are encrypted using both REST technology (AES-256) and transit technology (TLSv1, TLSv1.1). Client requests to the API are encrypted using TLSv1.2 and a HTTPS connection, including user passwords.

6.7.9 System Stability

In addition to data security, it is extremely important for future providers to provide customers with a stable system of the highest quality. This is because, as described in the previous chapters, focus is beginning to shift away from the ERP systems that previously acted as system stabilizers. This stabilizing factor therefore needs to be replaced, and the following sections detail how appropriate measures could look.

6.7.9.1 Preventative Mechanisms

Cache/Transaction Functionality

Incoming and outgoing data are stored in a cache before they are processed, and all jobs to be processed are stored in a processing queue. Only when a transaction (job) has been successfully completed can it be marked as such. Jobs that were not processed due to system failure or connection termination are executed when the system resumes.

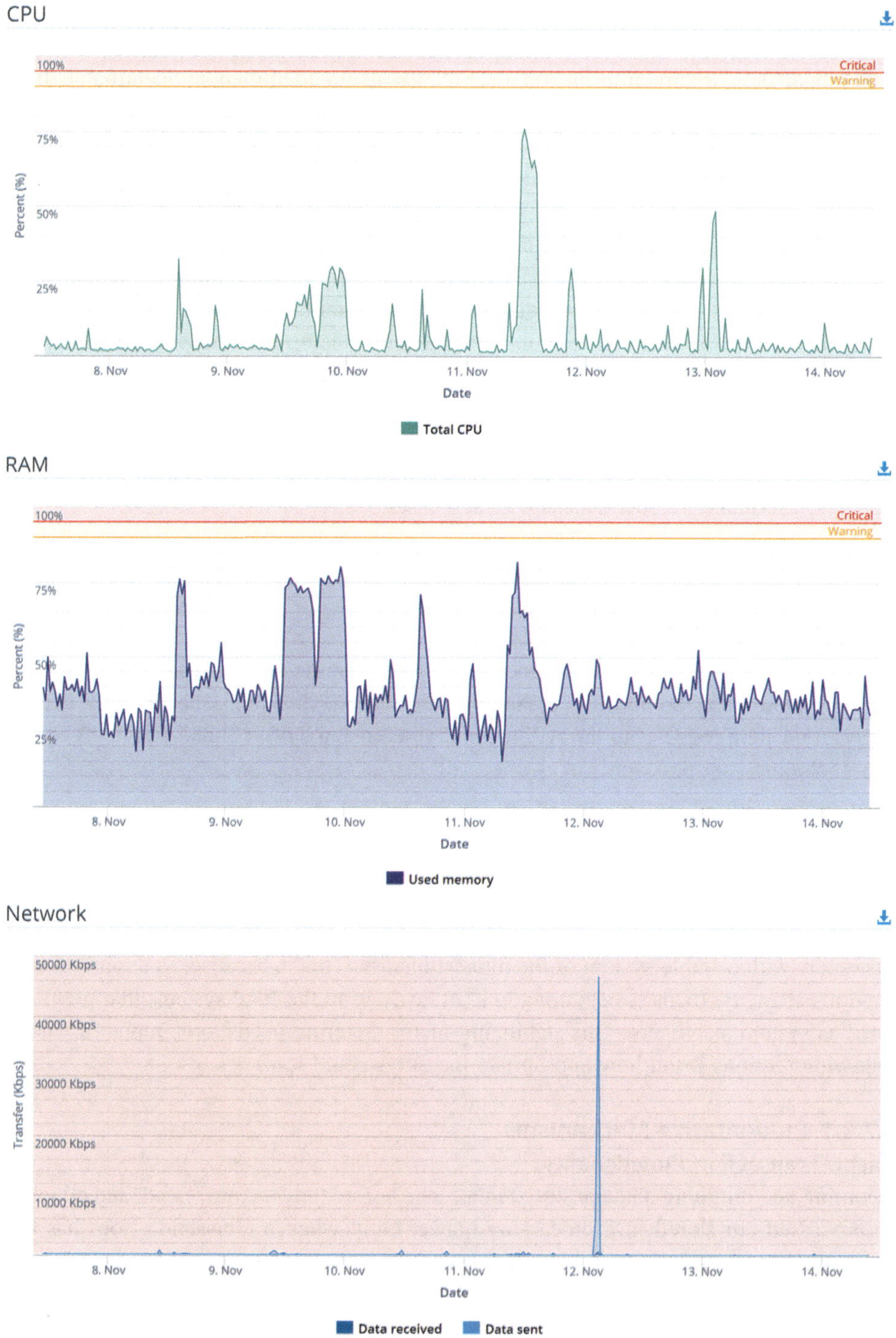

Fig. 6.27 Sample processor, memory, and network usage monitoring. (Source: 1&1 IONOS SE—Server monitoring)

Multiple-Bulkhead Mechanisms

Future systems will be built using a 'bulkhead' or 'fire lane' system. If one bulkhead is breached, the next takes effect. Any security leaks/penetrations that occur can be identified by a monitoring mechanism (see Fig. 6.27). The vulnerability can be selected using information collected in the customer's system, technology, and database. The affected area is determined and, if necessary, a partial lockdown is performed. If no identification is possible, an automatic lockdown takes place. For security reasons, we can only provide a superficial description of the mechanisms involved.

6.7.9.2 Technical Measures

Backup Systems (Database)

Databases are permanently backed up at predefined intervals, so that if a database is lost or fails, the next older version is restored, either at the push of a button or fully automatically.

Redundant System (Proxy Server, Load Balancing)

Upstream mechanisms (proxy server, load balancing) permanently calculate the load and availability of the running systems. The proxy server can thus selectively forward requests to the available system with the lowest load. Requests are not forwarded to heavily loaded servers, unavailable servers, or servers undergoing maintenance.

Monitoring

Load distribution, availability, security indicators, firewall indicators, processes, and services are permanently monitored to enable a timely and proactive response to future issues such as a full hard disk, or current situations such as a hacker attack. In addition, the system can react to past events such as the failure of certain functions. Future monitoring proactively reports various escalation levels (such as notes, warnings, or error messages) to the service team in real time.

Dynamically Growing Systems

Existing cloud IT infrastructure technologies mean that issues such as scaling performance requirements are no longer a problem. Cloud technologies make it possible to expand RAM, processor performance, and hard disk space at the push of a button. Even technical system management is now conveniently available as a service from cloud providers via an easy-to-monitor web interface. The administration of individual hardware and operating systems is a thing of the past, as these are now universally available on a managed basis.

Automatic Delivery of IT Infrastructure Systems

Future systems are delivered centrally via swarm technology. A template system is defined, and new systems are created (or older systems are maintained) fully automatically.

Version Management

Future software infrastructure will be documented using version management tools. This makes every code change traceable. A wide variety of versions, parallel development processes, and version branches can be used to advance a huge set of statuses and development projects while still complying with the required quality assurance processes. For example, an error in a productive system can be corrected in real time using a hotfix, and this fix can be automatically incorporated into any other parallel version of the same code.

6.7.10 Quality Assurance Measures

Stability can be ensured with the help of continuous quality assurance measures. In the future, managed technologies and services will be available that will perform these tasks and ensure the required degree of system stability.

6.7.10.1 Error Tracking

Software is not infallible, but rather buggy and error-prone. Even in productive systems, it is inevitable that users trigger unforeseen errors through a combination of factors that wasn't adequately tested at the development stage. In such cases, it is extremely important that the software manufacturer can react to errors sufficiently quickly to prevent the user from suffering any kind of loss.

Figure 6.28 shows an active error response triggered by a previously unknown combination of user factors.

The data with information on the application, input data, browser used, and version level is forwarded to a specially-trained task force team that then reproduces the error and creates a hotfix. The requirement is that hotfixes in productive systems are applied within 30 min of the error occurring, and that the user automatically receives an e-mail when the error is fixed. Errors must be solved without active communication with the user. In the past, users usually had to open a support ticket and then manually cooperate in the support feedback loop.

6.7.10.2 Continuous Integration (CI)

In the past, software was delivered on a CD with a specific, static version status. Today, software is highly dynamic and changes permanently. At large corporations like Facebook, Google, and Amazon, hundreds of software changes are made every minute without the user noticing. The current trend is for software to be dynamic and subject to permanent change, expansion, and improvement.

Before software can be delivered, you have to check that it can be integrated with the existing code. If a feature fails, the integration cannot be performed and a correction is due. If you take this approach, it is possible to continuously incorporate changes and improvements.

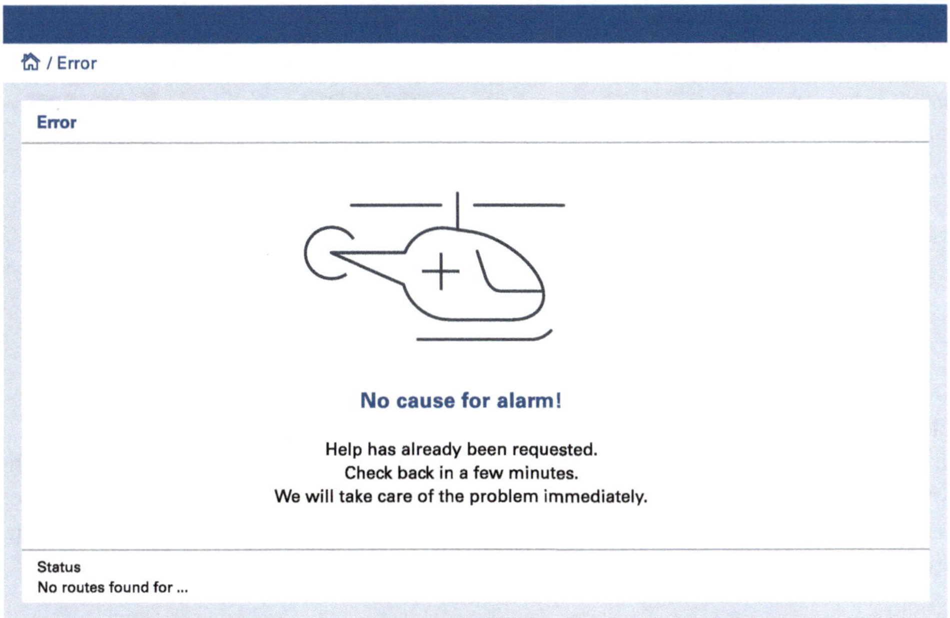

Fig. 6.28 Error tracking output in a web application interface. (Source: H&F Solutions GmbH/ www.hf-solutions.co)

Example

Innovative car manufacturers already practice continuous integration today. They are able to install new software updates (driver experience, new safety functions, and so on) while you are driving. Old-school, non-innovative manufacturers still require you to take your vehicle to the workshop to make any necessary changes. ◄

Code Styling

Since programming code can be created in many different ways, software code will in future be checked against internal style specifications that enable the software team to create a uniform style. Such technologies are able to automatically fix coding errors and adapt the existing code to match predefined standards.

Analysis and Measurement of Code Quality

What parameters would you use to define a good developer? By the number of lines of code he has programmed, or perhaps by the quality of the code? Today it is possible to automatically analyze developer quality using parameters such as code redundancy, simplicity, and structure. Using these kinds of metrics, developers can be motivated to write better code in the future.

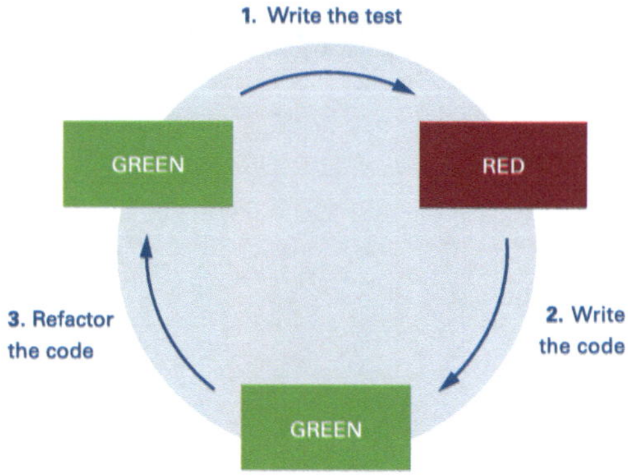

Fig. 6.29 The creation cycle in process-driven software development. (Source: H&F Solutions GmbH/www.hf-solutions.co)

Identifying Errors/Tests

In the future, new code will be checked automatically before being imported into the working environment. The focus here is on the integration and interaction of the modified and/or newly created code. Predefined tests check the behavior of the code, and manual testing becomes a thing of the past.

Check Whether Maintenance Updates Are Available

Continuous integration (CI) automatically checks whether any updates or fixes are available for integrated third-party software. Any manual maintenance effort therefore only applies to in-house systems.

6.7.10.3 Automated Tests

Today, automated tests help us to keep the code quality stable over the entire system. Today's leading platforms apply a huge range of predefined tests that check for potential errors for every code change (see Fig. 6.29). We distinguish here between individual tests, integration tests, and performance tests. These tests are performed on a separate test system to avoid over-burdening the development and production servers.

Measurement of Test Coverage (Code Coverage)

A measurement of the test coverage in terms of depth and quality provides an accurate overview of the degree to which new and existing code can be scaled. The greater the test coverage, the greater the scalability.

Test-Driven Development (TDD)

In the future, developers will be asked to first think about how a new requirement can be tested before any actual code is written. This enables us to check whether the code contributes to the success of the overall system during development, or even before any actual development takes place. A traffic-light system could be used to provide the necessary monitoring. The optimal procedure involves writing the test first, then writing the actual code, and finally checking and, if necessary, refactoring it. Ideally, the theoretical traffic light is always green. If the tests created this way work, they are then integrated into the code too.

Behavior-Driven Development (BDD)

In this case, it is not the developer who writes the test cases, but rather the user. Test cases are formulated as text and then formalized in such a way that they can be translated into executable programming/testing language. This procedure closes another of the gaps (or "media interruptions", as they are also known) that cause a lot of headaches in the increasingly networked world.

UI Testing

User interface tests are performed directly at the front end of your application. If you want to deliver high-quality products, automated testing is essential in this area too. Today, RPA bots are the tool of choice for this kind of testing, and are capable of successful testing even if the dialog interface changes dynamically.

Continuous Deployment (CD)

Today, continuous deployment is fully automated in staging environments that include levels such as test, pre-release, and release environments. Differing deployments or version statuses are delivered using a timestamp. A "current" folder points to the last deployed release folder and, if necessary, the pointer ("") can be switched within a few milliseconds to another release folder in order to publish an older version. This functionality is often referred to in context as a "rollback facility". When a new version is deployed, the pointer is not switched from the current to the new version until the deployment is complete. This avoids the possibility of errors occurring during long delivery processes, or the use of a deployment that is not yet ready. Following just a single change to the program code, orchestrated swarms automatically organize delivery to multiple instances/machines.

Use of Maintained Software

When using third-party software such as libraries, only applications that guarantee long-term support (5 years or more) and where the software is externally maintained and improved should be used. You also need to make sure that the software in use can receive continuous hotfixes and other updates. Your goal should be to concentrate on your own core software and for any external tools to be maintained by a large community. The software tools that are not part of your core business should function with a high degree of automation in the course of their everyday operation. This is why you should only use tools that are in continuous development by hundreds of community developers.

Dealing with Unforeseen Events

Every day, many companies are confronted with hacker attacks. Just as there are plenty of great options for successfully performing innovation strategy work, there are also many ways to adequately protect yourself. Most hacker attacks are trivial and their consequences can be quickly mitigated. But even harmless hacking is an annoyance that shouldn't really exist.

In the summer of 2020, however, a serious case occurred at *Garmin*. An encryption Trojan took all of the company's customer data and its homepage down for several days and, in the end, the entire site had to be completely recreated and rebuilt. The hackers' aim wasn't to steal the data, but 'only' to encrypt it and hold it to ransom. Unfortunately, in many companies the topic of IT security is not given sufficient consideration due to the costs involved and/or a simple lack of interest. The following measures are the minimum necessary to protect your company:

- **Decoupled security mechanisms (backup)**
  Backup systems such as data backups should be decoupled in such a way that a hacker cannot access them directly. Today's cloud providers offer services that regularly and automatically back up and store data that can then only be accessed in read-only mode. At this point, a concept is required that actively decouples backup data from the productive system. A simple variant that can be implemented immediately is to perform daily backups to a separate magnetic tape drive.
- **Multi-stage bulkhead system (preventative measures)**
  A security concept must allow for a subsequent safety system to kick in when a bulkhead is breached. For more details, see Sect. 6.7.9.1 above.
- **Setup speed (automation, orchestration)**
  Similar to the methods used for cloud scaling, a mechanism should be established that makes it possible to set up security systems fully automatically. In addition, a concept and a methodology should exist that make it possible to read data from the decoupled system at the push of a button so that data can be continuously imported, even in the event of a system failure. In a worst case scenario, the dependency of the system setup is then only physically limited by its own performance and no longer by the human factor.
- **Task Force Team**
  A task force team should be defined in advance that is available on call to identify any security leaks and apply appropriate remedial measures.
- **Task Force Mechanism**
  Establish an on-call response system for your security task force. This team of security experts must be able to respond to unforeseen events together with the software engineering team. This means that these people must be available around the clock to respond to system stability threats and events. To do this efficiently, you also need to introduce an escalation process for the service team that automatically hands over event management to the security task force if the escalation level requires it.

6.7.11 Process Security

Successful companies must have the goal of permanently improving process security. This requires a holistic approach based on the interplay of the following crucial factors:

Human Factors

- Continuous staff training
- Use of experts
- Balanced mix of employee soft skills

Technical Factors

- OKR (Objectives and Key Results) methodology
- Use of current standards (security, technology, methodology, and so on)
- Enhancement and improvement of quality assurance measures
- Verification and control of the planned security technology
- Automation and avoiding the human factor (for security issues)
- Validation and testing security measures
- Benchmark your security technologies against other high-end tech companies

If you apply this mixture of factors, your company will be well equipped to successfully implement the requirements of your current and future strategies. We wish you every success in the implementation of your own strategic topics.

The Most Important Points at a Glance

Once you have all the appropriate innovation strategies, methods, and tools at your fingertips, there is only one crucial building block missing for the overall success of integrated networking, namely: the generation of knowledge. In the future, approaches will emerge that anonymously store knowledge and make it available to companies. After all, if ten suppliers have already connected to a producer of industrial goods, the eleventh supplier shouldn't have to go through the same complicated connection process all over again. This supplier should be able to use the (presumably) 99% identical steps immediately and connect in no time at all. However, this scenario is only possible if a particular group of stakeholders pool their knowledge. As with many other aspects of a business, it is sufficient if you do this for all non-critical standard processes. This chapter finishes up by describing how to build an interface for linking to just such a community. ◄

7 Outlook

Abstract
Our previous book *The ERP Fallacy* created the basis for this book, which gives you plenty more valuable and practical tips and information. Nevertheless, even armed with the content of this book, your journey has only just begun. You too are facing countless new experiences, and nobody really knows whether they are going to turn out better or worse than those you have already had. We will be continuing our journey with further publications, and we will continue to change the future. There are good reasons to be excited about what's coming down the line. Please contact us directly with any questions or queries you may have.

P. Futterknecht, T. Hertfelder, *Data, Disruption & Digital Leadership*,
https://doi.org/10.1007/978-3-658-41601-0_7

Printed by Printforce, the Netherlands